BURTON ON BURTON

Burton on Burton

Revised Edition

Edited by
Mark Salisbury

Foreword by Johnny Depp

faber and faber

First published in the United Kingdom in 1995
by Faber and Faber Limited
3 Queen Square London WC1N 3AU
A Revised Edition first published in 2000
This Revised Edition first published in 2006
Printed in England by CPI Mackays, Chatham ME5 8TD

Stills appear courtesy of BFI Stills, Posters and Designs, Alan Jones and the Kobal
Collection. Copyright for the stills are held by: the Walt Disney Company Inc.
(*Vincent, Hansel and Gretel, Frankenweenie, Tim Burton's The Nightmare Before
Christmas* and *Ed Wood*); Warner Bros (*Pee-Wee's Big Adventure, Batman, Batman
Returns, Mars Attacks!, Charlie and the Chocolate Factory* and *Corpse Bride*);
Amblin Entertainment (*Family Dog*); The Geffen Company (*Beetlejuice*); Twentieth
Century Fox (*Edward Scissorhands, Planet of the Apes* (1968), *Planet of the Apes*
(2001)); De Laurentiis (*Danger Diabolik*); Paramount Pictures (*Willy Wonka and
the Chocolate Factory*); Paramount Pictures & Mandalay Pictures (*Sleepy Hollow*);
Sony Pictures Entertainment (*Big Fish*); Charles H. Schneer/Columbia Pictures
(*Earth Versus the Flying Saucers*); and Hammer Films (*Dracula Has Risen From
the Grave*)

A CIP record for this book
is available from the British Library

ISBN 978-0-571-22926-0

Contents

To Laura and Milo, the diamonds in my sky

Acknowledgements

The first edition of *Burton on Burton* was published in 1995 and was comprised of interviews that took place between 1988 and 1994, followed by a revised edition in 1999 which coincided with the release of *Sleepy Hollow* and which featured material gathered from interviews between January and April 1999. All additional material for this second revised edition is comprised of interviews undertaken between January 2001 and March 2005: on the set of and during post-production on *Planet of the Apes*, during post-production on *Big Fish*, on the set of *Charlie and the Chocolate Factory*, as well as several in-depth sessions in London between January and March 2005 while Burton was editing *Charlie* and *Corpse Bride*.

As always, my principal debt of gratitude is to Tim Burton who has been a wonderful champion and supporter of this project from day one, and who has patiently and willingly submitted himself to many, many hours of questioning for more than a decade now, generously providing his time, his opinions and some wonderful artwork – thank you.

My sincere thanks too to his long-serving right-hand man, the incomparable Derek Frey, whose tireless enthusiasm is second to none, and who is as charming as he is efficient. For your help in arranging interviews, for checking details, for collating illustrations, and for much more besides, I salute you.

To Johnny Depp, my thanks and appreciation for providing another of your penetrating and very personal forewords and offering a very loving, moving and incredibly heart-felt take on this book's subject that is priceless. You made me wait man but, boy, was it worth it . . .

Throughout this undertaking, numerous people have provided assistance, guidance and support. Many have been thanked previously, but for this edition I'd like to single out Richard D. Zanuck for his wonderful old school manners, generous hospitality, amazing Hollywood stories, and a lovely tea at Claridges; the ever-charming Sarah Clark, who made my many *Charlie and the Chocolate Factory* visits so delightful; Peter Mountain for his fantastic cover shot; Allison Abbate, my most agreeable

Corpse Bride host; and Christi Dembrowski, for her constant nudging, and help with extraction . . .

Thanks too to Walter Donohue, wise 'old' man of Faber and Faber for his flexibility with deadlines and much more besides, Richard T. Kelly who held the fort during a very difficult period, Eileen Peterson, Helena Bonham Carter, John August, Alex McDowell, Mike Johnson, Felicity Dahl, Kathy Heintzelman, DP extraordinaire Emmanuel Lubezki, Brenda Berrisford, and Jayne Trotman.

And finally, my love and heartfelt appreciation to the ever wonderful Laura. For reasons far too numerous to mention, you are, quite simply, the best.

Foreword

by Johnny Depp

In the winter of 1989, I was in Vancouver, British Columbia, doing a television series. It was a very difficult situation: bound by a contract doing assembly-line stuff that, to me, was borderline Fascist (cops in school ... Christ!). My fate, it seemed, lay somewhere between *Chips* and *Joanie Loves Chaachi*. There were only a limited number of choices for me: (1) get through it as best I could with minimal abrasion; (2) get fired as fast as I could with slightly more abrasion; (3) quit and be sued for not only any money I had, but also the money of my children and my children's children (which, I imagine, would have caused severe chafing and possible shingles for the rest of my natural days and on through the next few generations of Depps to come). Like I said, this was truly a dilemma. Choice (3) was out of the question, thanks to extremely sound advice from my attorney. As for (2), well, I tried and they just wouldn't bite. Finally, I settled on (1): I would get by as best I could.

The minimal abrasion soon became potential self-destruction. I was not feeling good about myself or this self-induced/out-of-control jail term that an ex-agent had prescribed as good medicine for unemployment. I was stuck, filling up space between commercials. Babbling incoherently some writer's words that I couldn't bring myself to read (thus having no knowledge of what poison the scripts might have contained). Dumb-founded, lost, shoved down the gullets of America as a young Republican. TV boy, heart-throb, teen idol, teen hunk. Plastered, postered, postured, patented, painted, plastic!!! Stapled to a box of cereal with wheels, doing 200 mph on a one-way collision course bound for Thermos and lunch-box antiquity. Novelty boy, franchise boy. Fucked and plucked with no escape from this nightmare.

And then, one day, I was sent a script by my new agent, a godsend. It was the story of a boy with scissors for hands – an innocent outcast in suburbia. I read the script instantly and wept like a newborn. Shocked that someone was brilliant enough to conceive and then actually write this story, I read it again right away. I was so affected and moved by it that strong waves of images flooded my brain – dogs I'd had as a kid, feeling freakish and obtuse when I was growing up, the unconditional love that only infants and dogs are evolved enough to have. I felt so attached to this story that I was completely obsessed. I read every children's story, fairy tale, child-psychology book, *Gray's Anatomy*, anything, everything … and then, *reality* set in. I was TV boy. No director in his right mind would hire me to play this character. I had done nothing work-wise to show that I could handle this kind of role. How could I convince this director that *I was Edward*, that I knew him inside and out? In my eyes, it was impossible.

A meeting was set up. I was to see the director, Tim Burton. I prepared by watching his other films – *Beetlejuice, Batman, Pee-Wee's Big Adventure*. Blown away by the obvious gifted wizardry this guy possessed, I was even more sure that he would never see me in the role. I was embarrassed to consider myself as Edward. After several knock-down-drag-'em-outs with my agent (thank you, Tracey), she forced me to have the meeting.

I flew to Los Angeles and went straight to the coffee-shop of the Bel Age Hotel, where I was to meet Tim and his producer, Denise Di Novi. I walked in, chain-smoking, nervously looking for the potential genius in the room (I had never seen what he looked like) and BANG! I saw him sitting at a booth behind a row of potted plants, drinking a cup of coffee. We said hello, I sat down and we talked … sort of – I'll explain later.

A pale, frail-looking, sad-eyed man with hair that expressed much more than last night's pillow struggle. A comb with legs would have outrun Jesse Owens, given one look at this guy's locks. A clump to the east, four sprigs to the west, a swirl, and the rest of this unruliness to all points north and south. I remember the first thing I thought was, 'Get some sleep', but I couldn't say that, of course. And then it hit me like a two-ton sledgehammer square in the middle of my forehead. The hands – the way he waves them around in the air almost uncontrollably, nervously tapping on the table, stilted speech (a trait we both share), eyes wide and glaring out of nowhere, curious, eyes that have seen much but still devour all. This hypersensitive madman *is* Edward Scissorhands.

After sharing approximately three to four pots of coffee together, stumbling our way through each other's unfinished sentences but somehow still understanding one another, we ended the meeting with a handshake and a 'nice to meet you'. I left that coffee-shop jacked up on caffeine, chewing insanely on my coffee-spoon like a wild, rabid dog. I now officially felt even worse about things because of the honest connection I felt we had had during the meeting. Mutually understanding the perverse beauty of a milkcow creamer, the bright-eyed fascination with resin grapes, the complexities and raw power that one can find in a velvet Elvis painting – seeing way beyond the novelty, the profound respect for 'those who are not others'. I was sure we could work well together and I was positive, if given the chance, I could carry out his artistic vision for Edward Scissorhands. My chances were, at best, slim – if that. Better-known people than me were not only being considered for the role but were battling, fighting, kicking, screaming, begging for it. Only one director had really stuck his neck out for me and that was John Waters, a great outlaw film-maker, a man both Tim and I had huge respect and admiration for. John had taken a chance on me to spoof my 'given' image in *Cry-Baby*. But would Tim see something in me that would make him take the risk? I hoped so.

I waited for weeks, not hearing a thing in my favour. All the while, I was still researching the part. It was now not something I merely wanted to do, but something I *had* to do. Not for any ambitious, greedy, actory, box-office-draw reason, but because this story had now taken residence in the middle of my heart and refused to be evicted. What could I do? At the point when I was just about to resign myself to the fact that I would always be TV boy, the phone rang.

'Hello?' I picked up.

'Johnny … you are Edward Scissorhands,' a voice said simply.

'*What?*' flew out of my mouth.

'*You are Edward Scissorhands.*'

I put the phone down and mumbled those words to myself. And then mumbled them to anyone else I came in contact with. I couldn't fucking believe it. He was willing to risk everything on me in the role. Head-butting the studio's wishes, hopes and dreams for a big star with established box-office draw, he chose me. I became instantly religious, positive that divine intervention had taken place. This role for me was not a career move. This role was freedom. Freedom to create, experiment, learn and exorcize something in me. Rescued from the world of mass-product, bang-'em out TV death by this odd, brilliant young guy who had spent his youth drawing strange pictures, stomping around the soup-bowl of Burbank, feeling quite freakish himself (I would learn later). I felt like Nelson Mandela. Resuscitated from my jaded views of 'Hollyweird' and what it's like to not have any control of what you *really want* for yourself.

In essence, I owe the majority of whatever success I've been lucky enough to have to that one weird, wired meeting with Tim. Because if it weren't for him, I think I would have gone ahead and opted for choice (3) and quit that fucking show while I still had some semblance of integrity left. And I also believe that because of Tim's belief in me, Hollywood opened its doors, playing a strange follow-the-leader game.

I have since worked with Tim again on *Ed Wood*. This was an idea he talked to me about, sitting at the bar of the Formosa Café in Hollywood. Within ten minutes I was committed to doing it. To me, it almost doesn't matter what Tim wants to film – I'll do it, I'm there. Because I trust him implicitly – his vision, his taste, his sense of humour, his heart and his brain. He is, to me, a true genius and I wouldn't use that word with too many people, believe me. You can't label what he does. It's not magic, because that would imply some sort of trickery. It's not just skill, because that seems like it's learned. What he has is a very special gift that we don't see every day. It's not enough to call him a film-maker. The rare title of 'genius' is a better fit – in not just film, but drawings, photographs, thought, insight and ideas.

When I was asked to write the foreword to this book, I chose to tell it from the perspective of what I honestly felt like at the time he rescued me: a loser, an outcast, just another piece of expendable Hollywood meat.

It's very hard to write about someone you care for and respect on such a high level of friendship. It's equally difficult to explain the working relationship between actor and director. I can only say that, for me, Tim need do nothing more than say a few disconnected words, tilt his head, squint his eyes or look at me a certain way and I know exactly what he wants from the scene. And I have always done my best to deliver that to him. So, for me to say what I feel about Tim, it would have to be on paper, because if I said it to his face he would most probably cackle like a banshee and then punch me in the eye.

He is an artist, a genius, an oddball, an insane, brilliant, brave, hysterically funny, loyal, nonconformist, honest friend. I owe him a tremendous debt and respect him more than I could ever express on paper. He is him and that is all. And he is, without a doubt, the finest Sammy Davis Jr impersonator on the planet.

I have never seen someone so obviously out of place fit right in. *His* way.

Johnny Depp
New York City
September 1994

Tim Burton and Johnny Depp on the set of *Edward Scissorhands*

Tim Burton, Johnny Depp and Sarah Jessica Parker on the set of *Ed Wood*

Foreword to the Revised Edition

by Johnny Depp

Many a moon has passed since the days of my brief brush with TV stardom, or whatever one might dare call it. I mostly think of them as the do-or-die years: picture, if you will, the confused young man hurtling dangerously towards the flash-in-the-pan at sound-breaking speed. Or, on a more positive note, forced education, with decent dividends in the short term. Either way, it was a scary time when so-called TV actors weren't eagerly received into the fickle fold of film folk. Fortunately, I was more than determined – even desperate – to break away from my ascent/descent. The chances were nearly impossible, until the likes of John Waters and Tim Burton had enough courage and vision to give me a chance to attempt to build my own foundation on my own terms. Anyway, no time to digress . . . this has all been said before.

I sit here, hunched at the keyboard, banging away on a ratty old computer, which does not understand me at all, nor I it, especially with a zillion thoughts swirling through my skull on how to proceed with something as personal as an update on my relationship with old pal Tim. He is, for me, exactly the same man I wrote about nearly eleven years ago, though all kinds of wonderfulness has flowered and showered the both of us, and caused radical changes in the men we were and the men we've become – or, at least, the men we've been revealed as. Yeah, you see, Tim and I are dads. Wow. Who'd have ever thought it possible that our progeny would be swinging on swing-sets together, or sharing toy cars, toy monsters, even potentially exchanging chicken pox? This is a part of the ride I had never imagined.

Seeing Tim as proud Papa is enough to send me into an irrepressible weeping jag, because, as with almost everything, it's in the eyes. Tim's eyes have always shone: no question about it, there was always something luminous in those troubled/sad/weary peepers. But today, the eyes of old pal Tim are laser beams! Piercing, smiling, contented eyes, with all of the gravity of yesteryear, but bright with the hope of a spectacular future. This was not the case before. There was a man with, presumably, everything – or so it seemed from the outside. But there was also something incomplete and somehow consumed by an empty space. It is an odd place to be. Believe me . . . I know.

Watching Tim with his boy, Billy, is an enormous joy to behold. There is a visible bond that transcends words. I feel as if I'm watching Tim meet himself toddler-size, ready to right all wrongs and re-right all rights. I am looking at the Tim that has been waiting to shed the skin of the unfinished man that we all knew and loved, being reborn as the more complete radiant hilarity that exists full-blown today. It is a kind of miracle to witness, and I am privileged to be near it. The man I now know as a part of the trio of Tim, Helena and Billy is new and improved and completely complete. Anyway, that's enough of that. I'll step off the Kleenex box and get on with things, shall I? Onwards . . .

In August of 2003 I was in Montreal, working on a film called *Secret Window*, when I received a phone call from Tim asking if I could make it down to NYC for dinner the following week to discuss something. No names, no title, no story, no script – nothing specific. And, as always, I said that I would be there happily, 'I'll see you then', that type of deal. And go I did. When I arrived at the restaurant, there was Tim, tucked away in a corner booth, half in darkness, nursing a beer. I sat, we enjoyed for the first time the fantastic, 'How's the family?' exchange, and then zoomed immediately to the subject at hand. Willy Wonka.

I was stunned. Amazed, at first, by the outrageous possibilities of Tim's version of the Roald Dahl classic, *Charlie and the Chocolate Factory*, but even more floored that he was, in actual fact, asking me if I would be interested in playing the role of Wonka. Now, for any kid who grew up in the 70s or 80s, the first film version starring Gene Wilder (who was a brilliant Wonka) was an annual event. So there was the kid in me who was giddy that I should be, in this case, the chosen one for the part. But there was also the 'thespian' in me who understood very, very well that every actor and their mother and that mother's brother's uncle's third cousin's pet iguana's goldfish would have hacked each other up into tiny morsels – or at best, gladly knocked each other off in a more civilized fashion – clamouring, gagging for the chance that was being presented to me by one of the people I admire most. I was also keenly aware of the many battles with many studios that Tim had had to endure over many years to secure my involvement on the various films we'd already done together, and it made every kind of sense to me that he'd probably need to take the gloves off for this one. I couldn't believe my luck . . . I still can't.

I think I probably let him finish a sentence and a half before I blurted out the words, 'I'm in.' 'Well', said he, 'think about it and let me know . . . '

'No, no . . . if you want me, I'm there.' We finished our dinner with more than a few titbits and amusing ideas about the character of Wonka and, of course, traded the occasional nappy-changing story, as grown men who are dads are wont to do. We ventured out into the night with a handshake and an embrace, as grown men who are pals are wont to do. And I then handed him the complete set of *Wiggles* DVDs, as grown men probably shouldn't do, but do anyway and deny later. We said goodbye and I then wandered off back to my day-job. Several months later, I found myself in London to begin the shoot.

Our early discussions of Wonka had been incorporated and we were ready to play. The idea of this solitary man and the extreme isolation he'd inflicted upon himself – and what effect this might have – was a colossal playground. Tim and I had explored many areas of our own pasts with regard to the various layers of Wonka: two grown men in serious consultation, debating the merits of Captain Kangaroo versus Mr. Rogers, even spicing things up with a dash of, say, a Wink Martindale, or Chuck Woolery, two of the finest game-show hosts ever to crack the boards. We were navigating through territories that would eventually wind up bringing us to tears, laughing like teenage school chums. Sometimes we even travelled into the arena of 'local' kiddie-show hosts, who in some cases could be defined as being just this side of mimes, or carnival clowns. We braved some treacherous possibilities and discarded all things unnecessary. My memories of the process are a gift that I'll treasure always.

The experience of shooting the film with Tim was as good as anything gets. To me, it felt as if our brains were connected by a blistering hot wire that could have generated sparks at any minute. There were moments in certain scenes where we'd find ourselves precariously high on an unbelievably thin thread, trying to work out just how far the limits were, which would only give birth to more absurd notions and mirth.

To my surprise, while shooting *Charlie* he invited me to play another part in his stop-motion feature *Corpse Bride*, which he was working on simultaneously. The size and scope and commitment level of these projects if taken on one at a time would have been enough to drop a horse. Tim glided effortlessly from one to another. He is an unstoppable force. There were plenty of times when I was unable to fully grasp his inexhaustible, almost perverse energy.

All told, we worked hard and had an absolute ball. We laughed like mad children about everything and nothing, which is always about something. We shamelessly swapped imitations of some of our favourite entertainers of days gone by, such brilliant individuals as Charles Nelson Reilly,

Georgie Jessel, Charlie Callas, Sammy Davis Jr (always), Shlitzy (from the Tod Browning film *Freaks*), et cetera. The list could go on and on and on, ad infinitum but, the names would get more and more obscure and our readers might just derail. We'd dive into these deep philosophical conversations concerning whether or not the guests of the Dean Martin Roasts were actually in the same room together when the show was taped – and became really super-worried that maybe they weren't.

His knowledge of film is staggering, far into the obscure and downright scary. For example, in conversation one day at work I happened to mention that my girl, Vanessa, has a thing for disaster films, and preferably bad ones. Right away, Tim's side of our gabbing became incredibly animated, the hands waving and zigzagging dangerously through the air. He rattles off a list of things I'd never heard of in my life. We settled on a couple of humdingers that Tim tracked down from his personal library for us – titles like *The Swarm* and *When Time Ran Out*. And then, for good measure, he'll break out something a bit more soothing like *Monster Zero*, or *Village of the Damned*. The point is, his relationship with cinema is not, even in the slightest sense, jaded. He has not tired or bored of the process. Each outing is as exciting as the first.

For me, working with Tim is like going home. It is a house made of risk, but in that risk, there is comfort. Great comfort. There are no safety-nets, for anyone, but that is how you were raised in that house. What one has to rely on is simply trust, which is the key to everything. I know very deeply that Tim trusts me, which is an amazing blessing, but that is not to say that I am not always paralytic with the fear of letting him down. In fact, that is first and foremost in my thinking as I am approaching the character. The only elements that keep me sane are my knowledge of his trust, my love for him, and my profound and eternal trust in him, coinciding with my hefty yearning to never disappoint him.

What more can I say about him? He is a brother, a friend, my godson's father. He is a unique and brave soul, someone that I would go to the ends of the earth for, and I know, full and well, he would do the same for me.

There . . . I said it.

Johnny Depp
May 2005
Dominica, West Indies

Introduction to Revised Edition

In the decade or so since the first edition of *Burton on Burton* was published, Tim Burton has transformed from being a visionary director with the Midas touch to becoming an identifiable brand; the term 'Burtonesque' being ascribed to any filmmaker whose work is dark, edgy or quirky, or a combination thereof. It's a transformation that's brought its own benefits – Hollywood clout, for one – but also its own, unique set of difficulties, not least in the expectations that both studios and audiences now have of him and his output. Burton remains a filmmaker whose modus operandi is based entirely on his innermost feelings. For him to commit to a project it's necessary for him to connect emotionally to his characters, be they original creations – the razor-fingered innocent of *Edward Scissorhands* – adapted from comic books – the masked vigilante of *Batman* – or people from real life – the delusional director in *Ed Wood* – connections that, as he is the first to admit, are sometimes far from obvious. *Edward Scissorhands*, for instance, began as a cry from the heart, a drawing from his teenage years that expressed the inner torment he felt at being unable to communicate with those around him, especially his family; while so many of his films reflect upon his childhood in suburbia.

Growing up in the Los Angeles suburb of Burbank in the 1950s and 1960s, in the shadow of the Warner Bros lot, Burton sought solace from the bright and sunny outside world in the dark of the movie theatre, connecting psychologically to those images that flicked on the big screen. His passion was monster movies, his idol Vincent Price, to whom he paid tribute in his stop-motion short *Vincent* and cast as the inventor father-figure in *Edward Scissorhands*. But while many of his work's recurrent themes and images appear, on the surface, to be a director graciously paying homage to his youthful inspirations – notably James Whale's 1931 *Frankenstein* – the reality is much more complex. 'The image isn't always literal,' he once said, 'but linked to a feeling.'

Burton's characters are often outsiders, misunderstood and misperceived, misfits encumbered by some degree of duality, operating on the fringes of their own particular society, tolerated but pretty much left to their own devices. And in many ways he embodies that contradiction himself. Although Burton continues to hold his position at the very top of the Hollywood A-list, a director whose very name will guarantee not only an audience but a studio green-light, in almost all other respects he and Hollywood maintain a respectful distance from one another. His films may well have reaped in excess of a billion dollars worldwide, but they're as far from being slaves to common-denominator commercialism as he is from fully embracing the Hollywood studio system in which he has continued to operate since his beginnings as an animator at Disney in the 1980s. Despite the enormous budgets entrusted to his care, Burton's voice has remained as original and uniquely creative as ever. He may use Hollywood's money, he may make their summer blockbusters and their tent-pole pictures, but he makes them *his* way. And that's what makes them so appealing and intriguing.

When Burton was announced as the director of a new version of *Planet of the Apes*, there were equal amounts of feverish excitement to those who questioned his motivation and the wisdom of remaking such a classic and much-loved film. Burton was only too aware of the potential pitfalls – 'I knew I was walking into an ambush' – and his 're-imagining' of the material, as Twentieth Century Fox dubbed it, proved to be something of a poisoned chalice. The original *Planet of the Apes* had been released in 1968 into a radically distinct era and political climate – the war in Vietnam, race riots at home – working as both marked social commentary and top-notch entertainment. The world was a different place back then. In 2000, Fox weren't interested in social comment; they wanted a franchise. Burton's film was green-lit without a completed script and rushed into production to meet a summer release date. The compromises were there for all to see, and the finished film, despite some typically imaginative and stylistic flourishes, as well as Rick Baker's terrific make-up, was a marked disappointment even to die-hard Burton fans. The experience, as he relates in the chapter devoted to the film, was fraught with difficulties, not least in his dealings with the studio. As for that necessary personal connection, *Apes* offered several familiar themes – that of reversal and of the outsider – as well as a chance to work with Charlton Heston, star of the original film. But, as Burton later reveals, his heart wasn't quite in it: he admits to being 'more intrigued by the idea of it than I was the actual thing.'

Burton bounced back with *Big Fish*, his most mainstream and, ironically, most personal film to date. Adapted by John August from a novel by Daniel Wallace, *Big Fish* was perfect material for Burton, playing not only with the very notion of storytelling itself but making exquisite use of his flair for fables. More importantly, Burton connected to its central theme of a son trying to reconcile with his dying father, and the script gave him a means to address his feelings about the death of his own father, who had passed away in 2000. *Big Fish* centres around the relationship between Edward Bloom, a former travelling salesman who has always found a deeper truth in fantasy than in reality, and his estranged son Will, who grew up to detest his father for constructing elaborate myths but who eventually comes to realize that they reveal the true man after all. The film was a triumphant blend of the fantastical and the sentimental, the emotional and the magical, with Burton, working with his best script since *Ed Wood*, presenting a bright, heroic, mythical America, one populated by werewolves and giants, Siamese twins and outsize catfish, an America where the romantic and the brave always win out in the end. As Peter Travers of *Rolling Stone* noted: 'The tension inherent in this fable brings out a bracing maturity in Burton and gives the film its haunting gravity. As the son learns to talk to his father on the father's terms and still see him clearly, *Big Fish* takes on the transformative power of art.'

There was a real sense of inevitability and providence when Burton signed on to direct a new version of Roald Dahl's children's classic *Charlie and the Chocolate Factory*. Two massively creative talents with a similarly malevolent wit and subversive streak, Burton's and Dahl's worlds had collided once before when he produced *James and the Giant Peach*. Even more thrilling was the news that the film would reunite Burton with Johnny Depp for the first time since *Sleepy Hollow*. Their ongoing relationship has produced their finest work on both sides, although their pairing, inevitably, brings with it a degree of expectation that Burton finds disconcerting. 'Early on in your career you struggle to get things done but there's the amazing freedom that comes with lack of expectation', he says. 'It's harder to surprise people when they have certain expectations.'

And yet the combination has once again produced something not just surprising, but without compare. As Depp explains in his Foreword and Burton in the chapter on the film, to create their Willy Wonka they drew upon their childhood memories of children's TV hosts and the result is genuinely startling, weird and even a little creepy – but one that would have had Roald Dahl himself, had he lived, cackling. But while Burton's version of *Charlie and the Chocolate Factory* is an intensely faithful adaptation of Dahl's world, it's also quintessentially Burtonesque at the same time, a hippy-trippy riot of glorious colour, amazing design and delightful imagination. For fans of the book, and there are millions, it does everything you expect – but in ways you don't.

While *The Nightmare Before Christmas* wasn't a Pixar-sized hit on its initial release, in the years since it's become a perennial holiday favourite for many, and has spawned a sideline in merchandise and toys that shows no sign of diminishing. Burton had long looked for another project to draw on his love of stop-motion animation, in particular the movies of Ray Harryhausen, and with *Corpse Bride* he's created a fable that is timeless in tone and style. In a world dominated by computer-imagery, Burton keeps coming back to this painstakingly detailed medium, a resolutely hand-crafted art that, for him, contains real emotion. 'It's kind of an unspoken, subconscious thing which is why I like it,' he says, 'it's something you can't quite put words to, there's a certain magic and mystery, tactile. I know you can get that on computers and get *more* on computers in a certain way, but there's that handmade quality that gives it an emotional resonance, for me anyway. I don't know if it's because I have nostalgia for it, but I do really believe there is that in the medium.'

Inspired by a 19th century Eastern European poem, *Corpse Bride* tells of Victor, a shy, nervy groom who unwittingly finds himself hitched to the eponymous 'corpse bride' on the eve of his wedding to his fiancée Victoria, and winds up trapped in the Land of the Dead. Within this, there's much that is recognizable from Burton's oeuvre: the story thematically echoes *Beetlejuice* and *Sleepy Hollow*, Victor, voiced by Johnny Depp, is a typical Burton protagonist, while the inversion of the two worlds – the land of the living being 'deader' than that of the dead – is comfortingly familiar. It's also not without coincidence, too, that Victor looks just like the little boy from *Vincent* all grown up – meaning he looks a lot like Burton. 'That's not lost on me, he says. I definitely felt the same thing, and said as much to myself after the fact. Any project you try to make personal.'

Mark Salisbury

Childhood in Burbank – Cal Arts

*Tim Burton was born on 25 August 1958 in Burbank, California, the first
son of Bill and Jean Burton. His father worked for the Burbank Parks and
Recreation Department, while his mother ran a gift shop called Cats Plus
in which all the merchandise featured a feline motif. They had one other
child, Daniel, who is three years younger and works as an artist. The
Burtons' house was situated directly under the flight path of Burbank
Airport and Tim would often lie in the garden, gaze up at the planes flying
overhead and time the exhaust fumes floating down from them. Between
the ages of twelve and sixteen, he moved in with his grandmother, who
also lived in Burbank, and then later into a small apartment above a
garage which she owned, paying the rent by working in a restaurant after
school. Situated within the Los Angeles city limits, Burbank was then, as
it is now, an outpost of Hollywood. Warner Bros, Disney, Columbia and
NBC all have their studios there, but in every other way Burbank is an
archetypal working-class American surburb. It was an environment, however, from which Tim Burton felt alienated at an early age, one that he
would later portray in* Edward Scissorhands. *Indeed, it's easy to see the
young, introverted Tim Burton in Edward's stranger-in-a-strange-land,
removed from his hilltop castle home to a pastel-coloured version of suburbia. As a child, Burton was, by his own admission, moderately destructive. He would rip the heads off his toy soldiers and terrorize the kid next
door by convincing him that aliens had landed. He would seek refuge
from his surroundings in the movie theatre or sit in front of the television
watching horror movies.*

If you weren't from Burbank you'd think it was the movie capital of the
world with all the studios around there, but it was and still is very suburban. It's funny, the areas around Burbank have gotten less suburban, but
somehow Burbank still remains the same. I don't know how or why, but
it has this weird shield around it. It could be Anywhere USA.

As a child I was very introverted. I like to think I didn't feel like anybody different. I did what any kid likes to do: go to the movies, play,

draw. It's not unusual. What's more unusual is to keep wanting to do those things as you go on through life. I think I was the quiet one at school. I don't have a real perception of myself. I don't really remember. I kind of floated through things. I didn't consider them the best years of my life. I didn't cry at the prom. I didn't think it was going to be all downhill. I *had* friends. I never really fell out with people, but I didn't really retain friends. I get the feeling people just got this urge to want to leave me alone for some reason, I don't know why exactly. It was as if I was exuding some sort of aura that said 'Leave Me The Fuck Alone'. For a while I looked like I could have been on a casting call for *The Brady Bunch*: I had bell-bottom pants and a brown leisure suit. But punk music was good, that helped me, it was good for me emotionally. I didn't have a lot of friends, but there's enough weird movies out there so you can go a long time without friends and see something new every day that kind of speaks to you.

There were five or six movie theatres in Burbank, but systematically they got taken away. And so for a few years when I was a teenager, there weren't any. But there used to be ones where you could see these weird triple bills like *Scream Blackula Scream*, *Dr Jekyll And Sister Hyde* and *Destroy All Monsters*. Those were the good days of cinema, those great triple bills. And I would go to the cinema on my own, or with a couple of kids in the neighbourhood, whatever.

Recently I went back to Catalina Island. I hadn't been there since I was a kid. I used to go there a lot, and there is this really cool theatre there, The Avalon, and it was done out in these incredible art deco shells. I remember seeing *Jason and the Argonauts* there. I remember both the theatre and the movie, because they seemed to be as one, the design of the theatre, that movie, and the kind of mythology it evoked. It was incredible. That was one of the first movies I remember. It was sometime early, somewhere before I was fifteen.

There was also a period in time when they'd show movies on television on Saturday afternoons, movies like *The Brain that Wouldn't Die*, where the guy gets his arm ripped off and rubs his bloody stump along the wall before he dies, while a head on a plate starts laughing at him. They wouldn't show that on TV now.

I've always loved monsters and monster movies. I was never terrified of them, I just loved them from as early as I can remember. My parents said I was never scared, I'd just watch anything. And that kind of stuff has stuck with me. *King Kong*, *Frankenstein*, *Godzilla*, the *Creature from the Black Lagoon* – they're all pretty much the same, they just have different

Fighting Ray Harryhausen's skeletons in *Jason and the Argonauts*

rubber suits or make-up. But there was something about that identification. Every kid responds to some image, some fairy-tale image, and I felt
most monsters were basically misperceived, they usually had much more
heartfelt souls than the human characters around them.

Because I never read, my fairy tales were probably those monster
movies. To me they're fairly similar. I mean, fairy tales are extremely vio-
lent and extremely symbolic and disturbing, probably even more so than
Frankenstein and stuff like that, which are kind of mythic and perceived
as fairy-tale like. But fairy tales, like the Grimms' fairy tales, are probably
closer to movies like *The Brain that Wouldn't Die*, much rougher, harsher, full of bizarre symbolism. Growing up, I guess it was a reaction against
a very puritanical, bureaucratic, fifties nuclear family environment – me
resisting seeing things laid out, seeing things exactly as they were. That's
why I think I've always liked the idea of fairy tales or folk tales, because
they're symbolic of something else. There's a foundation to them, but
there's more besides, they're open to interpretation. I always liked that,
seeing things and just having your own idea about them. So I think I
didn't like fairy tales *specifically*. I liked the *idea* of them more.

For a while I wanted to be the actor who played *Godzilla*. I enjoyed

3

those movies and the idea of venting anger on such a grand scale. Because I was quiet, because I was not demonstrative in any way, those films were my form of release. I think I was pretty much against society from the very beginning. I don't know any children, I don't have any children and I don't like the phrase 'remaining like a child', because I think it's kind of retarded. But at what point do you form ideas and at what point are you shaped? I think these impulses to destroy society were formed very early.

I went to see almost any monster movie, but it was the films of Vincent Price that spoke to me specifically for some reason. Growing up in suburbia, in an atmosphere that was perceived as nice and normal (but which I had other feelings about), those movies were a way to certain feelings, and I related them to the place I was growing up in. I think that's why I responded so much to Edgar Allan Poe. I remember when I was younger, I had these two windows in my room, nice windows that looked out on to the lawn, and for some reason my parents walled them up and gave me this little slit window that I had to climb up on a desk to see out of. To this day I've never asked them why; I should ask them. So I likened it to that Poe story where the person was walled in and buried alive. Those were my forms of

Godzilla venting his anger

4

Vincent Price

connection to the world around me. It's a mysterious place, Burbank.

Vincent Price was somebody I could identify with. When you're younger things look bigger, you find your own mythology, you find what psychologically connects to you. And those movies, just the poetry of them, and this larger-than-life character who goes through a lot of torment – mostly imagined – just spoke to me in the way Gary Cooper or John Wayne might have to somebody else.

Together with a group of friends I would make Super 8 movies. There was one we made called *The Island of Doctor Agor*. We made a wolfman movie, and a mad doctor movie, and a little stop-motion film using model cavemen. It was really bad and it shows you how little you know about animation at the beginning. These cavemen had removable legs – one was in the standing position, and the other was in a walking one – and we just changed the legs. It's the jerkiest animation you'll ever see. I used to love all those Ray Harryhausen movies – *Jason and the Argonauts*, *The Seventh Voyage of Sinbad* – they were incredible, I loved stop-motion animation as a kid. And as you get older, you realize that there's an artistry there too, and that's what you're responding to.

5

I got through school, but I wasn't interested in the curriculum. I'm of that unfortunate generation that grew up watching television rather than reading. I didn't like to read. I still don't. So what better way to get a good grade than to make a little movie? I remember one time we had to read a book and do a twenty-page book report, but I decided to do a movie called *Houdini* instead. I shot myself on black and white Super 8, speeded up. It had me escaping from the railroad tracks and then being dumped in a pool and escaping again – all these stupid Houdini tricks. It was really fun to do. I didn't read any book, it was just me jumping around in my backyard. It was an easy way to get an A, and I certainly got a higher grade than if I had attempted to talk my way through a written report. That was in early junior high. I must have been about thirteen. And then I did one on psychology for high school. I just took a lot of pictures of books and played them to Alice Cooper's 'Welcome To My Nightmare'; deeply psychological. And I shot a bean bag chair in stop-motion attacking me in my sleep. That was the ending, I think.

I never actually thought about making films for a living. Maybe somewhere deep inside, but I never consciously said I wanted to be a filmmaker. I liked doing it. It helped me get through school. Before Universal Studios became what it is now, they used to have a tour which was very low key and I remember being young and going to see the streets where they shot *Dracula* and *Frankenstein*. It was a powerful feeling, and I think that enhanced the romantic aspects of it. I never consciously thought of making films; it's something I lucked into after a couple of years at Disney. Maybe I was just protecting myself, because I don't like to make proclamations. I prefer to be a bit more stream-of-consciousness about things.

While he showed no particular aptitude for schooling, Burton's artistic potential soon began to reveal itself. In the ninth grade he won ten dollars and first prize in a community competition to design an anti-litter poster which adorned the side of garbage trucks in Burbank for two months. At Christmas and Hallowe'en he would earn extra money by painting and decorating Burbank residents' windows with either snowscapes or jack-o'-lanterns, spiders and skeletons, depending on the season.

In some ways I'm all over the place. I can get hyper and kind of unfocused about things. But there are things that help focus you, and make you feel good. If I'm doing a drawing I can become focused, and, in a funny way, it's a calming experience. And that's something I've never forgotten. I like to draw very much, and as a kid that's all you do in class all day. It's great. If you go to a kindergarten class all the children draw the same, no one's better than another. But something happens when you get older. Society beats things out of you. I remember going through art school, and you've got to take life drawing, and it was a real struggle. Instead of encouraging you to express yourself and draw like you did when you were a child, they start going by the rules of society. They say, 'No. No. You *can't* draw like this. You have to draw like *this*.' And I remember one day I was so frustrated – because I love drawing, but actually I'm not that good at it. But one day something clicked in my brain. I was sitting sketching and I thought, 'Fuck it, I don't care if I can draw or not. I like doing it.' And I swear to God, from one second to the next I had a freedom which I hadn't had before. From that point on, I didn't care if I couldn't make the human form look like the human form. I didn't care if people liked it. There was this almost like drug-induced sense of freedom. And I fight that every day, someone saying, 'You can't do that. This doesn't make any sense.' Every day it's a struggle. It's just a question of trying to maintain a certain amount of freedom.

In 1976, when Burton was eighteen, he won a scholarship to attend the California Institute of the Arts (Cal Arts), a college in Valencia, California founded by Walt Disney, with a programme that had been set up the previous year by the Disney Studio as a training school for prospective animators.

In high school I had a teacher who was encouraging, and I got a scholarship to Cal Arts. At Cal Arts we would make Super 8 movies: we made a Mexican monster movie and a surf movie, just for fun. But animation – I thought that might be a way to make a living. Disney basically had had the same animators since *Snow White* and they had taken a very leisurely approach to training new people. I joined the second year of the Disney-funded programme; they were trying to teach all these eager young new recruits to be animators. It was like being in the Army; I've never been in the Army, but the Disney programme is probably about as close as I'll ever get. You're taught by Disney people, you're taught the Disney philosophy. It was kind of a funny atmosphere, but it was the first time I had been with a group of people with similar interests. They were similar outcast types, people who were ridiculed for their liking of *Star Trek* or whatever.

You had access to Disney propaganda material. So, if you wanted to see the way Snow White was drawn, you could see the lines under the dress. You were taught by Disney artists, animators, layout people; you were taught the Disney way. At the time there wasn't the diversity in animation that exists now, so Disney, even as low as it was, was a very romantic ideal, and I would say 90 per cent of the class had aspirations to work there.

At the end of the year, everybody would do a little piece of animation and the Disney review board would come out to view them. It was like a draft. They would review all the films, and they would take people to work at the studio from any class, freshman, on up to the final year, with special consideration for those at the end. But they didn't care. If somebody showed particular promise, then they would get picked. So there was always a lot of competition and speculation about who was going to get picked. It was very intense, and there were always a few surprises each year. I was there three years. I don't know if I would have gone there a fourth, because during the last year I spent almost every day in the financial aid office, because they gave me a scholarship and then they took it away; it was an expensive school, and I could only afford it with that scholarship. As the years went on, the competition, the films, would get more elaborate, there was sound, music, even though they were basically pencil tests. The last one I did was called *Stalk of the Celery Monster*. It was stupid, but I got picked. It was a lean year, and I was lucky, actually, because they really wanted people.

Disney and *Vincent*

Burton joined Disney in 1979 and went to work as an animator on the studio's The Fox and the Hound.

Disney and I were a bad mix. For a year I was probably more depressed than I have ever been in my life. I worked for a great animator, Glenn Kean. He was nice, he was good to me, he's a really strong animator and he helped me. But he also kind of tortured me because I got all the cute fox scenes to draw, and I couldn't draw all those four-legged Disney foxes. I just couldn't do it. I couldn't even fake the Disney style. Mine looked like road kills. So luckily I got a lot of far-away shots to do. But it was not good; it was like Chinese water torture. Perhaps it was just the film I was working on. Imagine drawing a cute fox with Sandy Duncan's voice for three years. It's not something that you can relate to very much. I didn't

The Fox and the Hound

have the patience for it, I couldn't do it – which was probably a good thing.

But what's odd about Disney is that they want you to be an artist, but at the same time they want you to be a zombie factory worker and have no personality. It takes a very special person to make those two sides of your brain coexist. So I was very emotionally agitated at that time and couldn't really function very well. I learned how to sleep sitting up with a pencil in my hand. It was so bad. For a while I would sleep a good eight to ten hours a night, and then I would go to work and sleep a good two hours in the morning, and then two hours in the afternoon, sitting up straight, so if anybody walked in I had my pencil at the ready.

I was very strange back then. I could see I had problems. I was always perceived as weird. I would sit in a closet a lot of the time and not come out, or I would sit up on top of my desk, or under my desk, or do weird things like get my wisdom teeth out and bleed all over the hallways. But I've gotten over that. I don't sit in a closet any more. I was kept at arm's length, but at the same time they let me be. I guess I did enough work not to get fired. I just had to do it fast, and because I couldn't draw it anyway, it didn't matter how much time I spent on it. It was probably better if I didn't spend too much time on it. I was weird at that stage. I was having emotional problems. I didn't know who I was.

But because I did these other kinds of drawings, people would see them and I got to do other things. The company was in a kind of screwy stage at that time. They were making things like *Herbie Goes to Monte Carlo*; nobody knew what was going on there. It was like a hermetically sealed world, and I got to move around a little bit in this weird sort of 'non-structure' structure. I got to try different things, to do concepts for live-action and animated projects.

There used to be this guy at Disney in the early days who was paid to come up with ideas and just do drawings. The animators liked his stuff, and he would draw whatever he wanted, like a hand with an eyeball on it. And I worked myself into that kind of position, as a sort of conceptual artist, which was really great. Then it started to turn fun again because I got to do whatever I liked, just sniff magic markers all day.

I was hired as a conceptual artist on *The Black Cauldron*, which was great because for several months I just got to sit in a room and draw any creature I wanted to: witches, furniture, just things. But then, as the film started to get closer to being a reality, they put me with this guy, Andreas Deja, who's a good strong animator in the old, character-driven style, a style completely different from mine. They said to me, 'Tim, we like your

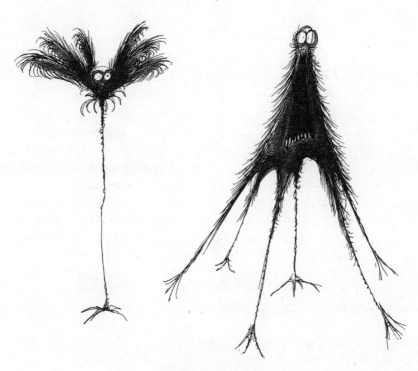

The Black Cauldron

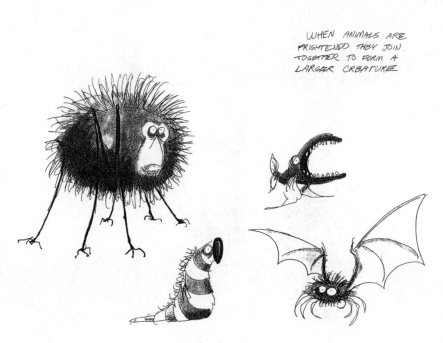

The elements ...

ideas, but Andreas is more what we want.' I guess they wanted us to mate and have offspring of some kind. He would sit on one side of the room and I would sit on the other. It was like a friendly version of *The Odd Couple*.

So he ended up doing his thing and I did mine. I didn't see the movie, but they didn't use one single concept of mine. I basically exhausted all of my creative ideas for about ten years during that period. And when none of it was used, it was kind of funny. I felt like a trapped princess. I had a great life, in a way. I was able to draw anything I wanted, but it was like working in this completely sealed environment in which you would never see the light of day. But there was always something that made it worthwhile, like doing the *Vincent* short and then the *Frankenweenie* one. Those things were unheard of. So I was lucky enough that everything led to a little higher level.

I did some conceptual work over ten years ago on that Barry Levinson movie *Toys*. I don't think he even knows that I worked on it, but the guy at Disney asked me to do some conceptual stuff. There were still the remnants from the old days at Disney, there were still people who would say, 'Let's do another *Fantasia*', guys from the old school where they didn't

... joined together

have scripts, just a couple of zany gag men in a room who'd say, 'Let's get Louie Prima in here and work up a little number.' Those guys were still around. It was cool.

I remember when they were doing that movie *Tron*. I was just a lowly in-betweener at the time, and there were all these computer guys pitching stuff that only now they are able to do, and not even all of it. It seemed like a company in puberty really, that awkward stage where you're still stuck in the past. I remember when I first got to Disney they were still talking about Walt and it was like this weird mantra: 'Walt would have done this.' And it was like, 'How do you know?' Then, it seemed to me, they realized they needed to come into the twenty-first century but they didn't quite know how to do that. The movies that they made then were awkward. My impression was of a company being run by people who were the third or fourth on the tier – when the talented people left, retired or died they were left in charge.

While working as a conceptual artist, Burton found himself two allies in the shape of Disney executive, Julie Hickson, and Head of Creative

Trick or Treat

Trick or Treat

Development, Tom Wilhite, who had begun to see in his drawings a
rather unique talent that while not typically Disney was one they felt
deserved to be nurtured. And so in 1982 Wilhite gave Burton $60,000 to

produce Vincent, *a stop-motion animated short based on a poem Burton had written in verse in the style of his favourite children's author Dr Seuss.*

I had been working there about a year to a year and a half, maybe two years – I'm not very good with time. But by that stage I had worked on *The Black Cauldron*, I had worked on a thing called *Trick or Treat* for which I don't think there was even a script, just a concept: a haunted house, kids, Hallowe'en. I had written this *Vincent* story, and I was bored, I was about ready to walk. I couldn't take it any more. But there were a few people there who were very supportive of me, and they gave me a little money to do *Vincent* under the guise of it being a stop-motion test. It was very very nice of them to do that, and that kept me going for a while.

I had written *Vincent* originally as a children's book and was going to do it that way first. But then I got the opportunity to make it as a stop-motion film. I wanted to do that kind of animation because I felt there was a gravity to those three-dimensional figures that was more real for that story. That was really important to me, I wanted it to feel more real.

Together with fellow Disney animator Rick Heinrichs, stop-motion animator Steven Chiodo and cameraman Victor Abdalov, Burton toiled away for two months and came up with the five-minute film. Shot in stark black and white in the style of the German expressionist movies of the 1920s, Vincent *relates the story of seven-year-old Vincent Malloy, a somewhat disturbed child who fantasizes that he is Vincent Price. Flitting between the reality of his banal suburban existence and his fantasy world, Vincent imagines himself in a series of situations inspired by the Vincent Price/Edgar Allan Poe films that had had such an affect on Burton as a child, including experimenting on his dog – a theme that would subsequently reappear in Burton's next project* Frankenweenie – *and welcoming his aunt to his home while simultaneously conjuring up the image of her dipped in hot wax. The film ends with Vincent lying on the ground in the dark quoting Poe's 'The Raven'.*

Vincent Price, Edgar Allan Poe, those monster movies, those *spoke* to me. You see somebody going through that anguish and that torture – things you identify with – and it acts as a kind of therapy, a release. You make a connection with it. That's what the *Vincent* thing really was for me. The

'The Raven'

film just goes in and out of Vincent's own reality. He identifies and believes that he's Vincent Price, and you see the world through his eyes. It clicks in and out of reality so to speak, and it ends with a quote from 'The Raven'. The people at Disney thought he died, but he's just lying there. Who's to say whether he's really dead or beautiful in his own little dream world? They wanted it to have more of an upbeat ending, but I never saw it as being downbeat in any way. It's funny, I think it's more uplifting if things are left to your imagination. I always saw those tacked-on happy endings as psychotic in a way. They wanted me to have the light click on and have his dad come in and go, 'Let's go to a football game or a baseball game.' That was my first encounter with the happy ending syndrome.

I never directly linked the shots in *Vincent* to any specific films. There are no real shots from those Poe movies per se. It's just more a matter of growing up and loving those movies than it is direct linkage in terms of shots. There's a *House of Wax* thing, there's some burying alive, some experiments, but I was more concerned with trying to get the stop-motion to work.

17

House of Wax

Anyone who has seen Vincent *can be in no doubt that the title character, a pasty-faced youth with black, straggly hair, bears a striking resemblance to his creator.*

Well, I never consciously go, 'I'm going to do a drawing that looks like me', but yeah, it's certainly based on feelings that I had, for sure. But anything, even things that are perceived as commercial, like *Batman*, anything that people would find no personal, redeeming qualities in, for me, I've got to be in it to some degree. Even if it's just a feeling. You invest so much in it, there has to be something you identify strongly with. And *Vincent* is certainly more pointedly specific to the way I felt. People would say, 'That's you Tim', but what am I supposed to say? I don't like to think about that. I like to think about it in terms of a concept. I'm very wary of analysing it too intellectually. I find it gets in the way of the more spontaneous, which I prefer to be if I can. If I start to think too much about it, it's not good. But *Vincent*'s one that I feel really good about letting speak for itself, because it's just what it is. It's very hard in

Hollywood because people like things literal. They don't like it when you leave things open for interpretation, but I like that very much.

The film's expressionistic set design and photography seems reminiscent of Robert Wiene's The Cabinet of Dr Caligari.

I certainly saw pictures of it, in any monster book there were pictures of it. But I didn't see it until fairly recently. I think it probably has more to do with being inspired by Dr Seuss. It just happens to be shot in black and white, and there's a Vincent Price/Gothic kind of thing that makes it feel that way. I grew up loving Dr Seuss. The rhythm of his stuff spoke to me very clearly. Dr Seuss's books were perfect: right number of words, the right rhythm, great subversive stories. He was incredible, he was the greatest, definitely. He probably saved a bunch of kids who nobody will ever know about.

Vincent

SO THEN HE AND HIS
HORRIBLE ZOMBIE DOG,
COULD GO SEARCHING FOR
VICTIMS IN THE DENSE
LONDON FOG.

P-2665A R-1

WHERE HE'D BE LEFT TO REFLECT
ON THE HORRORS HE'S INVENTED,

Vincent

20

Vincent

21

Vincent

22

Vincent

23

Vincent *was narrated by Burton's childhood idol Vincent Price and marked the beginning of a friendship between the director and the actor that lasted until Price's death in 1993.*

We sent Vincent Price the storyboards and asked him to do the narration, and he was incredible. It was probably one of the most shaping experiences of my life. Who knows what it's going to be like? You grow up having a feeling about someone, then you meet them, and what if the guy goes, 'Get the the fuck out of here. Get away from me, kid.' But he was so wonderful, and so interesting as a person in what he liked in terms of art and stuff. He was very supportive. I always had the feeling he understood exactly what the film was about, even more than I did; he understood that it wasn't just a simple homage, like 'Gee Mr Price, I'm your biggest fan.' He understood the psychology of it, and that amazed me and made me feel very good, made me feel that someone saw me for what I was, and accepted me on that level.

It's a scary proposition meeting somebody who helped you through childhood, who had that affect on you, especially when you're sending them something that's showing that impact in a kind of cheesy, children's book kind of way. But he was so great. Those kinds of things are very important to keep you going, emotionally, especially when you run into so many shady characters. Some people are just nice, but he seemed to truly get it. Again, there's a reason why you respond to certain people on the screen – there's some sort of light there, they project something beyond even what their character is.

Vincent *was theatrically released for two weeks in one Los Angeles cinema with the teen drama* Tex, *starring Matt Dillon. But before it was consigned to the Disney vaults, it garnered several critical accolades when it played at festivals in London, Chicago and Seattle, winning two awards at Chicago and the Critics' Prize at the Annecy Film Festival in France.*

Disney were pleased with *Vincent*, but they didn't know what they were going to do with it. It's like, 'Gee, what shall we worry about today, this five-minute animated short film or our $30 million dollar movie?' I felt very happy to have made it. It's cathartic to make anything, to get it done, so that was good, and it got a good response from people who saw it. It was a little odd, though, because Disney seemed to be pleased with it, but at the same time kind of ashamed. I just think they didn't know what to do with it. There's not really a market for a five-minute animated film, and the company was in a strange state of flux, so it didn't rate really high on their priority scale. Plus, I didn't even know whether I was an employee then.

Hansel and Gretel, Frankenweenie and Aladdin's Lamp

Still employed at Disney, Burton next directed a live-action, all-Oriental version of the Grimms' fairy tale Hansel and Gretel *which was produced for $116,000 for the studio's then embryonic cable network The Disney Channel. Written by its executive producer, Julie Hickson, the show lacks* Vincent's *emotional depth, but is a perfect illustration of Burton's outré imagination, deviating from the original Grimms' tale in a variety of uniquely Burtonesque ways, climaxing with a kung-fu fight between Hansel and Gretel and the wicked witch, who is played by a man.*

The Disney Channel had just started and they had a fairy-tale series, and I had this idea of doing *Hansel and Gretel* using only Japanese people and giving it a little bit of a twist. I had a bunch of drawings and they let me do it. Everything, especially early on, was based on drawings. I had a room filled with drawings, and I think that was the thing that made them feel comfortable about me, to some degree. Even though, visually, the drawings aren't easy to imagine in three dimensions, or in any other form than those drawings, I think it made them feel I wasn't completely insane, and that I could actually do something. And again, as a company, they were just kind of floundering around a little bit at that point. Up until very recently, I could never imagine a scenario where I would get to do these things in a studio situation. It was unheard of. I mean now they have those new programmes where studios foot the bill, or they'll invest in film schools. Disney, I think, now tests potential directors by giving them a scene and having them shoot it. But at that time there was no real precedent for what I was doing, and so I was always very aware that the situation I was in was fairly unique. So even when I felt bad, I still felt pretty good.

It follows the fairy tale fairly closely except that it's done with Japanese people. I have always been drawn to the Japanese sense of design. Growing up with *Godzilla* movies, their sense of design and colour really appealed to me, and it has a slight martial arts twist. I liked those martial arts movies, and if you like something, then you like to see it. That was always my attitude. I've never been able to predict or think what an audience would like to see. I've always felt: how can anybody else want to see it if I don't want to? And if I want to see it, and nobody else wants to, then at least I get to see it. So, there's one person who'll enjoy it.

Hansel and Gretel *marked the first time that Burton had worked with actors, albeit a cast of total non-professionals.*

It was pretty amateurish, but that was more to do with me than with them. But I enjoyed doing it, and I learned a lot from it. It's funny, if you've never made a movie with actual people, you think you can do it, you don't see any reason why you can't. It looks very easy. But there is something about it that's abstract. So it was a good learning experience for me. Being an animator, early in my life I rarely spoke to people. I was not a good communicator. I never spoke much – even now – but it used to be worse. I would never finish my sentences; my mind would kind of race

Hansel and Gretel

The witch's house

ahead. It was not like we were doing a Shakespeare play where there was a foundation to it. It was hard to describe to people, and I wasn't very good at it. I think I've got a little better each time I've done it. Obviously, it's a medium where you have to communicate with a large number of people, so that was really the first time I experienced that side of it. I had done it with those Super 8 movies, but this was different, and I think it helped me with the next thing. When I did *Frankenweenie*, I had already learned a lot of stuff from *Hansel and Gretel* in terms of how to deal with people.

Despite its low budget, Burton employed a series of ambitious special effects, including stop-motion animation courtesy of his Vincent collaborators Heinrichs and Chiodo, as well as a number of on-set visual gags. And by changing Hansel's and Gretel's father's profession from a woodcutter to a toymaker, Burton indulged in his passion for toys and gadgetry – a trait present in almost all his subsequent work – filling the screen with Japanese 'Transformer' toys.

Gingerbread
Man

'A weird little puppet who forces Hansel to eat him'

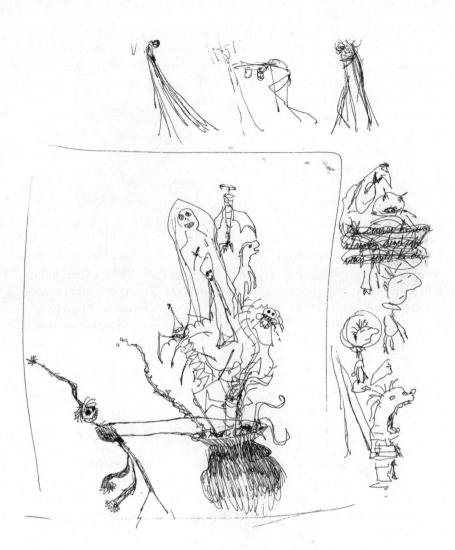

Hansel and Gretel

We had front projection, stop-motion, every FX known to man, but extremely, extremely, extremely crude. It was a great way to try things out. I have always been interested in the combination of live-action and stop-motion animation, stemming from the Harryhausen movies I saw as a kid. This was a very 'designed' kind of thing. It's weirdly ambitious on the one hand, and on the other it's really cheesy and cheap. I don't know where that thing with the toys comes from, however, except that I've always liked toys. I don't recall having an extreme toy fixation or toy fetish. I always saw them as an extension of my imagination – at least that's the way I used them, as a way to explore different ideas. There was a little duck toy that turns into a robot and a gingerbread man. He was a weird little puppet who forces Hansel to eat him.

But there really was no money to make it. I think it showed one night, Hallowe'en, at 10.30 p.m., which for The Disney Channel is like the 4.30 a.m. slot. So, that one didn't go over too big. But there are little moments in it that I like. It was like one of those scary children's shows I grew up watching.

I honestly don't ever recall thinking that I wanted to be a director after I'd made *Hansel and Gretel*. The one thing I did know – and I think I knew this early on, right after the animation experience – was that, whatever I do, it's just got to be more *me*. I can't just pull it together, I'm not proficient enough as an illustrator to fake it. So I didn't say, 'Well, I want to be a director', because that wasn't where my head was. It was more that I was just doing this work, and enjoying it, and I thought the main thing was to create images. It's still true, actually. I think it has less to do with 'I am now a director or a movie maker', and more to do with the joy of creating. And this can be in many forms: images, feelings, *things*, just creating anything.

After that I just kept on developing things, and at that point I was developing *The Nightmare Before Christmas* concept. Often when I was developing something it wasn't a case of 'Now I'm going to develop this', but there would be drawings and the seed of a thought. Things would come out more from a series of sketches. It would be a case of 'This character's kind of interesting', and then discovering what it meant, and uncovering the psychology behind it. Things came about a bit more organically in this period of time. It was not like 'Okay, now I'm doing this, and then I'm going to develop that'; it was much more like a weirdly organic process. It wasn't clean-cut.

Burton's third directorial outing was Frankenweenie, *a stunning twenty-five-minute black and white reworking of James Whale's 1931 version of* Frankenstein *and its 1935 sequel,* The Bride of Frankenstein. *Written by Lenny Ripp from Burton's story,* Frankenweenie *was produced by his champion at Disney, Julie Hickson, and financed by the studio to the tune of almost $1 million. Burton was twenty-five at the time.*

Frankenweenie came out of some drawings and some feelings, and then thinking that maybe this could be good, maybe we could do it as a featurette. I think it was originally intended to go out with *Pinocchio* on its re-release. That whole period of time was very organic. From my thinking of the ideas, to the decision to finance them, none of it could have been planned. When they said yes, I was amazed. I don't think Tom Wilhite was even the head of the department that made the decision to make *Frankenweenie*, it was somebody else. It was odd, none of it made any sense. To this day I'm really bad if people ask, 'How did you become this?' I really have no answer. There's no point A to point B kind of history to it. There's no kind of training that I could look at. It was a completely surreal fluke, the whole thing.

Frankenweenie, *which Burton feels could have been stretched out to feature length if he had been given a few extra days' shooting, updates Mary Shelley's classic story to modern-day suburbia, and follows the adventures of ten-year-old Victor Frankenstein (Barrett Oliver) as he reanimates his pet dog, a bull terrier named Sparky who has been run down and killed in a car accident, in his parents' attic. The film opens with Victor showing his parents a Super 8 movie he's made entitled* Monsters From Long Ago, *featuring Sparky, dressed up as a prehistoric monster and being attacked by a creature straight out of a Godzilla movie. Later, after Sparky has been brought back to life, he is covered in stitching, with a bolt on either side of his neck, a homage to Jack Pierce's make-up for Boris Karloff as the Creature in Whale's* Frankenstein *films.*

You have a dog that you love, and the idea of keeping it alive was the impulse for the film. Again, growing up watching those horror movies, for some reason I was always able to make direct links, emotionally, between that whole Gothic/*Frankenstein*/Edgar Allan Poe thing and growing up in suburbia. *Frankenweenie* was just another outgrowth of that.

But it's very, very important to me, even though there are feelings from *Frankenstein*, that I do not make direct linkage to it. In anything I have ever done, people have always said, 'That's like this sequence in that movie', and it may well be true. But something that's always been very important to me is not to make a direct linkage. If I was to sit down with somebody, and we were to look at a scene from *Frankenstein* and say 'Let's do that', I wouldn't do it, even if it's a homage or an inspired-by kind of thing. In fact, if I ever use a direct link to something, I try to make sure in my own mind that it's not a case of 'Let's copy that'. Instead it's,

Frankenweenie: Victor

33

Frankenweenie: Sparky

'Why do I like that, what's the emotional context in this new format?' That's why I always try to gauge if people get me and are on a similar wavelength. The writer Lenny Ripp was that way. He got it. He didn't want to sit there and go over *Frankenstein*; he knew it well enough. It's more like it's being filtered through some sort of remembrance.

For *Frankenweenie*, I didn't look at anything. I remember thinking the skies in *Frankenstein* were really cool because they were painted. But I didn't go and look at the film because I didn't want to say, 'Do it like that.' I wanted to try to describe it the way I remembered. So I would

Sparky, covered in stitching

describe something, and say, 'It was like a painted backdrop, but the clouds were more pronounced. It was a much more intense, wild sky.' Then when I finally looked at *Frankenstein* I saw that the sky was not quite the way I had described it. That was my impression, but I would still rather go with that. I feel when somebody is just borrowing something, they don't have any feeling for it themselves.

Much like Whale's Frankenstein *(and indeed like* Edward Scissorhands)*,*

35

Sparky and his bride

Frankenweenie *climaxes with the inevitable showdown between the mob – or in this case, Victor's frightened and angry neighbours – and 'the monster' – Sparky – at a miniature golf course which resembles the setting from Whale's movie. It then culminates in Sparky finding true love in the shape of a poodle whose hairdo resembles that of Elsa Lanchester in* The Bride of Frankenstein. *These references, according to Burton, were again less of a direct link to Whale's films, than a reaction to what he saw around him in Burbank.*

What was great was that you almost didn't even have to think about it, because growing up in suburbia there were these miniature golf courses with windmills which were just like the one in *Frankenstein*. These images just happened to coincide, because that was your life. There were poodles that always reminded you of the bride of Frankenstein with the big hair. All those things were just *there*. That's why it felt so right or easy for me to do – those images were already there in Burbank.

Frankenweenie *marked the first time Burton had worked with a professional cast – which included Shelley Duvall and Daniel Stern as Victor's*

The Bride of Frankenstein

parents, and director Paul Bartel as his teacher – and yet he managed to elicit a number of tender, sympathic performances, from Barrett Oliver, as Victor, in particular.

They were all great. I've been very lucky in that way with actors. I've rarely had experiences where you meet people and it's like the clichéd, horrible, bite-your-head-off kind of thing. It's really shaped my attitude about working with people, actors especially. They need to feel the same about me as I feel about them. If they don't like me, if they're not into me, then I don't want to work with them. All of these people, they knew I had never done anything before, but they liked the idea. They felt that I cared – it's just a little thing, but it's important to me, because there are lots of great actors and you have to connect with them and they need to connect with you. That whole thing of seeking attention, I have never been into that. It's so hard to make something that everybody should be trying to work in the same spirit. And those people were great; everybody was for the project. I think what they did was make me feel comfortable, and I started to learn that you have to communicate with people.

Frankenweenie: Daniel Stern, Shelley Duvall, Barrett Oliver, and Sparky

Frankenweenie *shares with* Vincent *a strong emotive core, a result of their profoundly personal origins. Yet Burton, much like he would later do with* Edward Scissorhands *and* The Nightmare Before Christmas, *passed on the task of writing the screenplay to someone else.*

I never considered myself a writer, even though I do write things. I wrote *Vincent.* Some time I may try it more. But I feel whether or not you write it, you have to feel like you wrote it. I mean, everything I do, I feel like it's me. I guess it was easier and more fun and I could, hopefully, see it a little more clearly by having somebody else write it. I've always felt as long as they get me and get what it is that I feel, then they can bring something to it themselves. Then it's better. It opens it up a little bit more.

Originally intended to be shown with Pinocchio *on its re-release in 1984,* Frankenweenie *was shelved by Disney when it received a PG rating.*

Perception is the one thing that I can't think about, because if I do, it drives me crazy. I can't find logic in how things happen. For instance, it freaked everybody out that *Frankenweenie* got a PG rating, and you can't

38

release a PG film with a G-rated animated film. I was a little shocked, because I don't see what's PG about the film: there's no bad language, there's only one bit of violence, and the violence happens off-camera. So I said to the MPAA, 'What do I need to do to get a G rating?' and they basically said, 'There's nothing you can cut, it's just the tone.' I think it was the fact that it was in black and white that freaked them out. There's nothing bad in the movie. There was a test screening where they showed *Pinocchio* and then *Frankenweenie*. If you ask any child, there are some very intense, scary things in *Pinocchio*. Our perception after not seeing it for a long period of time is that it's a children's classic. It's the same way people feel about fairy tales. When you hear the words 'fairy tale', the first thing that comes to mind is a cute children's story, which is not the way it is. It's the same with *Pinocchio*. It is pretty soft, but there are some intense moments. I remember getting freaked out when I was a kid; I remember kids screaming. And in this test screening kids started crying at certain parts. For kids, it's more horrific than anything in *Frankenweenie*, but because it wasn't a tried and true children's classic with the Good Housekeeping seal of approval, everybody got all freaked out and said, 'We can't release this.'

It was right at the time when the company was changing, when the people who are there now came in. So it met with the same response as *Vincent* in a way, which was 'Oh, this is great, but we have no plans to release it. *Ever.*' I remember being very frustrated because the old regime was out, the new one was in, and again, a thirty-minute short is not a high priority for people who are just coming into a studio and trying to make something of it.

By that point I was really tired of Disney. I felt like 'Okay, this has been really, really great, I'm very, very lucky. Nobody's had the opportunities that I've had. I feel great that I've been able to do this.' But it was a case of doing a bunch of stuff that nobody would ever see. It was kind of weird.

Frankenweenie *did receive a small release in the United Kingdom on a double bill with Touchstone Pictures'* Baby: Secret of the Lost Legend, *and was finally made available on video in the US by Disney prior to the release of* Batman Returns *in 1992. Impressed by his visual style and his dealings with actors, Shelley Duvall invited Burton to direct an episode of Showtime's* Faerie Tale Theatre *series that she hosted and executive-produced. Burton's forty-seven-minute episode,* Aladdin and his Wonderful Lamp, *was his first experience of working with video tape and again featured model and effects work from Rick Heinrichs and Steve Chiodio.*

Right after *Frankenweenie*, Shelley Duvall asked me to do one of the episodes for her *Faerie Tale Theatre*, which was really nice because they basically hired name directors like Francis Coppola and I felt honoured. It was interesting, but it was another case of me being in over my head because it was a tape show with three cameras. Again, some of it is okay and some of it is not. Some of it looks like a bad Las Vegas show. And that's just because when I'm bad, I'm *really* bad. I can't rise above it. I want to keep growing. Everybody wants to stretch. But if I'm not there, if I don't feel right, then I can't fake it too well.

But Shelley created a great atmosphere for that show. She got people there doing it for no money. She was good that way. It was hard work: one week, three cameras; it was intense, and what I realized was that I'm not a very good director-for-hire. I learned that early on. That's why I'm very firm and say, 'Look guys, if you're going to let me do this, then let me do this and I'll try to do the best I can. But it's not going to help to treat me like you might treat a director-for-hire because, you know what, I'll do a really lousy job, and we don't want that.' So I've always tried to protect myself in that sense, and I'm actually in awe of those old directors that could do a Western and then a thriller. It's very admirable, and I'm fascinated by it. I just know I'm not that type.

Aladdin's cast featured James Earl Jones (who provided the voice of Darth Vadar in the Star Wars *trilogy) in two roles, including that of the genie of the lamp, and Leonard Nimoy (*Star Trek's *Mr Spock) as the villainous Moroccan magician intent on possessing the lamp.*

It's surreal to work with those people who you've watched as you grow up, especially when you first get into it. But my first experience with Vincent Price on *Vincent*, that was the ultimate. My mind had been blown once before, so now these were kind of great little explosions. Again, I got a chance to see great actors at work; every actor has a different way of working and so I was observant and learnt from that.

While Aladdin *is reminiscent of* The Cabinet of Dr Caligari *with its skewed set design, it features a number of other images that have, in one form or another, found their way into Burton's subsequent work – bats, skeletons, skulls, spiders and topiaries.*

Once that stuff is inside you, you don't know how long it's going to take to exorcize it. I remember thinking, 'You know what, I've done this. I don't feel this inside me any more. I don't need to see another skeleton.' But then there are times where it's, 'You know what, I just love those skeletons. I thought I was through with them, but I just love them.'

You never know when something is going to be exorcized out of you; those movies are a part of you, part of your make up. That imagery becomes a part of you; it's not even something you think about too much. I try not to think, 'Have I done this before?', because I actually find it's interesting for me to look back and see connections. I haven't really done too much of that, but I do it a little bit. After I did three movies I started to see thematic kinds of things. The process I pretty much go through is: 'Oh, that must mean something to me, deeply.' I find you learn more about yourself if you don't intellectualize right away, if you try to go more intuitively, and then you look back and see what themes and images keep coming up. Then I start to get psychologically interested in discovering what it means, where it's founded. And I find that I learn more about myself. I don't trust my intellect as much, because it's kind of schizy; I feel more grounded going with a feeling.

Pee-Wee's Big Adventure

Having finally left Disney, and with Frankenweenie *receiving good word of mouth within industry circles, it was only a matter of time before Burton secured a feature to direct. What nobody, least of all Burton himself, could have predicted, however, was that the project would be so in tune with his artistic and creative sensibilities. Pee-Wee Herman, aka comedian Paul Reubens, a weirdly asexual, grey-suited personality with a red bow-tie, rouged cheeks and a beloved bicycle, had achieved cult status with his children's TV show* Pee-Wee's Playhouse. *Warner Bros were looking to turn Pee-Wee from TV star to film sensation, and in Burton, who was only 26 at the time, they found the perfect man to do it.*

I was just waiting around, and there was this woman at Warner Bros, Bonnie Lee, she was sort of a friend, and she brought me to the attention of the people over there, and I got the *Pee-Wee* movie fairly easily. That was the easiest job I have ever got, I mean, any job, even a restaurant job, and any movie before or since. Bonnie showed *Frankenweenie* to the Warner Bros people. They showed it to Paul Reubens and the producers of the movie, and it was like, 'Do you want to do this movie?' and I said, 'Yeah.' It was great. It was perfect, because I liked the material, and I felt very comfortable that I would be able to support it because Paul's character was so strong. He *was* Pee-Wee.

I also just liked the fact that he was into his own thing: his bike. In most movies the plot device has to be something that is of importance, and what was of importance to him was his bike.

It's hard for me to imagine a first movie, unless I had created it myself, that I could have related to as well as I did to *Pee-Wee*. It was so easy to realize it because I could feel it very easily. It was all scripted, except for tiny bits here and there. Some of the visual jokes weren't scripted, like when he's in the bathroom and he looks out through the fish tank window. But since the character was so strong it allowed us to focus on certain visual things.

I loved the movie and felt so connected to it because there was a lot of

Pee-Wee's Big Adventure: Paul Reubens and bicycle

imagery that I liked. I could add, but I wasn't imposing my own thing on it completely. I got to take the stuff that was there and *embellish* it. There were a few things that I added, but I was just lucky to be so clearly in synch with Paul. It would have been a real nightmare if I hadn't been in synch with him; I would have been fired because he was the star and it was his movie.

I remember seeing Paul's show and loving it because it really tapped into the permanent adolescence thing, and I completely connected with that. It was good for me too, because at that point in my life I really wasn't the best communicator, and it would have been a nightmare if we hadn't been so in synch. What he liked, for the most part, I liked; what I liked, for the most part, he liked. So we just did it.

'It really tapped into that permanent adolescent thing'

I've always felt close to all the characters in my films. I've always felt I *had* to be, because when you're doing something you're putting your life into it, and there has to be aspects to all the characters that are either a part of you, or something you can relate to, or something that is symbolic of something inside you. I *have* to connect. The Pee-Wee character was just into what he was doing, and when you grow up in a culture where people remain very hidden, it was nice that he didn't really care about how he was perceived. He operated in his own world, and there's something I find very admirable about that. He's a character who is on his own, who is able to operate in society, and yet he's also sort of an outcast. Again, it's that whole theme of being perceived as this weird thing. In some ways, there's a freedom to that, because you're free to live in your own world. But it's a prison in a way. It's how I felt when I was an animator at Disney.

Written by Phil Hartman, Michael Varhol and its star Paul Reubens, Pee-Wee's Big Adventure *centres around Herman's quest to retrieve his stolen bike, a search that takes him on a road trip across America, from a dinosaur park in Palm Springs, down to the Alamo and back to Burbank,*

*encountering all manner of American film archetypes, including a biker
gang, an escaped prisoner and a waitress out to better herself. It was a
journey which allowed Burton to indulge in his penchant for stop-motion
animation. Firstly, in a dream sequence in which a Tyrannosaurus rex –
animated by regular collaborator Rick Heinrichs – chows down on Pee-
Wee's bike, and secondly, in the film's most memorable sequence, when
Pee-Wee encounters Large Marge, a ghostly female truck driver whose
face distorts in front of his eyes.*

There's an energy with stop-motion that you can't even describe. It's to do
with giving things life, and I guess that's why I wanted to get into animation originally. To give life to something that doesn't have it is cool, and
even more so in three dimensions, because, at least for me, it feels even
more real. With the Large Marge thing or the dinosaur – any time we
could throw in some stop-motion, the better. We would have had a lot
more if they'd have let us.

The movie-making process is weird, because the Large Marge sequence

Transformation: Large Marge

The dinosaur dream

was in the script originally, and there was lots of talk about how to do it; we even talked about not having anything, just Paul screaming, and let that be the joke. It's funny, whenever I see the movie with an audience that sequence almost always gets the biggest laugh. You can tell that was the thing that kept people going for the whole movie, it carried people along, and it's so scary because I almost cut out the best thing before an audience saw it. It was a special effect and those are the first things to go.

I completely storyboarded *Vincent*. I storyboarded at least half of *Frankenweenie* and a friend of mine did the rest, while on *Pee-Wee* I got a guy to board it. From movie to movie they've gotten boarded less and less and what I've done since then is little sketches. On *Pee-Wee*, because it was my first film, they wanted to know that I'd got the shot list, that I could make the day. So it was helpful, and I liked that. It was my background, so I felt comfortable. Again, since I wasn't very good at speaking, this visual representation was helpful.

A lot of people in the movie were from improv groups like The Groundlings, and I started to get really into it, because when people are good at improv, it's really fun and it's kind of liberating. And so I started to feel that I was going to storyboard less because it's more fun to build up to a spot and let it happen on the stage. You have to have enough of an idea to know what you're doing, but as much as you plan, there's something about the reality of being on the set with the actors, costumes, lights and the rest of that environment that changes things. Not so much on the *Pee-Wee* movie because that was kind of *there*, but in later movies, it's like 'This line may sound good, but it's being said by a guy in a bat-suit, so I don't know if it's a good line.' You may think it's a good line, but it's not until you get on that stage, at that moment, with these weird characters that it's right. So I loosened that up a lot. On *Beetlejuice* it was even more so because Catherine O'Hara and Michael Keaton are so good at improv.

It started with Paul and one of the writers, Phil Hartman, who is on *Saturday Night Live* now. Those guys were really good and funny, and working on that movie was a lot like being in animation and having a story meeting; even though the script was really good, we'd sit around and come up with ideas. It was very exciting to me to be around them because they were funny. In improv, they base everything on knowing what their character is and letting it go from there. In *Pee-Wee* it was a case of having the elements there already: he's got these bunny slippers and there's a little toy carrot, so you have the slippers go and sniff the carrot. One thing that was completely improvised was that whole thing in the Alamo with the guide. That was the first time that there was a good chunk of improvisation and the girl who did that, Jan Hooks, was really good and ended up on *Saturday Night Live*. All these people from The Groundlings, people from improv, I have a real respect for them because it's the way I like working: it starts with a very good foundation and then kind of goes free.

Pee-Wee's Big Adventure *climaxes with a bicycle ride on the Warner Bros backlot. It's almost Felliniesque in content and tone as Pee-Wee Herman, reunited with his beloved red and white bicycle, is pursued through a series of soundstages disrupting the filming taking place on each one. The movies in question reflect Burton's preoccupations and interests: a beach movie, a Christmas number, a Japanese monsterfest with Godzilla – though, he says, the majority of the films were in fact present in the original script.*

I think I added a couple. But all those genres were stuff that I liked very much; that monster fighting Godzilla was the Giddra, otherwise known as Monster Zero. Working on the Warner Bros backlot was kind of magical. Shooting on a soundstage *is* magical. That magic has worn off a little since then, unfortunately, because of the business side surrounding Hollywood, the torture aspects of it. I kind of get freaked out when I go to studios now because there's a negative as well as a positive side, whereas before there just used to be a positive one.

While Burton had previously used composers Michael Convertino and David Newman to score Frankenweenie *and* Aladdin, *to provide the music for* Pee-Wee's Big Adventure *he chose Danny Elfman, lead singer with the cult group Oingo Boingo Band, who had never scored a film before.*

Before I was in the movies I'd go see them in clubs. I had always liked their music. Of all the groups that I went to see, which was mainly the punk kind of stuff, which I love, I always felt that because they had more people in the band and used weirder instruments, the music seemed to be more story-oriented in some way, more filmic. So when the *Pee-Wee* movie came about, it was great, because being low-budget they were more willing to take a chance. They took a chance on me, they took a chance on Danny. Their attitude was to surround me with a bunch of old pros, but music was the one area which that didn't carry over into. Hearing the music played by an orchestra was probably one of the most exciting experiences I've ever had. It was incredible and so funny to see Danny because he'd never done anything like that. It's always magical when you've never done something. I guess it's like having sex: it can be great, but it's never quite the same as that first time. Music is always important, but that was really the first time where it was like a *character*, definitely a character.

Danny was great because he had never done this and so it was good for me because I got to go through the process. He got a tape of the film and I would go over to his house, and he'd play little things on his keyboard so I could see it right there. We were definitely on the same wavelength. It was good because what he couldn't verbalize, or what I couldn't verbalize, didn't matter because it was there and he got it. It was pretty much like, 'It's great, it's perfect', and it's so much easier when that's the case. I've always tried to be very sensitive; if you find the right people, you're almost on a different level.

Because it was a low-budget movie it wasn't high on Warner Bros' priorities, but at the same time *The Goonies* was being shot across the way and they had these huge sets, and, I don't know, they may have been on schedule, maybe it was just me who wasn't, but the executives passed by that stage every day and would come down and start yelling at me, 'What are you doing? You're taking all this time?' They were on our case, but it didn't teach me anything, except to have a worse temper and go faster. It's at that stage that you learn that movie-making is not an exact science. The thing that has always bothered me is that nobody was irresponsible. It was like, 'I wish this was going faster', but we were dealing with animals and elements and FX. We weren't doing anything crazy, we weren't overshooting. I even cut stuff out as we were going along because we didn't have time. But we were just a small thing. It's show-business hierachy, in a way. They won't torture A list people, but they'll torture the B list, because they can.

To be a director you can't have any fear. At best, you probably have to have a very healthy balance of not being an egomaniac, but with enough security in yourself to just go for it. Also, I think the unknown helps. Actually, you get more freaked out as you go along and the experiences pile up on you; you find yourself getting weirder. I found that on my first feature, I was the most secure and unfreaked out than at any other time since. I had the greatest time.

I was the worst in school for learning anything. If somebody tells me something, I have some reaction against hearing it, I just will not listen. It's why I'm so bad with names. I don't know where that's from. It probably comes from some weird internal protection. In school I retained *nothing*. All I remember from school are the names of certain clouds. I don't remember dates, I don't remember anything. So I didn't come away from *Pee-Wee* thinking I had learned this or I had learned that, because that experience was probably the purest experience I have ever had, and part of that was me being fairly naïve about the whole situation. I've found that there are a lot of unpleasant things involved in movies and it's best not to dwell on them. It's funny about selective memory because on every movie I've done I've gotten very sick, because I've put a lot of myself into it. I've gotten sick and I've had to keep going and finish the movie, and yet I wanted to die. But those things kind of fade away after a while. It's a good thing. That's why I never like jumping from one movie to another, because it's too much of a harsh experience. Luckily it leaves you, so that you can do it again, but it does get harder and harder.

That's why I think I always liked Fellini movies because he seemed to capture the spirit and the magic of making a movie. It is something that is beautiful and you want to obtain it because it gives you the energy to keep going. But there are a lot of negative sides to it, nothing *really* negative, but it's a harsh experience. The things you learn about movie-making are fine, as you go along you learn about lenses. It's taken me a while, but I gather information each time. You just try to keep learning on a basic technical level. But on the other side, the Hollywood side, there's nothing really to learn that's of any value. A lot of it is not based on logic, and that can be disturbing. If you're trying to find a foundation for something, it's a disturbing thing, so I try not to think too much about it, because I feel more irrational from movie to movie.

Released in the summer of 1985 Pee-Wee's Big Adventure *was a surprise box-office success, though critical opinion was mixed.*

The reviews on *Pee-Wee's Big Adventure* were *really* bad. I remember one review, and I'll never forget this, which said, 'Everything is great, the costumes are brilliant, the photography is great, the script is fabulous, the actors are all great, the only thing that's terrible is the direction.' One said, 'On a scale of one to ten, ten being best, *Pee-Wee's Big Adventure* gets a minus one.' It's the first minus one I remember seeing. It was on a lot of the ten worst films of the year lists. It's funny, I look at the movie and I don't think it's bad. I love it. There may be some weak passages, but it's really not that bad. It was kind of devasting; I had never really been through that before. There were a couple of good reviews, but for the most part they were pretty bad. Not just on the fence bad, but *bad* bad.

But I think it affected me in a positive way. I've always gotten enough good and bad reviews. I've known people who've gone through that first film thing when they get 'They're the next Orson Welles', and that can kill you. I'm glad I didn't get that. I much prefer the kind of raking over the coals I got because it's a mistake to believe any of it. A lot of the criticism I got was that the film was just images, and I'm thinking, 'It's a movie for Christ's sake, it's not a radio programme, it's a visual thing, so what's wrong?'

Having a background in animation sort of broadens the scope of what you can do visually. Cinema is a visual medium so everything that you do – even if it's not blurting out to the audience on a completely conscious level: 'This is what I am' – everything is meaningful in terms of the look of things. So I always felt having that background in animation was a good tool for me to explore visual ideas and apply them to live action.

The thing I liked about Fellini was that he created images that even if you didn't know what they meant literally, you *felt* something. It's not creating images to create images. And even though I didn't fully understand a lot of what he was saying, I could feel a heart behind it. That's what his work meant to me, that things don't have to be literal, you don't have to understand everything. Even though it may be an extreme image, something that's out of the realm of people's perception of reality, you *feel* something. It's that whole sort of unspoken thing that I find beautiful. That's the magic of movies.

Pee-Wee made money, which was the main thing in Hollywood at that stage of the game. I care about money, which is why I get so intense when these people are on my case saying I don't make commercial movies, because I've always felt very responsible to the people who put up the money. It's not like you're doing a painting. There is a large amount of money involved, even if you're doing a low-budget movie, so I don't want to waste it. In a non-exact science, kind of weird world, you try to do the best you can. I've never taken the attitude of the artiste, who says I don't care about anything, I'm just making *my* movie. I try to be true to myself and do only what I can do, because if I veer from that everybody's in trouble. So I try to maintain that integrity. And when there is a large amount of money involved, I attempt, without pretending to know what audiences are all about, to try and do something that people would like to see, without going too crazy.

You try your best, but it's such a surreal thing. I thought the movie industry was bad, but when you look at other worlds, like fashion or advertising or the art world, it's even more cut-throat and even more full of pretension and bullshit. I think the good thing about the movie industry which protects you from that is that there are so many things that can go wrong, so many elements: the reviews, the box office, and then there's the movie itself. There are so many things that can punch away at you and force you to have a little bit of humility, that it kind of keeps you grounded.

I had a good experience on *Pee-Wee*, I enjoyed it. It was surreal: a lot of the reviews were bad and then the movie did fairly well, which was great. It's hard to imagine a better, more grounding experience in a way because it left me realizing that you've got to just try and hope for the best, maintain some integrity and try to punch through it.

I don't even think they asked me to do the next *Pee-Wee* movie, but it's not something I wanted to do. It was my first movie and I could already see the rut that Hollywood puts people in. You do two *Pee-Wee* movies, and then that's you, which was different for me than it was for Paul. For him that's fine, because that's his character.

Later that same year Burton directed The Jar, *an episode of* Alfred Hitchcock Presents, *a revamped version of the sixties TV series which had been updated by US network NBC and which featured colourized versions of Hitchcock's prologues and epilogues. Scripted by horror novelist Michael McDowell, from Ray Bradbury's original teleplay,* The Jar *starred Griffin Dunne as the owner of the titular container whose misshapen contents have a persuasive effect on those who behold them and featured a score from Danny Elfman and special effects by Rick Heinrichs.*

That was another tough one. I've learned from things like *The Jar* and *Aladdin* that when I get into situations like that it's very dangerous. If I can't do exactly what I want to do – that's not to say that what I want to do is going to work out every time – things just don't work out quite as well. I need that deep connection.

The next year Burton was called in by Brad Bird, who he had worked with on The Fox and the Hound, *to contribute a number of designs to* Family Dog, *an animated episode of Steven Spielberg's television series* Amazing Stories *which Bird was directing, and which was originally part of a showreel the pair had produced during their time at Disney. The episode was subsequently turned into a series by Spielberg's company Amblin for which Burton served as executive producer.*

My involvement was pretty much from a design point of view; I did storyboards and designed some more characters, because I just love the idea of

Family Dog

trying to do something from a dog's point of view. I don't know why, but I always relate to dogs. Edward Scissorhands is like a dog to me.

Beetlejuice

The success of Pee-Wee's Big Adventure at the American box office meant that Burton was now considered a 'bankable' director. He had begun working on a script for Warner Bros for a proposed Batman movie with screenwriter Sam Hamm, but while the studio was willing to pay for the script's development they were less willing to green-light the project. Meanwhile, Burton had begun reading through the scripts that had been sent his way, and was swiftly becoming disheartened by their lack of imagination and originality. That is, until record industry mogul turned film producer David Geffen, whose company had a distribution deal with Warner Bros, handed him a script called Beetlejuice, written by Michael McDowell, who had provided the script for The Jar. It was, in retrospect, quintessential Burton material: ghoulish, bizarre, highly imaginative with the potential for outrageous set design and innovative special effects. Described by McDowell as 'a feel-good movie about death', it featured Alec Baldwin and Geena Davis as Adam and Barbara Maitland, a happily married New England couple who are killed when their car plunges into the river and who wind up haunting their own home. But when a pretentious New York family – Catherine O'Hara, Jeffrey Jones and Winona Ryder – move in, their quaint spooking techniques prove ineffectual and the Maitlands call in the services of Michael Keaton's bio-exorcist Betelgeuse (pronounced Beetlejuice) to get rid of the intruders.

I didn't work for a long time between *Pee-Wee's Big Adventure* and *Beetlejuice* because I just didn't want to do the things they were offering me. I was being offered any bad comedy. It was a case of, you do a bad comedy, you get offered *all* the bad comedies. I even got offered *Hot to Trot*, a talking horse movie! Stuff I had passed on before I even started working on *Beetlejuice* had been made and had come out. That's how long a period of time it was.

It was David Geffen who asked me if I wanted to do *Beetlejuice*. I loved it because I had read a lot of scripts that were the classic Hollywood 'cookie-cutter' bad comedy. It was really depressing. Then this script came through the door, and after Hollywood hammering me with the concept of story structure, where the third act doesn't work, and it's got to end with a little comedy, or a little romance, the script for *Beetlejuice* was completely anti all that: it had no real story, it didn't make any sense, it was more like stream of consciousness. That script was probably the most amorphous ever. It changed a lot, but the writer Michael McDowell had a good, perverse sense of humour and darkness, and that was the good thing about it. It had the kind of abstract imagery that I like, with these strange characters and images floating in and out.

We worked on the script for a long time, and some of it came to something, some of it didn't. I wanted to cast Sammy Davis Jr as Betelgeuse, but they nixed that idea. We went through a lot of things; Michael McDowell and (producer) Larry Wilson worked on the script for a while, but they got beaten down by the constant questioning. I mean, for a lot of the time on *Beetlejuice* I felt like I was in court giving depositions. I remember having script meetings that lasted for like twenty-four hours over the course of two days, and by the end of it we were questioning every element of the script which, for me, is not necessarily that productive.

It was time to bring in a fresh fighter, so to speak, in the shape of Warren Skaaren, because Michael and Larry were burnt out. Warren was known at that point as a script doctor, as a sort of straight arrow. And because I was perceived as a crazy kind of loose cannon, I went along with it because I wanted to get it done. If they perceived him as the logical one that was fine with me. So we worked on the script for a long, long time, but the fact of the matter is, a lot of the stuff in the film is improvised, a lot of it was just me going over to Michael Keaton's house and the two of us coming up with jokes. Michael was just so much fun. He would say things like, 'How about some teeth?' and he would put in some teeth and his voice would start to change. It was a building process. It was really fun because we were essentially creating a character. It was the first time I had done that because the Pee-Wee character was *there*. This time I got to be there, watching, creating, being a part of that.

Casting is always a very case-by-case thing for me. It's hard because it's like a puzzle. You go with one person, then you try to find another person, but you don't want to go too much in a certain direction because then it starts looking like TV. Michael Keaton was actually Geffen's idea. I hadn't seen him in anything, which was good, because I don't like seeing people in other things. I prefer to just meet them. I met Michael and that's when I started to see the character of Betelgeuse. I didn't know him that

Beetlejuice: Michael Keaton and Winona Ryder

well, I didn't know his work, but he's crazy. Michael is manic, a livewire, and he's got these great eyes. I love people's eyes, and he's definitely got a wild pair.

I grew up watching Lon Chaney and Boris Karloff. There's a freedom to those performers, even though most people think they're so loaded up with make-up you can't see them, which is an odd thing to me. I've found that when you put make-up on people it actually frees them. They're able to hide behind a mask and therefore show another side of themselves, which is great. What it did for Michael was it allowed him to play some-body who wasn't a human being, and the idea of playing someone who isn't human, behind some cheesy make-up, is very liberating. You don't have to worry about being Michael Keaton, you can be this *thing*. That was very magical to me. And ever since, any time an actor is able to immerse himself behind something, I just love it, because you get to see another side of him. Be it Johnny Depp in *Edward Scissorhands* or Jack Nicholson as The Joker, it's fascinating. It taps into some other side of them. It's like at Hallowe'en, people dress up and it allows them to get a little wilder, they become something else. That's one of the aspects of film-making that I've constantly enjoyed, the transformation of people. For Betelgeuse we wanted Michael to look like he'd crawled out from under a

Sketches for Winona Ryder's character, Lydia

rock, which is why he's got mould and moss on his face.

A lot of the people didn't want to do the movie. The only person who initially really wanted to do it was Geena Davis. The others may have wanted to, but it didn't seem like they did. I understand why, nobody knew what it was, and all I'd ever done was *Pee-Wee's Big Adventure*, and even though it was okay and did fairly well, it was not *Citizen Kane*, I wasn't Preston Sturges, and even the final script is not really about *anything*. But that's what's great about it. We would talk about things that it was about. But it was more like junior high psychology than the Hollywood meaningful-one-sentence kind of pitch. Everybody would read the script, and just go, 'Do I want to do this? I don't know. What is it?' But it was hard to describe because it's the *look*, it's the *feel*, and you can't really describe that until you're in there, doing it. But everybody obviously came on board and was there one hundred per cent. Michael got into it because we talked and he started to think about it in a certain way. But I can see why people weren't lining up to sign on.

Catherine O'Hara was from the SCTV improv troupe which was very popular at the time, and those people were very good at doing characters. I had asked about Winona Ryder because I had seen her in *Lucas* and she had a really strong presence, but I'd heard she didn't want to do it because of the satanic thing. I thought she must be a religious person or something, but then I found out that it wasn't true, because when I met her she wanted to do it and she was great.

Having previously been locked so much into the design ethic predetermined by Paul Reubens's character for Pee-Wee's Big Adventure, Beetlejuice *finally afforded Burton the budget to meld to his unique imagination and hire the artists he wanted to work with, including visual effects supervisor Alan Munro, who initially began storyboarding the film, and production designer Bo Welch, with whom Burton would later collaborate on* Edward Scissorhands *and* Batman Returns.

If you read the *Beetlejuice* script you could imagine it done many different ways, and I think that's what freaked people out. If you're talking about death, you could imagine it in a cruel and horrific way – either that or you could go for the *Heaven Can Wait* approach with clouds and the guy walking along surrounded by fog. With *Beetlejuice*, I had the opportunity to hire a designer who I wanted, and to do more what I wanted to do. I hadn't really seen any of Bo's work, but I just liked him. He cared. It's funny, there are a lot of people who get so freaked out by the movie industry that they just become a part of it, there's no joy in it for them any more, so it's nice to work with people – and this may sound corny – who want to do a good job, who care, and who have an artistic sensibility. It shouldn't be that big a deal, but I guess it is.

I would do a few sketches, then we'd look at things. You start out with a concept, and then build upon that. I always had my own ideas about the way it should be: if there's darkness there should be colour and light. *Beetlejuice* was a real mix of colour and dark to me, and I wanted to temper a lot of the darker aspects and make it a bit more colourful. Again, I never think about it, it's just something I do. It's like, this person would look good with blue skin – it's just a feeling. And you come up with jokes. I would come up with sketches and the effects guy would come up with some sketches. For example, we had this waiting room in the afterlife and I always had it in mind to poke fun at death, and it was a case of thinking what kind of people are we going to put in here? Let's have a guy who's been in a shark attack, a skin diver with a shark on his leg. So, we'd come up with sketches like the magician's assistant who's just been sawn in half, or a guy who's been burnt to death while smoking in bed. We tried to portray the afterlife as a cheap science fiction movie; not as clouds in a beautiful sky, but as an IRS office. I got more of an opportunity to do my thing.

The Waiting Room: poking fun at death

Returning behind the camera were cinematographer Thomas Ackerman, who had previously shot Frankenweenie, *and Rick Heinrichs, who was employed as visual effects consultant. Heinrichs, like Burton, had gradu- ated from Cal Arts to a career at Disney, and had been his regular design collaborator ever since* Vincent.

We started out when we were both at Disney. Rick was a sculptor and I had all these weird drawings which nobody believed could be brought into the third dimension. Rick's one of the best sculptors I've ever worked with. He was the only person who I really felt could take an idea, a draw- ing of mine, and bring it into the third dimension. He wanted to get into the art director end of things. He did some stuff on *Edward Scissorhands*, was art director on *Batman Returns* and visual consultant on *The Nightmare Before Christmas*. But I think it was good for us to do other things. It's like Dean Martin and Jerry Lewis, Rick became so associated with me that it was very important for him to expand his horizons a bit. I think it's been very good for him, and when the time arises we will proba- bly do stuff together again.

The Waiting Room: burned to death smoking in bed

Transformation: Barbara Maitland

Beetlejuice's budget was $13 million with just one million of that given over to special effects work, a paltry sum considering the scale and scope of the effects called for by the script, which included stop-motion, replacement animation, make-up effects, puppetry, blue screen and false perspective. It was always Burton's intention, however, that the special effects be cheap, creaky illusions rather than state-of-the-art effects, a feeling in keeping with the tone of the script, his early work on Hansel and Gretel *and* Pee-Wee's Big Adventure, *and a throw-back to the* Godzilla *movies he loved so much as a child.*

We wanted the effects to be kind of cheesy, and they were. We just tried to be fairly matter-of-fact about it. I didn't want to make too much of a show

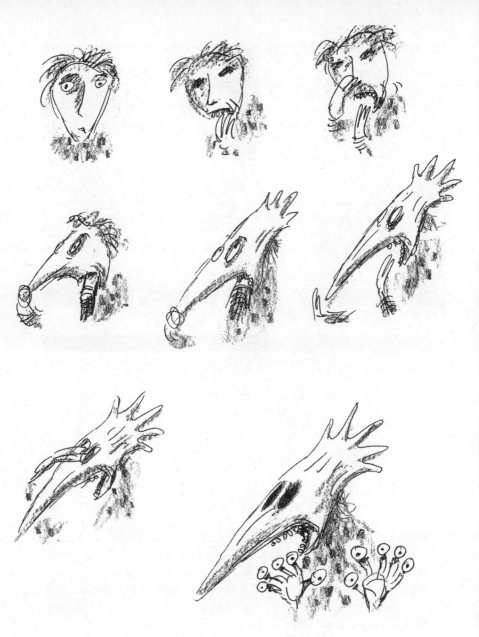

Transformation: Adam Maitland

of it, in a way. Growing up watching the kinds of movies that I did, like Harryhausen, *The Fabulous World of Jules Verne* and *Baron Münchausen*, I always found the effects to be a little more human. There's a certain sort of handmade quality about them, which is probably why I like folk art.

The Maitlands transformed

The handmade feel Burton was after is more than apparent in the sequences in which Geena Davis and Alec Baldwin pull their faces apart and distort their features – effects that are more outré than gruesome.

'We wanted the special effects to be kind of cheesy'

We tried to take the edge off it being gruesome by making them real in their own context. We did a snake in *Beetlejuice* which just didn't work – it looked *too* fake – so I always had my own personal set of standards of what I thought was believable in this world, and what didn't quite make it. It was very much a personal thing.

It worked in *Beetlejuice*, and I continued that philosophy in *Batman*, which was a mistake. It disturbed people. In *Batman* I always loved that whole thing of The Joker pulling out a gun and shooting the Batplane down. But again it's perception. I was doing a giant big-budget movie and people expect a certain kind of thing with that. So while that concept works in *Beetlejuice* and *Pee-Wee,* it doesn't necessarily work when people perceive the movie as a big blockbuster.

Beetlejuice *features a number of visual references that surface continually in Burton's work: these include a model town, characters patterned with black and white stripes, and a graveyard setting.*

There was a graveyard right next to where we lived, about a block away, and I used to play there. I don't know exactly why it keeps showing up, except for the fact that, again, it's part of your soul; it was a place where I felt peaceful, comfortable; a whole world of quiet and peace, and also excitement and drama. It's all those feelings mixed into one. I was obsessed with death, like a lot of children. There were flat tombs, but there was also this weird mausoleum with weird gates on one side. And I would wander around it any time of the day or night. I would sneak into it and play, and look at things, and I always felt really good there.

As for model towns, I used to draw big tableaux of flying saucers attacking an army. They were very elaborate, almost like miniatures in a way. Also when we were shooting those Super 8 movies we used to make miniatures. Again, I don't know why, but all those movies I used to like as a kid had them. It's like stop-motion animation, there's a certain energy and vibe which is quite strong. A lot of it has to do with those *Godzilla* movies.

As far as the black and white stripes are concerned, that one I have never been able to figure out. I guess there must be some sort of prison element involved in there somehow. I *am* drawn to that image, I always have been, it's in a lot of drawings as well, but I don't know why.

Throughout the film Betelgeuse transforms into various guises, the most extreme of which is seen towards the film's climax when Keaton appears wearing a merry-go-round hat, featuring various demonic carousel creatures revolving around its rim, and fifteen-foot-long hammer-weight arms. Designed by Burton and built by special make-up effects artist Robert Short, Keaton's headpiece was topped off with a skull that looks remarkably like Jack Skellington, the main character from The Nightmare Before Christmas.

I would just doodle those things all the time and the images would reoccur in other forms. But I hadn't noticed that until now. I also had bat ears on the thing too and, at the time, I had no idea I was going to be doing *Batman*. Often these images are planted early on, and then later come to be real, which is interesting to me. It shows how the subconscious works.

It was Danny Elfman who again provided the music for Beetlejuice, *creating a fantastical score that was, as with* Pee-Wee's Big Adventure, *as much of a character as Keaton's bio-exorcist. But the soundtrack also featured two calypso songs from Harry Belafonte, including the 'Banana Boat Song', which became the film's unoffical theme tune.*

That was something Warren Skaaren put into the script – the people reacting to a musical number – and he had picked this *Big Chill/* yuppie kind of Motown music that was very happening at the time. I didn't want to do it. So I just started listening to a bunch of music, and I liked the Belafonte songs. There was something about Adam and Barbara being on vacation and this kind of calypso music which I liked.

There was a weird incident with *Beetlejuice*. We did some test screenings without the score, and the film got some really low marks. Then we showed it with the score and it got really high marks, and one of the things people liked from these test screenings was the score. But then somebody at the studio said that the score was 'too dark', which was odd because these are the people who live and breathe by these audience research screenings and here they were contradicting the only positive thing from the screening.

The test screenings also suggested to Burton a new coda. Since the response to the afterlife waiting room scenes was so enthusiastic, Burton included an epilogue featuring Betelgeuse foolishly angering a witch doctor, who then sprinkles a powder over Keaton's head causing it to shrink.

66

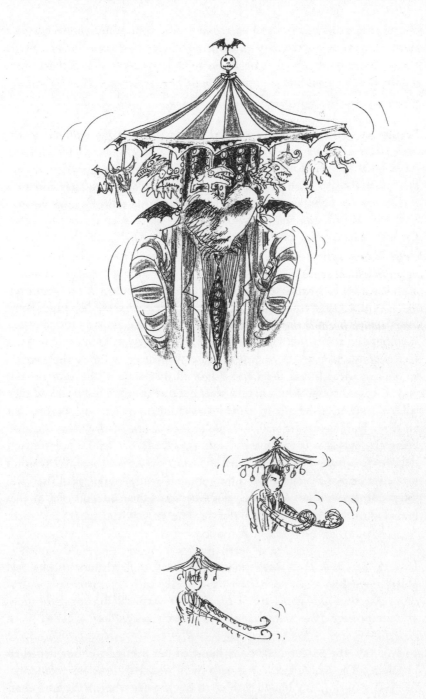

Transformation: Betelgeuse

We never really had an ending, so we shot some different things and showed preview audiences a couple; they chose that one. But the movie was so random, in a way, it never really had an ending. It still hasn't, but it's the best we could do.

Beetlejuice opened in America on April Fool's Day 1988 and was a surprise success, taking $32 million in its first two weeks, eventually grossing more than $73 million. The film won an Oscar for Ve Neill, Steve La Porte and Robert Short for make-up, and seemed to vindicate Burton's theory that audiences could handle films that break with Hollywood conventions. Weird was good, weird was acceptable, weird was successful. Critical reaction too was enthusiastic: Pauline Kael called the movie 'a comedy classic'.

That did a lot for me, because the fight in script meetings had always been to make it more literal, and while I do believe that there has to be some foundation to make sense of it, the thing that I was most gratified about was that audiences could go along with something that didn't follow what you're constantly getting hammered into your head by the studios, which is: it's got to be literal. *Beetlejuice* proved that it didn't have to be that way. I went through a lot of scary stuff because it didn't test well and they wanted to change the title to make it something more benign, and I fought all that. They wanted to call it *House Ghosts*, and it came very close to being changed. I was at a meeting and they said, '*Beetlejuice* doesn't test, but *House Ghosts* is going through the roof.' As a joke I said, 'Why don't we call it *Scared Sheetless*?' and they actually considered it until I said I'd jump out the window. But to give Warner Bros their due, they left it as it was. They didn't have to, so I was very, very grateful.

If there was one consistent criticism levelled at Beetlejuice *it was that Davis's and Baldwin's characters were boring in comparison with everything else that was going on in the film. It was as if Burton paid more attention to the other characters and the film's design than to them.*

I never saw the Maitlands as one hundred per cent good; they had their problems. The whole gist to me with them was that these are people that like being boring. It's like that thing in old movies where the bland characters need to get goosed a little; they need to get their blood going a little

The Maitlands

bit. Alec kind of bad-mouthed the movie and me and while I think he did a good job, I don't think he saw it for what it was. I don't know what he saw. To me they always were kind of nice, but there was a lot of criticism that they were bland and everything else was great. But if you didn't have those bland characters for Betelgeuse and those afterlife characters to bounce off of, it wouldn't be what it is. That was the point, in a way.

Batman

The movie rights to Bob Kane's comic strip character had been secured from DC Comics in 1979 by producers Benjamin Melniker and Michael Uslan, who had hired Superman screenwriter Tom Mankiewicz to write a script which focused on the Dark Knight's origins. Eventually, Melniker and Uslan relinquished production duties to Peter Guber and Jon Peters, and throughout the early eighties a number of film-makers, including Joe Dante and Ivan Reitman, were linked to the property, though it remained in development until a satisfactory script was found. Following the success of Pee-Wee's Big Adventure, the project, which was in development at Warner Bros, was offered to Burton. His Frankenweenie producer, Julie Hickson, wrote a thirty-page treatment, before Burton brought in Sam Hamm, a comic book fan and screenwriter with only one produced credit, Never Cry Wolf.

They had had the project for ten years and had had several directors attached to it. After Pee-Wee, they asked me if I was interested in directing Batman, and I was. But they didn't give the okay officially until after the first weekend's grosses from Beetlejuice came in. It was kind of charming in a way, because Sam and I would meet on weekends to discuss the early writing stages, and we had a great script, but they kept saying there were other things involved. They were just waiting to see how Beetlejuice did. They didn't want to give me that movie unless Beetlejuice was going to be okay. They wouldn't say that, but that was really the way it was. So, after that first weekend, it got the magical green-light.

Hamm and Burton fashioned a dark, brooding, deeply psychological story for the Caped Crusader which, like Mankiewicz's script, pitted him against The Joker but was set in a dark, hellish vision of Gotham City that eschewed the campness of the Batman TV series of the sixties and instead went back to Kane's original comic strips of the forties. Helping sell Warners on the script's noirish approach was the comic book/graphic

Tim Burton

novel explosion of the mid-eighties, and the resurgence of interest in Batman that had been initiated by comic book artist/writer Frank Miller's The Dark Knight Returns, *a graphic novel which delved into the darker side of Batman's psyche, and Alan Moore's* The Killing Joke, *which featured Batman battling against The Joker.*

I was never a giant comic book fan, but I've always loved the image of Batman and The Joker. The reason I've never been a comic book fan – and I think it started when I was a child – is because I could never tell which box I was supposed to read. That's why I loved *The Killing Joke*, because for the first time I could tell which one to read. It's my favourite. It's the first comic I've ever loved. And the success of those graphic novels made our ideas more acceptable.

71

So, while I was never a big comic book fan, I loved Batman, the split personality, the hidden person. It's a character I could relate to. Having those two sides, a light side and a dark one, and not being able to resolve them – that's a feeling that's not uncommon. So while I can see it's got a lot of Michael Keaton in it because he's actually doing it, I also see certain aspects of myself in the character. Otherwise, I wouldn't have been able to do it. I mean, this whole split personality thing is so much a part of every person that it's just amazing to me that more people don't consciously understand it. Everybody has several sides to their personality, no one is one thing. Especially in America, people often present themselves as one thing, but are really something else. Which is symbolic of the Batman character.

While the casting of Jack Nicholson as The Joker received almost unanimous acceptance, that of Michael Keaton in the dual role of Bruce Wayne and Batman sparked off an unprecedented amount of controversy. It was producer Jon Peters who first suggested Keaton for the role, and when the news was announced Bat-fans the world over were horrified, with 50,000 letters flooding into Warner Bros' offices to protest at the decision. In fact, the negative reaction reached such proportions that Warners' share price slumped, outraged fans tore up offending publicity material at comic conventions and the Wall Street Journal *covered the crisis on page one. One appalled aficionado wrote in the* Los Angeles Times *that, 'By casting a clown, Warner Bros and Burton have defecated on the history of Batman.' Even Adam West, who had camped up the Caped Crusader in the TV series of the sixties, thought himself a better choice than Keaton.*

In my mind I kept reading reviews that said, 'Jack's terrific, but the unknown as Batman is nothing special.' So I saw a zillion people and the thing that kept going through my mind when I saw these action-adventure hero types come into the office was, 'I just can't see them putting on a bat-suit. I can't see it.' I was seeing these big macho guys, and then thinking of them with pointy eyes, and it was, 'Why would this big, macho, Arnold Schwarzenegger-type person dress up as a bat for God's sake?' A bat is this wild thing. I'd worked with Michael before and so I thought he would be perfect, because he's got that look in his eye. It's there in *Beetlejuice*. It's like *that* guy you could see putting on a bat-suit; he does it because he *needs* to, because he's not this gigantic, strapping macho man. It's all

Adam West: TV's Batman

about transformation. Then it started to make sense to me. All of a sudden the whole thing clicked, I could see the pointy ears; the image and the psychology all made sense. Taking Michael and making him Batman just underscored the whole split personality thing which is really what I think the movie's all about.

With all this controversy, the studio was a little apprehensive. It was like, 'That wasn't what we were thinking.' But they quickly understood.

Obviously, there was a lot of negative response from comic book people. I think they thought we were going to make it like the TV series, and make it campy, because they all thought of Michael from *Mr Mom* and *Night Shift* and stuff like that. But that never bothered me because I knew we weren't doing that. Whatever the movie would be, I knew we weren't making a joke of the material.

When I was at school I went to a comic book convention in San Diego a few months before *Superman* was due to be released, and someone from Warner Bros came down and gave a presentation, and the fans tore him to shreds. That was the first time I really saw the intensity and passion that comic book fans have. They didn't like the fact that Superman changed into his costume on the edge of a building. This one guy stood up and said, 'I'm going to boycott this movie and tell everyone you are destroying the legend', and there was this huge round of applause. I never forgot that.

I remember when I first met Bob Kane, he was very pleased with what Sam Hamm and I had done with the script, but he was as freaked out as the rest of them about certain choices in it. Michael Keaton is not the image of Bruce Wayne, but in the comic books the image of The Joker is this really thin so-and-so, so it's a bit elitist to say Jack Nicholson's perfect. Well, he *is* perfect, but he's certainly not the comic book image. So people's bibles seemed to change. If you look at the *Batman* encyclopedia, the fucking thing changes every fucking week. Because, if you think about the reality of it, comic book writers say, 'God, what are we going to do this week? Let's change the history of how Robin was created.' There's no such thing as a bible. I always react against the single-mindedness that you find in Hollywood a lot. You can't think about it. I thought about being true to what I loved about the original idea, and I think in the spirit of it, it's close to Bob Kane. If you look at Michael, he's got all those wheels and that wild energy in his eyes which would compel him to put on a bat-suit. It's like, if he had gotten therapy he wouldn't be putting on a bat-suit. He didn't, so this is his therapy.

But there was no way to satisfy everybody. What you just had to hope for was that you were true to the spirit. And luckily comic books had gone through a phase where they had become much more acceptable. They had made things darker. They had taken Batman into the psychological domain. To me it was very clear: the TV series was campy; the regeneration, the new comics, were totally rebelling against that. I just had to be true to the spirit of it and what I got out of it: the absurdity of it.

Part of what interested me was that it's a human character who dresses up in the most extremely vulgar costumes. The first treatment of *Batman*, the Mankiewicz script, was basically *Superman*, only the names had been changed. It had the same jokey tone, as the story followed Bruce Wayne from childhood through to his beginnings as a crime fighter. They didn't acknowledge any of the freakish nature of it, and I found it the most frightening thing I'd ever read. They didn't acknowledge that he was a man who puts on a costume. They just treated it as if he's doing it for good and that was it. You can't do that. I never felt there had been a totally successful comic book movie ever made. At least not one that I had seen. I thought *Superman* was well done, but in terms of capturing the very specific feel of a comic book, it really didn't do it.

The Mankiewicz script made it more obvious to me that you couldn't treat *Batman* like *Superman*, or treat it like the TV series, because it's a guy dressing up as a bat and no matter what anyone says that's weird. And you've got to go along with that, to some degree. If you want it to be bright and light you either do *Superman* or Cotton Candy Man, you don't do *Batman*.

The TV series was something else, and I grew up on that. I remember running home to be there on opening night on TV. I was prepared. But they'd *done* that, so there was no point in doing that again. And then, as the movie got closer, the comic book explosion clicked in, which I thought was very healthy for everybody because comics, even though I still didn't really read them, are part of American mythology.

Batman *was filmed at Pinewood Studios in England during the winter of 1988/9 where the entire backlot was turned, at a cost of $5.5 million, into a vision of Gotham City that was described in Sam Hamm's script as 'if Hell had sprung up through the pavements and kept on going'. The man responsible was British production designer Anton Furst, who had previously worked on* The Company *of Wolves and* Full Metal Jacket, *and who Burton had tried to employ for* Beetlejuice.

To do a big movie you either do it in LA or you do it in London, due basically to the facilities. I mean, the dollar wasn't even great at the time, but at Pinewood there was nothing going on and it had a big outdoor area which we could build on. So it made sense. The characters were so extreme that I felt we had to set them somewhere that was designed for them. Because *Superman* had been filmed on New York locations, I don't think it captured the right comic book feel. I was very happy we did it at

Pinewood, just to get away from all that stuff with the casting and the hype and the pressure. The British press were intense too, but that didn't bother me as much. I liked being there, I liked working there, I liked a lot of the people, a lot of great artists; I made some friends and it was nice.

Design is very important to me and there are very few designers that I get excited about. Anton was a great designer. I had liked *The Company of Wolves*, and I thought he was one of the most individual ones around. I had met him before *Beetlejuice* and tried to get him to work on that, but he was working on something else. Because of my background, design is the one area I'm very critical about. Working with someone like Anton, who had a real talent, is a luxury. It excites me and it has always been important for me to like designers as friends.

For Gotham City we looked at pictures of New York. *Blade Runner* had come out, and any time there's a movie like that, that's such a trend setter, you're in danger. We had said early on that any city we were going to do was going to get the inevitable *Blade Runner* comparison. So we decided there was nothing we could do about it. We just said, 'This is what's happening to New York at the moment. Things are being added and built on and design is getting all over the place.' We decided to darken everything and build vertically and cram things together and then just go further with it in a more cartoon way. It has an operatic feel, and an almost timeless quality, which I think is similar to *Beetlejuice*.

Every time I do anything I start with the character. Batman's character likes the dark and wants to remain in the shadows, so it's a city at night without many day scenes. Everything is meant to support these characters, so every decision we make is based on that, running it by the character almost, and making sure it's okay with what that character's about.

In addition to the casting of Keaton, comic book fans were also outraged by the redesign of the bat-suit by costume designer Bob Ringwood, who changed its colour from blue to black and incorporated fake musculature into the design.

We just took off from the psychology of saying 'Here's a guy who doesn't look like Arnold Schwarzenegger, so why is he doing this?' He's trying to create an image for himself, he's trying to become something that he's not. Therefore, every decision that we made was based upon that. What's he trying to achieve? Why do you dress up as a bat? You're trying to scare criminals, you're putting on a show, you are trying to

Batman: the image

scare and intimidate people. The idea was to humanize the character.

Despite Warners' initial faith in Hamm's screenplay, the script went through another two writers – Beetlejuice's Warren Skaaren and Charles McKeown, co-writer of Terry Gilliam's The Adventures of Baron Münchausen *– and also required rewrites on set.*

I don't understand why that became such a problem. We started out with a script that everyone liked, although we recognized it needed a little work. Everyone thought the script was great, but they *still* thought it needed a total rewrite. Obviously it was a big movie, and it represented an enormous investment by Warners, so I understood why we had to make it right. But what made the situation worse was that there was all this fuss about making the script better and suddenly we were shooting.

There were so many changes and fixes that it was like unravelling a ball of yarn. It gets to a point where you're *not* helping it any more. We were shooting a scene leading up to the bell-tower and Jack's walking up the steps, but we didn't know why. He said to me that day, 'Why am I going up the steps?' And I said, 'I don't know, we'll talk about it when you get up the top.' You're always working on something, you're always trying to make it better, that happens all the way through, but in this case I felt I wasn't making it better. That pressure is really lousy because you don't have your own strong foundation to stand on like you usually do. I like improvising, but not that way. *Beetlejuice* was amorphous, but it didn't matter because it wasn't as expensive, and it wasn't as big a dinosaur.

The first time you direct a movie on that scale it's kind of surreal. You're not fearful because you don't know. You only have to fight things off after you've been through it once or twice. It's a weird kind of conditioning. If you give somebody a little electrical jolt, the first time they won't know what's coming. After that, they'll be thinking about that little jolt. It's a similar kind of thing.

I was very lucky because I didn't go into it with a fear of 'Oh my God, Jack Nicholson!' And he was great to me. He was very supportive. With Jack a lot of the work was done early on in terms of how he felt about me. He was very cool. He helped me a lot when there was trouble on the movie and the studio freaked out. He was very calming and helpful and would just say, 'Get what you need, get what you want, and just keep going.' He's so great. He'll do like six takes and each take he'll give it

The Joker

Batman: 'The duel of the freaks'

something else. He was fascinating that way, and you'd almost wish you could play all six takes in the movie. He was very exciting to watch.

Charles McKeown came in and we did some work on The Joker character. He was The Joker and he needed more jokes, not for the sake of more jokes, but because that was his character. He needed more of that identification. He's the best character and besides Catwoman he's the clearest villain. I just love the idea of a person who's turned into a clown and is insane. The film is like the duel of the freaks. It's a fight between two disfigured people. That's what I love about it. I was always aware of how weird it was, but I was never worried about it in any way. The Joker is such a great character because there's a complete freedom to him. Any character who operates on the outside of society and is deemed a freak and an outcast then has the freedom to do what they want. The Joker and Beetlejuice can do that in a much more liberating way than, say, Edward Scissorhands, or even Pee-Wee, because they're deemed disgusting. They are the darker sides of freedom. Insanity is in some scary way the most freedom you can have, because you're not bound by the laws of society.

We tried to put Robin in, to make that relationship work in a real way. In the TV series he's just *there*. We tried a slightly more psychological approach, but I felt unless you're going to focus on that and give it its

80

due, it's like 'Who is this guy?' Sam and I spent a lot of time going over that, anguishing over it. It's a good thing we didn't do it, because it would have cost a lot, and when we were getting ready to shoot the movie it was the easiest lift. Again, I just went back to the psychology of a man who dresses up as a bat; he's a very singular, lonely character, and putting him with somebody just didn't make sense. It didn't make sense in the next one either; we tried it there too. But it's just too much. There's too much material with these characters.

As with Pee-Wee's Big Adventure *and* Beetlejuice, *Burton called upon Danny Elfman to provide* Batman's *dark, orchestral score. This time, however, Elfman's soundtrack album was complemented by one from Prince, who had initially been commissioned to provide two songs for the movie.*

We needed two numbers – one for when The Joker goes into the museum, and the other for the parade sequence, and I actually used music by Prince for those scenes when we shot them. But what happened was it snowballed. It got bigger. He really got into the movie and wrote a bunch of songs. Guber and Peters had this idea of getting Michael Jackson to do the love theme, Prince to do The Joker theme, and Danny would just tie it all together. They can make that work for *Top Gun*, but my stuff isn't like that. It needs to be finessed a bit more. And I don't think those songs work. It doesn't have anything to do with Prince's music, it has more to do with their integration into the film. I liked them on their own, but I'm not proficient enough to make something like that work if it's not right.

I love Prince. I saw him twice at Wembley when I was shooting the movie. I think he's incredible. Here was a guy who was looking at a movie and doing his thing to it. It's like what comic book people do, it's their impression. I love that. I wish there was more of that kind of thing. It's cool to have crossover things like that. But I couldn't make the songs work, and I think I did a disservice to the movie and to him. But the record company wanted those things to be in there. Obviously, they made a lot of money from it, so I guess in that respect they achieved something. But I don't feel I made it work very well. The songs bring it too much into a specific time frame.

Batman *opened in the USA on 21 June 1989 and became the first film to* *break $100 million in its first ten days of release. It eventually became not only the top money-maker of 1989, with a worldwide gross in excess of $500 million, and the biggest film in Warner Bros's history, but also a multi-media merchandising and cultural phenomenon, the hype of which had never been seen before; until the release of* Jurassic Park *in 1993, it was the blockbuster against which all subsequent blockbusters had to be measured.*

The interesting thing about hype is that everyone thought the studio was creating it, when in fact you can't create hype; it's a phenomenon that's beyond a studio, it has a life of its own. The most negative thing to me was working on something that gained so much hype, because I'm the type of person – and there is a percentage of the population out there like myself – who if I hear too much about something gets turned off by it. And it was odd to be working on something that, if I was a normal person, I'd have gone, 'Shut the fuck up. I'm sick of hearing about this thing. I won't go see it, 'cos I've heard too much about it.' That was the most disturbing thing. But there was no way to control it. And then you get the inevitable backlash to that. My main concern was that the movie be judged on its own merits and not become this *thing*. But there's nothing you can do about it. It helped being in England, even with the press attention there, because it wasn't my country, and so I just focused on making the movie and didn't think too much about anything else.

Batman *won Anton Furst an Oscar for his design work, but was criticized in some quarters for being 'too dark'. Many critics also felt that Burton was more interested in The Joker than in the title character.*

That's not true, but there is an inherent problem with these characters. It was similar to the criticism that Adam and Barbara Maitland were boring. That's not true either. But there is an inherent difference in the characters of Batman and The Joker: The Joker is an extrovert and Batman an introvert. So no matter what you do, you can't match the energy, the balance. You have this character who always wants to remain in the shadows, to remain hidden. If these two were standing on the street, Batman would always be wanting to hide, whereas The Joker would be, 'Look at me. Look at me.' So that's part of what the energy of it was. I certainly wasn't less interested in Batman, it's just that he is who he is, and The Joker is who he is. Right or wrong, I sort of let these things play themselves out.

Some people got it, some people understood that. Obviously, a lot of people thought The Joker was the thing, but a lot of people found Michael to be more compelling because of that. He captured a certain subtle sadness in his character. It was as if he was thinking, 'Look at this guy. He gets to go out there and jump around and be a clown, and I have to remain in the shadows.' And there was a pent-up, bottled-up feeling to him which I think works with the Batman character.

It's funny, that whole dark and light thing. In fact, I've gotten more confused by it in a way. It was so weird on the second *Batman* because I would do those big press junkets where you're seeing a zillion people – every six minutes somebody new – and it became like a joke. I felt I was on *Candid Camera*, because one person would come in and go, 'The film is much lighter than the last one', and then the next person would come up and say, 'It's much darker than the first movie.' I felt like a psycho because I never think of things as dark or light. I've always felt that you couldn't even pull apart light and dark, they're so intertwined. I felt that way growing up, and I feel that way now. Sometimes I'll watch something that people don't see anything weird about and I'll find it deeply subversive and scary and dark. And then people will look at something that I've done and go, 'That's really dark', and I don't see it. It's like the end of *Vincent* when they said they wanted him to live and walk off with his dad. That felt darker to me, because the other ending felt more beautiful and more like what was in his mind, which is what the thing was about. It was about somebody's spirit, and to make it literal was, I felt, making it darker, ultimately. So what is perceived as light and dark is completely open to interpretation.

During the shooting of Batman, *Burton met Lena Gieseke, a German painter, and they were married in February 1989 while he was completing post-production in England.*

Edward Scissorhands

Following the enormous success of Batman, Burton was considered Hollywood's hottest young director. But rather than direct the Batman sequel that Warner Bros wanted, he opted to make Edward Scissorhands, a film he had long cherished, and one based on an image – a man with scissors in place of hands – that he had been toying with since childhood. Though Burton had been linked with Warners for his previous three films, he found the studio unreceptive to the idea, and sought out another studio which would allow him the freedom to make the film his way. He found it in Twentieth Century-Fox, which was then being run by former director Joe Roth.

Warners just didn't get it, which was good because I knew they didn't want to do it. I try to work with people who want to do what I want to do. Even now I try to gauge if people just want to do it because of me, or if they actually like it. It's helpful if they respond to the material because it's such a difficult process. So it was for the best, I think, because Warners weren't into it. Hollywood is so strange, though; for a community made up of so many freakish outsiders, it's oddly conservative.

Even though I have come up through the studio system, I haven't really felt like I have, and I don't think the studio people feel like I have either; they sometimes look at me with a sort of worried expression, often about what it is I want to do. But there's a great energy about that too, there's something that's great about operating within that system and then approaching things the way you want to. There's kind of a perverse charm to it.

Back when Burton had been in pre-production on Beetlejuice, he had commissioned Caroline Thompson, a young novelist, to write the screenplay for Edward Scissorhands. The pair had been introduced through their agent who thought they might get on. He was right. In Thompson, Burton found a kindred spirit who would later write the screenplay for another of

Johnny Depp as Edward Scissorhands

Burton's long-cherished projects, The Nightmare Before Christmas.

I had read her book, *First Born,* which was about an abortion that came back to life. It was good. It had sociological things that were thematic, but also had fantastical elements to it, which was nice, and the combination of

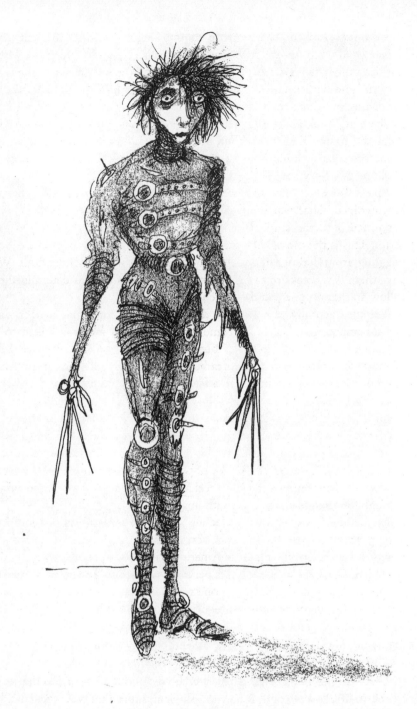

Edward Scissorhands

those things I liked. It was close to the feeling I wanted for *Edward Scissorhands*. I'm not the most communicative of people, especially when an idea comes from a feeling, so I was lucky to meet Caroline. She was very in tune with my ideas, which was good because the idea had been inside me for a long time, it was symbolic and not something I wanted to sit there and pick apart and analyse. I needed somebody who understood what the basic thing was about, so there wouldn't have to be a lot of grade school psychology going on in terms of discussing the project. I could be fairly cryptic and it still came across to her.

I paid Caroline a few thousand dollars to write it so there was no studio involved. That was good. Sometimes you just like to get it out. We submitted it to the studios as a package. It was like, 'Okay, this is the script. This is the movie. Do you guys wanna do it?' There wasn't a lot of haggling around about it, which is the best way to get anything done. We gave them two weeks to say yes or no. It was a route I was determined to follow so that no one could force changes on me.

The idea actually came from a drawing I did a long time ago. It was just an image that I liked. It came subconsciously and was linked to a character who wants to touch but can't, who was both creative and destructive – those sort of contradictions can create a kind of ambivalence. It was very much linked to a feeling. The manifestation of the image made itself apparent and probably came to the surface when I was a teenager, because it is a very teenage thing. It had to do with relationships. I just felt I couldn't communicate. It was the feeling that your image and how people perceive you are at odds with what is inside you, which is a fairly common feeling. I think a lot of people feel that way to some degree, because it's frustrating and sad to feel a certain way but for it not to come through. So the idea had to do with image and perception.

I remember growing up and feeling that there is not a lot of room for acceptance. You are taught at a very early age to conform to certain things. It's a situation, at least in America, that's very prevalent and which starts from day one at school: this person's smart, this person's not smart, this person's good at sports, this one's not, this person's weird, this one's normal. From day one you're categorized. That was the strongest impulse in the film. I remember sitting there as a child, looking at the teacher saying some other kid is stupid, and really he's not stupid, he's much more intelligent than a lot of others and has a lot more spirit, it's just that he's not conforming to the teacher's image. So I think the film is more of a reaction against that kind of categorization. I fell into the weird category because I was quiet, I was interiorized. People are categorized very easily,

Edward suburbanized

even in Hollywood. I talk to actors all the time who are categorized as dramatic and so can't do this or that. I don't know why people do it because it seems to me that nobody would like it done to them. It's kind of sad and frustrating at the same time, because somebody's saying you're this and somehow it's removed from you. And the more quiet somebody is, or the more different people feel you are, the more they like to do it.

On the surface Edward Scissorhands *appeared to be yet another of Burton's reworkings of* Frankenstein. *Edward, the unfinished creation of his inventor/father who dies before he can complete the job, is removed from his lonely existence in a hilltop castle by Avon lady Peg Boggs (Dianne Wiest) and finds himself living with her family in a pastel-coloured version of suburbia. There he becomes the source of fantasy, gossip, resentment, adoration and lust for the neighbours, who he wins over with his wildly kitsch topiaries, outlandish hairstyles and elaborate ice sculptures.*

First came the image, linked to those feelings of not being accepted. Then from that came the images of the ice and the hedges, just as a natural out-

Edward meets the Avon Lady (Johnny Depp and Dianne Wiest)

Edward and the hedges

growth of him being a helpful, handy household item. And then there was the world that he comes into; that came more from my memory of growing up in that world, in suburbia, and the feelings that were linked to it. Memory has a way of heightening itself. Any time you think back to something, the further away it is, the more extreme, the more heightened it becomes. The interesting thing about these neighbourhoods is that they're so close together you know everybody, but there's stuff underneath that you just don't know. Sexual stuff. There's a certain kind of kinkiness to suburbia. There was an undercurrent of it when I was growing up. I never saw it specifically, but you certainly got a feeling of it.

I grew up in suburbia and I still don't understand certain aspects of it. There's a certain kind of vagueness, a blankness, and I got this very strongly from my family. The pictures my family had on the walls, I never got the sense that they liked them, that they bought them, that somebody had given them to them. It was almost as if they had always been there, and yet no one had ever looked at them. I remember sitting there looking at some of these things going, 'What the hell is that? What are those resin grapes? Where did they get them? What does it mean?'

Growing up in suburbia was like growing up in a place where there's no sense of history, no sense of culture, no sense of passion for anything.

You never felt people liked music. There was no showing of emotion. It was very strange. 'Why is that there? What am I sitting on?' You never felt that there was any attachment to things. So you were either forced to conform and cut out a large portion of your personality, or to develop a very strong interior life which made you feel separate.

But the film is not autobiographical, because it was important for me to be as objective as possible. That's why I felt very lucky to have Johnny because he brought to it a lot of themes that are nearer his life which, when I started to talk to him, I liked very much. I could look at him and draw upon his world, in a way.

Johnny Depp, star of TV's teen detective show 21 Jump Street *and John Waters's* Cry-Baby, *had always been Burton's number one choice for the role of Edward Scissorhands, although he had initially met Tom Cruise in connection with the part.*

They are always saying, here is a list of five people who are box-office, and three of them are Tom Cruise. I've learned to be open at the initial stage and talk to people. He certainly wasn't my ideal, but I talked to him. He was interesting, but I think it worked out for the best. A lot of questions came up – I don't really recall the specifics – but at the end of the meeting I did feel like, and I probably even said this to him, 'It's nice to have a lot of questions about the character, but you either do it or you don't do it.'

I was glad Johnny did it. I can't think of anybody else who would have done it for me that way. I didn't really know him. I hadn't seen that TV show he'd been in, but I must have seen a picture of him somewhere. I like people's eyes a lot and, especially with a character like this who doesn't really speak, eyes are very important. We wanted him right from the beginning, but I was open about meeting other people because I think when I first started out I was a little snobby about the whole thing. I was, 'I don't like that person, I don't like this person', and sometimes I'd meet people and they were different from what I'd expected. So I've tried to become more open, because you can be surprised that way.

In America, Johnny is very much known as a teen idol and he's perceived as difficult and aloof; there are all sorts of things written about him in the press which are completely untrue. I mean, as a person he's a very funny, warm, great guy. He's a normal guy – at least my interpretation of normal – but he's perceived as dark and difficult and weird, and is judged by his looks. But he's almost completely the opposite of this perception. So the themes of *Edward*, of image and perception, of somebody being perceived to be the opposite of what he is, was a theme he could relate to. The words 'freakish' and 'freak' have so many interpretations, and in a weird way he sort of relates to freaks because he's treated as one. That flip-flopping and inverting of themes and perceptions was something he really responded to because he goes through that all the time. You pick up a tabloid and he's portrayed as the brooding James Dean type or whatever way people want to label him as, but he's not. People get judged by their looks a lot. It's fascinating; it's always been that way and it probably always will be. It's sad when you're judged by the way you look, and that sadness builds up in you because, at least for me, there was always a desire to connect with people – not everybody, but some people, one or two – and he's probably been through a lot of that kind of stuff, so he understood that side of it.

I think that a lot of the character is him. He has this kind of naïve quality which as you get older gets tested and has holes poked into it. It's hard to maintain that, because you don't want to shield yourself from society and the rest of the world completely, but at the same time you'd like to maintain a certain kind of openness and feeling that you had earlier on in your life. And I would imagine Johnny is somebody who would want to protect that to some degree.

Playing opposite Depp as Wiest's cheerleader daughter, Kim, was Winona Ryder, who had made such an impact in Beetlejuice, *and who, at the time, was romantically involved with her co-star.*

I like her very much. She's one of my favourites. Also she responds to this kind of dark material and I thought the idea of her as a cheerleader, wearing a blonde wig, was very funny. I think she might even say it's probably the most difficult thing she's ever done because she did not relate to her character. She was tortured by these people at school herself. It was so funny. I used to laugh every day when I saw her walk on the set wearing this little cheerleader outfit and a Hayley Mills-type blonde wig. She looked liked Bambi.

I don't think their relationship affected the movie in a negative way. Perhaps it might have if it had been a different kind of movie, something that was tapping more into some positive or negative side of their relationship. But this was such a fantasy. The fact that we were in Florida

Kim (Winona Ryder) and the ice

probably was helpful for the two of them to be together, because it was a pretty bizarre environment. But they were very professional and didn't bring any weird stuff to the set.

Everybody goes down to Florida for the weather. It's like a joke. I went there partially as a desire to get away from Hollywood and partially because the type of suburban neighbourhoods in California in which the film takes place were built in the fifties and they've all got very overgrown now. And Florida just happened to be a place where the neighbourhoods were new and had that flavour to them.

In typically Burtonesque fashion, the houses in this particular suburbia were slightly removed from reality by being painted various pastel shades.

It was seen from Edward's point of view, a slightly more romanticized view of the world. I like dark colours better, but they weren't too dissimilar from what was already there. And although the production designer Bo Welch painted all the houses different colours, it was important to me that the area still remain a community. We hardly touched the insides of the houses. What you see is pretty much what was there.

93

Sometimes people say, 'Are you going to do a real film with real people?' But to me the words 'normal' and 'real' have a thousand different interpretations. What's real? What's normal? And I think the reason I like fairy tales so much as a form – at least my interpretation of the form – what I get out of fairy tales, folk tales, myths, are these very extreme images, very heightened, but with some foundation to them. It means something, but is fairly abstract and if it's going to connect with you it will connect with you, and if it's not then it won't. I think that's the danger, especially in commercial film-making, because sometimes things will just leave people cold, it's not literal enough. A question they ask is 'Where did Edward get the ice?' Go see *Three Men and a Little Lady* if that's your thing. There's a certain amount of symbolism, a certain amount of interpretation and abstraction which I appreciate. I much prefer to connect with something on a subconscious level than to intellectualize about it. I prefer to intellectualize about it slightly after the fact.

I don't follow any script like the Bible because it changes in the process of the visualization of it. It is a different thing. I get out of a script the things I need. It's constantly changing, it's organic. So I just try to take the root and spirit of it. Sometimes I'll think there's a great line in a script, and then when a certain actor says it, it just doesn't come across. Whereas another actor could maybe say the line a better way. It's very much down to the elements involved at the moment you're doing it. Sometimes things just mutate. There's an excitement about that that I like. I don't mind if things change a little, I don't mind seeing how things work out, even from when you're shooting it, to when you see it on film. I remember Johnny was able to do something that amazed me. I was very close to him one day, watching him doing a scene, and the next day we saw it on film, and almost without doing anything he was able to do something with his eyes that made them glassy. It was as if he was about to cry, like one of those Walter Keane paintings with the big eyes. I don't know how he did it. It wasn't something we did with the camera or the lighting, it was incredible and that kind of excitement – weird little things, weird new images that surprise you – is very specific to film.

I love actors like Johnny and Dianne Wiest and Alan Arkin who are really doing a lot under the surface and doing a lot for the other characters; they're very unselfish. Those are the things that I enjoy the most when I see the movies years later. Dianne, in particular, was wonderful. She was the first actress to read the script, supported it completely and, because she is so respected, once she had given it her stamp of approval, others soon got interested. In many ways, she was my guardian angel.

Edward's isolation

In the film, Ryder's cheerleader, Kim, leaves her jock boyfriend, played by Anthony Michael Hall, to be with Edward, an event that many have postulated as Burton's revenge against those jocks he encountered at school.

I was always amazed by those guys in school. I would sit there thinking to myself: they've always got the girlfriends, they're always the image of things, and yet these guys are psychotic. If she stays with him, they'll get married straight out of high school, and he'll end up beating her up. It'll be that kind of situation. I resisted those kinds of labels because what others perceived to be the norm, often turned out to be the opposite. It's funny, I went back to a high school reunion and it was true – and this is pretty much across the board – that the people who were considered outcasts and freaks at high school – much more than me; I was considered quiet, so I sort of remained out of everything, but some people were really tortured – these people ended up being the most well-adjusted, really attractive (not just physically but attractive as people) and were doing really well. And the other people had faded. The presidents, the jocks, they had truly peaked in high school, and it was so shocking to

The Avon lady enters Edward's domain

see that. It confirmed your suspicions about things, because those who were tortured were forced to be their own people; they couldn't rely on society, they couldn't rely on the culture or the hierarchy to take care of them, so to speak, so they had to make themselves acceptable.

Hall's jock is subsequently killed, a scene that shocked a number of people who felt the whole tone of the movie had been radically altered.

That was perhaps some sort of junior high or high school revenge fantasy, I guess, somewhere deep inside. I don't know, perhaps I was just letting off steam.

In the small but pivotal role of Edward's inventor/father, Burton cast Vincent Price, with whom he had maintained a friendship since they worked together on Vincent.

When he did this, even though it was a small role, it had a lot of emotional impact for me, because he looks so amazing. When I see it and see him, it gives me a strong feeling. There are lots of layers of symbols and

Tim Burton and Vincent Price

Edward Scissorhands and his inventor/father

themes; his role probably had a lot to do with how I felt about him in terms of watching his movies and how he was my mentor, so to speak, through the movies. I was very happy that he did it and I got to know him a little better. After *Vincent* we had struck up a friendship, and I had always kept in touch with him, even loosely, when I was away in England making *Batman*. It was nice for me, because he was of the generation that, even if you didn't keep in touch regularly, you kept connected to in some way. He was really great that way.

After completing Edward Scissorhands *Burton began directing a documentary on his idol, who died in 1993, entitled* Conversations with Vincent *(working title).*

I knew he wasn't well. He hadn't been well ever since his wife died right after we were shooting the documentary. He was really into her and maybe the impulse to join her was there. I was sad. It's a loss, but he was an incredible person who had given a lot.

Depp's Edward is found living alone in the attic of a gothic castle, two settings that have regularly been the dwelling place of numerous Burton characters.

There's a sense of isolation in that. Symbolically I associate it with isolation. But it's also a reaction against the suburban home in some ways. It's like, if you've grown up and lived your whole life in one of those, you start imagining all sorts of things as a reaction against that. It was always a desire to be up, or out, or away, and in an environment that was not white like being inside a shoe box.

Edward Scissorhands *climaxes, much like James Whale's* Frankenstein, *and indeed much like Burton's own* Frankenweenie, *with a mob confronting the 'evil creature' – in this case, Edward – at his castle.*

Again, when you grow up watching these things you make analogies to your own life. I had always felt that growing up in those kinds of neighbourhoods the only time you'd ever see the neighbours all together was if there was an accident or something out front. Then the pull-out-the-lawnchairs kind of mob mentality would kick in. I was always fascinated by that, and how the parallel between surburban life and a horror movie was really closer than you might think. The mob mentality is in a lot of those horror movies.

With Edward Scissorhands finally unable to consummate his love for Kim because of his appearance, the film can also be seen as Burton's version of Beauty and the Beast, *a fairy-tale bookended by a prologue and an epilogue featuring Winona Ryder as an old woman telling her granddaughter the story of Edward.*

That's such a classic theme. Someone said there were only five stories, well, that's one of them. It's a theme that's in thousands of stories and any number of horror pictures. Obviously, I was conscious of it in a thematic way, but it's simply *there*, it's not something I dwelled on very much. It wasn't the overriding impulse to do the film, but it certainly was a part of it.

To create Edward's scissor hands, Burton employed Oscar-winning special effects artist Stan Winston, who would later go on to design The Penguin's make-up for Batman Returns.

Stan's the greatest. I love Stan. And part of his success is that he knows how to deal with people. A lot of people who do effects are very hard to communicate with. Stan's got such a big operation, and he's got a lot of great people working with him. He knows how to deal with me. He tries to get into the spirit of it, which is great. I give him my cheesy little sketches and he goes from there. I'm always appreciative of people who like to look at them, because obviously you can't just take my sketches and make them, there's another very crucial step where they're transformed into reality with an actor. But Stan would look at them and take them and do some illustrations and stuff. It was just a real pleasure. And he's got the cleanest studio I've ever seen in my life. I've never seen a cleaner special effects place. I used to joke with him about it because there's something wrong with that. It's like a museum. Everybody else's place, except for Rick Baker's, looks like my place, like a dump.

The scissor hands had to be large since I wanted Johnny to be beautiful and dangerous. We made him a pair and let him put them on and try to do something, and he learned better than just rehearsing what the feeling is like. Again, it was a case of becoming the character.

In 1989 Burton formed Tim Burton Productions with Denise Di Novi, a former journalist and the producer of Heathers, *as president of the company. Together they produced* Edward Scissorhands, Batman Returns *and* The Nightmare Before Christmas *before Di Novi left the company in 1992, though she has continued to work with Burton, co-producing* Ed Wood *and* Cabin Boy. Edward Scissorhands *marked Burton's first film as producer.*

Even when I wasn't really a producer, when you're doing something that you care about, those lines get very blurred. There's a little bit more responsibility to it, but it's not something that feels that different. A lot of it has to do with your attitude and how you go into something. If you go into something one hundred per cent, it doesn't matter if you're the director/producer. It doesn't feel that different from when you're directing it, anyway.

   Denise produced *Ed Wood*, but we've kind of split off a little bit. She's doing more things because I just want to focus on the things that I want to do and not do a whole bunch of other stuff necessarily. I needed somebody to help out and run things. Whereas at the beginning nobody pays any attention to you, once you get a little bit into it you find you're managing an office, because you get submissions, people calling, all that kind of stuff. I was looking to create some sort of semi-solid kind of thing. It's nice to have somebody who's with you, and who's just thinking about you.

Burton oversaw the transfer of Beetlejuice *into a children's cartoon TV series and made his first on screen appearance in Cameron Crowe's twentysomething movie,* Singles, *in which he played a director of dating agency videos referred to as 'the next Martin Scorsese'.*

That guy Cameron asked me to do it. He's a nice guy, and I just did it. I'd never done something like that before and I got to go to Seattle and that was fun. I was curious to see what it would be like to be a cheesy actor, and I certainly was.

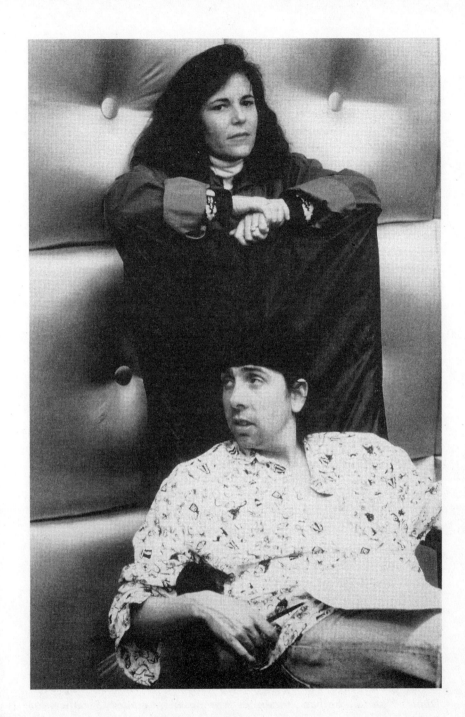

Tim Burton with Denise Di Novi

Batman Returns

While Burton was in Europe promoting the release of Edward Scissorhands, *he admitted that* Batman *was the one movie of his that he didn't feel close to and when, in 1991, he finally decided to direct the sequel, it was to enable him to connect with the material again.*

I didn't want to do the *Batman* sequel initially because I was kind of burnt out, and I didn't know what I could bring to it. It took me a long time to get interested in it again. Part of it was all those big weird circumstances: like not having a minute, working seven days a week under really harsh conditions, not having a chance to think, not having the script sorted out. It's the one movie that I feel more detached from than the others. I think any director will say that the first big movie you do is a little bit of a shock. But again, some of it has to do with how you feel at the time. I never walk into anything without feeling close to it; I *did* originally feel close to it, but it got away from me a little bit. That's how I felt at the time, but now, as everything gets further away, I get a slightly more romanticized vision of it: 'Oh those were the good old days, the first *Batman.*' So when I talked to you I was still suffering from that post-movie depression.

I think every movie that I've done has lots of flaws, it's just that I don't mind the flaws in the others as much as I mind the ones in *Batman.* I treat my films like my mutated children, in a way. They may have flaws, they may have weird problems, but I still love them. It takes me a good three years before I can distance myself from a film and then judge it. It wasn't until a couple of years ago that I could start to enjoy *Pee-Wee's Big Adventure.* The further away a movie is, the clearer it gets, and the more I enjoy it.

Initially Sam Hamm, screenwriter of Batman, *was hired to write* Batman Returns, *but when his script failed to meet with Burton's approval, Daniel Waters, who had written the mordant black comedy* Heathers *for Di Novi, was brought on board.*

Sam wrote one script, but the thing that started to get my interest going was the idea of Catwoman. I talked to Dan Waters loosely about it and he nailed Catwoman very quickly. And I realized I really like this material: I like Batman, I like Catwoman, I like The Penguin, I like their world. It's a good canvas of characters. I like their duality. And the thing that I really liked about *Batman* as a comic book property was that they're all fucked-up characters – that's what's so beautiful about them. Unlike other comics, they're just all fucked, the villains and Batman. But that's also part of the problem – I never see these people as villains.

Waters's script took off from Hamm's original and exploited Batman's vulnerabilities in a devilishly demented plot that pitted him against Catwoman, a PVC-clad anti-heroine engaged in a lust-hate relationship with the Dark Knight; The Penguin, a dark, mutated, nasty half-animal who was disposed of into the sewers as a baby by parents horrified at his flippers; and Max Shreck, the white-haired power-crazed industrialist who essentially acts as the catalyst for all the others. For many, however, it was a case of too many villains spoiling the Batman, with Keaton again forced to take a back seat.

I know. I think I probably got a little carried away. I just found interest in all of them, and I think I kind of evened them all out. I also wanted to have fun on the movie. I didn't have fun on the first one, and I wanted to get back to the feeling I had when I worked on *Beetlejuice*. But it certainly didn't turn out that way; it was the hardest one.

A lot of those characters from the comic strip – The Joker, Catwoman, Harvey Dent – are all very easy to identify in psychological profile. But characters like The Penguin and The Riddler are not so easy. It's like 'Who are these people?' Again, the idea of not knowing who you are, is, I think, why I like the Batman material. It's a very questioning kind of thing: who are we? Is what we perceive reality? But that's a dangerous kind of subject matter because it's very ethereal in some ways. So, we tried to give The Penguin a foundation and a psychological profile. I probably gave it too much, spent too much time on it. But I don't think there's anybody better than Danny at making the horrible acceptable.

I liked the fact that some people couldn't decide whether or not Catwoman was bad. She never was bad. When they were bad on the TV series they were never really bad. That's the thing, I never saw any of them as bad, and I never believe it when they say people are bad. I don't have that compass.

In the dual role of Selina Kyle, Max Shreck's mousy secretary who is transformed into Catwoman in a quite wondrously Burtonesque moment where she receives the life-force out of a number of alleycats, Burton initially cast Annette Benning, who had to bow out after falling pregnant. For Burton there was only one other choice for the role: Michelle Pfeiffer. But Sean Young, who had been cast in the part eventually played by Kim Basinger in the original Batman *until she broke her arm in a riding accident, believed the role should have gone to her and turned up on the Warner Bros lot dressed as Catwoman.*

She came to the studio and into my office. I wasn't there, but she had somebody out in the parking lot, a bodyguard or assistant, and when she saw somebody who looked like me she said, 'There he is, grab him.' I guess it was the publicist of the movie and it freaked him out. Then the people in my office told her it wasn't me, and she stormed over to Mark Canton's office where Michael Keaton was, and demanded to be in the film. After that she went on all these talk shows citing 'unfair Hollywood', which was so absurd, because the simple fact is that casting is just a choice. I'm not 'horrible Hollywood'. I'm not shunning her. But she made it into this big deal, which was absurd. She went on *The Joan Rivers Show* dressed as Catwoman, though her outfit seemed more appropriate for a female wrestling movie from what I saw, and said, 'Horrible Hollywood bigwigs wouldn't see me.' I hated being perceived in that way. I'm very sensitive when it comes to casting. I'm not the type of director who has mindless meetings with people. I don't like putting people through things; I don't want to waste their time. She made it into a big, stupid issue. I think she always wanted to play Catwoman, which is fine, it's a great role. I'd like to play Catwoman, but unfortunately it's just a simple choice and it's my choice, and it doesn't have anything to do with right or wrong. She's screaming 'Hollywood system' and I'm saying 'No, artistic choice'.

I met with Michelle. I hadn't really seen her in very much, but we had a nice meeting and I liked her. Certainly, you can look at Michelle and see she has a feline quality that you would expect in Catwoman, but I just met her and liked her. Again, that's all it is. It's a simple choice, a connection. She was into it. She's from Orange County, a kind of similar era and similar environment to mine and maybe I connected with her on that level. She's a talented actress and did great. I was impressed with her physical talents, the things that she could do. She was game for weird things; she put birds in her mouth, she endured a lot. She also did that weird thing with her eyes. It's not that shocking – given that these people

Catwoman

Michelle Pfeiffer: 'She has a feline quality'

are covered up with masks – that eyes play such an important part.

*In tune with Burton's fascination with duality, the film is full of warped
tensions, deep, dark dialogue and remarkably complex characters whose
other sides Burton twists into a bitter confection, with Batman and
Catwoman dangerously drawn to each other while suited up, yet
painfully unable to relate when freed from their costumes and their
masks.*

Masks in this country symbolize hiding, but when I used to go to
Hallowe'en parties wearing a mask it was actually more of a doorway, a
way of expressing myself. There is something about being hidden that in
some weird way helps you to be more open because you feel freer. People
would open up much more. They were always a little bit wilder, because
something about wearing a mask protected them. It's something I have
noticed in our culture and have felt myself. When people are covered, a certain weird freedom comes to the surface. It seems that the opposite should
be true, but I've found that it isn't.

Some actors have really tapped into the energy of dressing up. I've
always loved it on every movie I've ever done. Michael and I used to joke

Michelle Pfeiffer and Tim Burton

about it all the time and sometimes we'd just burst out laughing. You're in this costume and it's like a joke, it's unbelievable, and in some ways it's quite good because you can never take it seriously. There's something beautiful about that.

In one of the film's finest moments, Michael Keaton's Bruce Wayne is dancing with Michelle Pfeiffer's Selina Kyle at a masked ball when they both realize the other's secret identity, and Kyle, who has earlier admitted 'she's sick of masks', asks, 'Does this mean we have to start fighting?'

I think the actors got that very well, because they certainly had been going through it for some time. In some ways it's crazy, because there were so many restrictions with the kind of outfits, make-up and masks they were wearing – it's rather perverse how restricting in a physical sense it often is – that they began to feel that they were not emoting at all, but they were. So, by the time it got to the ball scene I think they could just feel it, it was just there.

Catwoman represents Burton's strongest female character; her relation-

Catwoman and Batman: sick of masks

ship with Keaton's Batman crackles with an intensity that is in marked contrast to that between Keaton and Kim Basinger's clichéd love interest, Vicky Vale, from the first movie.

Some of that is just the unfortunate conventions of movies. I mean, Catwoman is one of my favourite characters, but there is some truth to the criticism that certain characters are not as fleshed out or as wild as some of the others. But those characters are very important too; without the Adam and Barbara characters being kind of boring, Betelgeuse would have had nothing to play off against. Michael got the same criticism in *Batman*, but I always found him to be very compelling and real, which is particularly difficult in a fantastical setting. It's a very underneath the surface kind of service that those characters provide for the movies, and I find them to be more compelling than a lot of people do.

Although Warner Bros had, at great expense, kept the huge Gotham City set up at Pinewood Studios, Burton decided to film on soundstages on the Warners lot in Burbank instead. Bo Welch, Burton's production designer on Beetlejuice *and* Edward Scissorhands, *was employed to supervise the building of a new Gotham City, which retained Anton Furst's hellish feel, but which, according to Welch, was more American than the original's metropolis and contained 'more wit and irony'. Furst, who after* Batman *had been trying to get several directing projects off the ground and had designed Planet Hollywood in New York, was for contractual reasons unable to do the sequel. He committed suicide three months after* Batman Returns *began principal photography in September 1991.*

I decided to do it in LA just because it made more sense to do it there. I think it was felt that it could be kept more secure there, given what happened with the press on the first one. The dollar was probably even worse and it didn't make any sense to do it in England. Also, I wanted to do it in LA because I thought I could use more people that I know from here, actors like Paul Reubens, because to do it over there in England would mean taking some actors, but not all. I was really just looking for a different energy to it. It's closer to *Beetlejuice* in some ways than it is to the other *Batman*. There's a weirder energy to it than the first; the first *Batman* is, I think, a little more controlled. But I didn't think about that, I just tried to treat it like a regular movie and do the things that I wanted to see, which again, I realize, on something like this is a little dangerous. People would pick on certain things, like: 'What's that black stuff coming out of The Penguin's mouth?' I would say to them, 'I don't know, but I can send it in and have it analysed. He's filled with bile, he's a dark little character and he got a lot of things inside him, but I can get a chemical breakdown if you like.' It's good for me to be questioned about certain things; I think it's healthy for me not just to spin off into the cosmos, but people do it to ridiculous extremes.

Everything happens randomly on the set because there are so many things that can go wrong. I've probably been derailed more in terms of things that I've planned than those that I haven't, because so many things can go wrong. So I try in meetings with actors and everybody who is working on the film – costume designer, production designer – to make sure that everybody is on the same wavelength to some degree. So that when you get on the set it's like: here are all the realities of this day, of these people, of what we have, of what we don't have, the weather, the conditions, so let's try to make the best of it. And then, just hope. I don't do a lot of rehearsing. I get in there and block the scene and feel it out with people in their costumes and stuff, because everything suggests something and it's really hard to lock in, one hundred per cent, to what that is until all the elements are there together. So it gets to be much more of a last minute thing.

I would say I shoot an average of maybe five or six takes. That's if everything is okay technically. Often, I shoot more when there are technical problems or special effects involved. Usually I take it as it comes when I get on set. Sometimes if I do a little sketch, it will suggest a shot and I'll have something in mind. But usually I just go with it. Again, actors bring something to everything; each actor has their own set of issues, so something will be suggested by how they look in their costume. So, again, it's got to be right then and there on the set.

To transform Danny De Vito into The Penguin, Burton again called upon Stan Winston whose talented team of artists and technicians fashioned The Penguin's grotesque look from a sketch of Burton's. To create The Penguin's bird army, however, a combination of techniques were utilized, including men in suits, computer-generated imagery, robotic creatures and even real penguins.

The Penguin

I don't really like using real animals because they're in an unnatural setting. I love animals, and that's why I could never watch *Lassie*. I couldn't sleep on Sunday nights if I ever watched it because I don't like seeing animals in jeopardy. I worry more about them than I do the actors, or anybody else. I have a real strong sense of standards with that. There's a lot of added stress there I would rather not have. I love animals and I like learning about them and seeing them, but given that we didn't take them from the wild and torture them and stuff, it was okay.

Batman Returns *continued a trend that has followed through all the films Burton has directed, up to and including* Ed Wood, *in that all his*

Danny De Vito

The Penguin's army ...

... in action

films are named after the main character.

That's something I've never thought about, now that you mention it, and I have no real answer for that except that none of them really have a plot. They're all weird little character pieces, I guess, even though nobody would necessarily perceive them as that. I guess I have just been drawn to the names and who they are, even on a kind of symbolic level. Again, I don't think anybody would consider these pictures to be in-depth character studies, but in some ways they're alternative little character pieces.

Batman Returns opened in America on 19 July 1992 and shattered its predecessor's record for the most successful three-day opening in history with receipts of $47.7 million. The film eventually grossed $268 million worldwide, but was considered by many critics to be 'too dark'.

In retrospect I don't think Warners were very happy with the movie. That's my feeling. I had put them through a lot, but I was just trying to give them a good movie. The first one was very successful and there are all of those traps that go along with that, but I tried not to think too much about that and just make a good, fun movie. A lot of it was, I think, just the sheer size of the production. They always want you to go faster, they always want you to hurry up. These kind of productions are big; it's not an exact science and I was going through a lot at the time. It probably had more to do with personal things than anything else. There was the death of a friend of mine, I was having trouble in a relationship, and sometimes, consciously, you don't know until later what's wrong. I just thought it was the hellish shoot of this movie, which didn't help the situation at all.

But I really like the film. I like it better than the first one. There was a big backlash that it was too dark, but I found this movie much less dark than the first one. It's just the cultural climate. And they hear that. They listen to that. I guess they have to to some degree. I don't want to because I think it's dangerous and perverse. I think the culture is much more disturbed and disturbing than this movie, a lot more. But they just fixate on things and they choose targets. I like the movie and I don't feel bad about it, and in some ways it's a purer form of what the *Batman* material is all about, which is that the line between villain and hero is blurred. Max Shreck was like the catalyst of all the characters, which I liked. He was the one who wasn't wearing the mask but, in some ways he was. And the film, in some ways, is just a visual comment on the differences in perception of what is good and bad.

Critics of Burton's work have constantly pointed to what they term his inability to tell a coherent story, and with Batman Returns *he was again accused of sacrificing the narrative for the sake of the visuals.*

I guess it must be the way my brain works, because the first *Batman* was probably my most concentrated effort to tell a linear story, and I realize that it's like a joke. I realized from *Beetlejuice* that there are some people who can do that, and that's fine. In any of my movies the narrative is the worst thing you've ever seen, and that's constant. I don't know why people are so into that because there are lots of movies that have a strong narrative, and I love those. But there are other types as well. Do Fellini movies have a strong narrative drive? I love movies where I make up my own idea about them. In fact, there'll be movies that maybe aren't even about what I think they're about. I just like making things up. Everybody is different, so things are going to affect people differently. So why not have your own opinions, have different levels of things you can find if you want them, however deeply you want to go. That's why I like Roman Polanski's movies, like *The Tenant*. I've felt like that, I've lived it, I know what that's like. Or *Repulsion*, I know that feeling, I understand it. *Bitter Moon*, I've seen that happen. You just connect. It may not be something that anybody else connects with, but it's like *I* get that, *I* understand that feeling. I will always fight that literal impulse to lay everything directly in front of you. I just hate it.

Some people are really good at narrative and some people are really good at action. I'm not that sort of person. So, if I'm going to do something, just let me do my thing and hope for the best. If you don't want me to do it, then don't have me do it. But if I do it, then don't make me conform. If you want it to be a James Cameron movie then get James Cameron to do it. Me directing action is a joke; I don't like guns. I hear a gunshot and I close my eyes. But again it comes down to your interpretation of action. I mean, there's plenty of action in a *Godzilla* movie, but I don't know if people would consider that action.

The Nightmare Before Christmas

After completing Vincent *in 1982, Burton had begun work on another project based on a poem he had written, this time inspired by Clement Clarke Moore's* The Night Before Christmas. *Entitled* The Nightmare Before Christmas, *it told the story of the misguided passion of Jack Skellington, the Pumpkin King of Hallowe'entown, who stumbles upon a door to Christmastown, and is so taken by what he sees that he returns home obsessed with bringing Christmas under his control.*

The initial impulse for doing it was the love of Dr Seuss and those holiday specials that I grew up watching, like *How the Grinch Stole Christmas* and *Rudolph the Red-Nosed Reindeer*. Those crude stop-motion animation holiday things that were on year in, year out make an impact on you early and stay with you. I had grown up with those and had a real feeling for them, and I think, without being too direct, the impulse was to do something like that.

When I first wrote the poem I had Vincent Price in mind as the narrator. He was the overall inspiration for the project because initially I was going to do it with him narrating, like a more expanded version of *Vincent*. Back then I think I would have done it as anything – a television special, a short film – whatever would have gotten it done at the time. It was a funny project because everybody was really nice about it, but it was like being in that show *The Prisoner*; everybody's really nice, but you know you're never going to get out, it's not going to happen. I took it around the networks, did storyboards and sketches and Rick Heinrichs did a little model of Jack. Everybody said they liked it, but not enough to do it at that time. I guess that was my first real taste of that kind of show-business mentality – a nice big smile and an 'Oh yeah, we're going to do this'. But, as you proceed, it becomes less and less of a reality.

It was after *Vincent*, so I was really into stop-motion. I'd seen clay-mation, I'd seen stop-motion, the Harryhausen things. On *Vincent* we weren't trying to push the boundaries of great animation. What we were trying to do with it in a very simple way was be more specific with the design. To me, in claymation the design elements get lost. So what we wanted to do was what you do in a drawing, but just spring it to the third dimension. I always thought that *Nightmare* should be done better than *Vincent*, but at the time I was just thinking of that simple, emotional, trying to make it a well-designed type of animation. I think it's harder to do emotional stuff in three dimensions. In so many ways drawn animation is easier because you can truly do anything, you can draw *anything*. Three-dimensional animation has limitations because you're moving puppets around. But I think when it works it is more effective because it is three-dimensional, and it feels like it's *there*.

The characters that were designed for *Nightmare* had the added burden of not having any eyeballs. The first rule of animation is: Eyes for Expression. But a lot of the characters either don't have any eyes, or their eyes are sewn shut. I thought if we could give life to these characters that have no eyes, it would be great. So, after drawing all those foxes with their wet drippy eyes at Disney, there was a little subversion in having these characters with no eyes. It was funny to think of a character that had these big black holes and to try and make that work.

The idea behind *Nightmare* also came from a combination of feelings to do with love for those *Rudolph* things. Thematically that's something that I like, still respond to, and have responded to in other films about that type of character, somebody, like a Grinch, who is perceived as scary but isn't. Again, that goes back to the monster movies I liked as a kid. They were perceived as frightening and bad, but they're weren't. It's also true in society; people get perceived that way all the time. I felt that way and I never liked it, therefore I always liked characters who were passionate and felt certain ways, but weren't what they were perceived to be. Jack is like a lot of characters in classic literature that are passionate and have a desire to do something in a way that isn't really acknowledged, just like that Don Quixote story, in which some character is on a quest for some sort of feeling, not even knowing what that is. It's a very primal thing to me, that kind of searching for something and not even knowing what it is, but being passionate about it. There are just aspects to the character of Jack that I like and identify with. It means something to me.

When I developed it originally, it was during the period when Disney was actually changing over, and when I didn't know if I was still an employee or not. I was just hanging around. I always felt that it was one project that I would like to make, I felt so secure about it. There was talk of doing it as a kind of TV special, or doing it drawn. But I just didn't want to do any of that. So, I decided to bury it, but always with that feel-

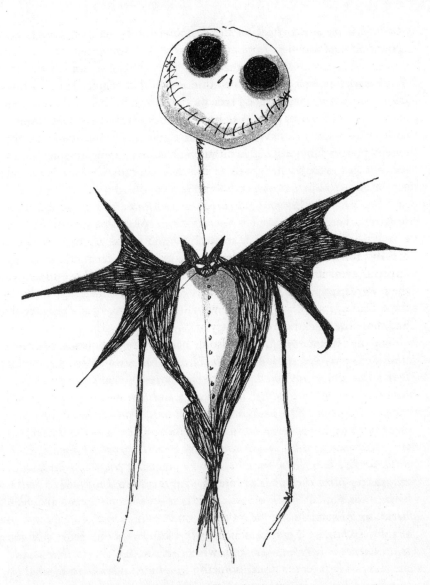

Jack Skellington: big black holes for eyes

ing that I would do it some time. It was weird, some projects you feel more like, 'Oh, I'd better do this now or never', but I never felt that way about *Nightmare*.

Over the years Burton's thoughts regularly returned to the project and in

1990 he had his agent check to see whether Disney still owned the rights to Nightmare *with a view to resurrecting it.*

I didn't even know if they owned it. So we tried to quietly say, 'Can we look around your basement?' And they did own it, because they own everything. There's this thing you sign when you work there, which states that any thoughts you have during your employment are owned by the thought police. Obviously, there's no real way of doing it quietly. We tried, but they were soon right there and they were fine – which is against their nature – so I'm very respectful and feel honoured that they let it happen. This was after *Edward Scissorhands* and *Batman*, and the reason it got made is because I've been lucky enough to be successful. That's really the only reason it got made. It certainly wasn't a case of the time being right. But I will say this about Disney, they at least understood our trying to push the envelope a little bit as far as the animation was concerned, they were responsive to that.

Recognizing the treasure locked in their vaults, Disney immediately leapt at the chance to work with Burton, and saw in his desire to produce a full-length stop-motion animated feature a way of further enhancing their reputation in animation. Though stop-motion had first been seen in 1907 in J. Stuart Blackton's The Haunted Hotel, *it was Willis O'Brien who pioneered stop-motion as an effects technique in 1925 in* The Lost World *and then, most memorably, in creating* King Kong *in 1933. He passed his mantle to Ray Harryhausen, who in turn created a coterie of fantastical creatures for films such as* Jason and the Argonauts *and the* Sinbad *series. The introduction of go-motion – a variation on stop-motion in which objects are blurred in the frame to produce a more realistic effect – in 1983 by Industrial Light and Magic for* Return of the Jedi, *and the advancement in computer-generated imagery, meant effects that would have previously been the domain of stop-motion could now be created by computer. This contributed to stop-motion's cinematic decline, though animators such as Nick Park in England, creator of the Oscar-winning* Creature Comforts, *and Henry Selick in the United States, with his commercials, idents for MTV and short films, kept the art very much alive and kicking.*

It's a funky old art form stop-motion, and even though new technology was used at times in *Nightmare*, basically it's artists doing it and painting sets and making things. There's something very gratifying about that, something I love and never want to forget. It's the handmade aspect of things, part of an energy that you can't explain. You can sense it when you see the concentration of the animators as they move the figures, there's an energy that's captured. It's like when you look at a Van Gogh painting. I remember the first time I saw one in reality. You've seen them in books, but the energy that's captured on the canvas is incredible, and I think that's something that nobody talks about because it's not something literal.

It's the same with this kind of animation, and I think that's the power of Ray Harryhausen. When it's done beautifully, you feel somebody's energy. It's something that computers will never be able to replace, because they're missing that one element. For as good as computers are and as incredible as it will get and is right now, it goes back to painters and their canvases. This project and these characters and these visuals, the only way that it could have been done was with stop-motion. Therefore, it's very specialized. I remember getting shots and each time I would see a shot I would get this little rush of energy; it was so beautiful. It's like a drug. And I realized if you did it in live-action it wouldn't be as good; if you did it in drawing it wouldn't be as good. There is something about stop-motion that gives it an energy that you don't get in any other form.

Despite Nightmare's *proximity to his heart, Burton passed on directing the project because of his commitment to* Batman Returns *and the painstakingly slow production period necessary to complete a project of this kind. Instead, he chose Henry Selick, whom he had first met at Disney in the late seventies and to whom he had shown his original* Nightmare *sketches in 1982. Since the early eighties, Selick had been living and working in San Francisco, an area that had become the centre for stop-motion animators. It was here that Disney's adult-orientated arm Touchstone Pictures and Burton set up Skellington Productions, and began work on* Nightmare *in July 1991.*

Henry is a real artist. He's truly the best. He had done a lot of great stuff for MTV and was doing a lot of great stuff for stop-motion animation. There was a whole group of really talented artists up there in San Francisco. It's just that, even more than with drawn animation, it's hard to find people who are really talented at it, because it's a much more rarified form, and such an intense process. So, they let us do it up in San Francisco.

When I wasn't shooting I would go up there because I loved it, but most of the time Henry would just send me stuff – there'd be a few shots during the week – and so over the period of a couple of years it all came together. I'm trying to think when it started, but I am the worst person when it comes dates. Have you noticed that? I just have the worst mind when it comes to that. Everything is true, it's just that the time frame is a little off-kilter. Anyway, I would get a reel and I had an editing room and I would edit some shots when I was working on the second *Batman* movie. At that stage, there's something about it taking so long that means you can just sit there and enjoy it, and look at the texture.

It was the hardest thing I ever worked on, in a way, because it just took so long, and there were a lot of people involved, a lot of artists. Hopefully, most people you work with are artists, but it's an intense thing, stop-motion animation, and the thing that I was looking for all the time was just the feeling of it. Everybody contributed something, everybody had ideas and stuff, but what I always tried to do was just go back to that initial feeling. And even though it expanded, I would try to keep it on a certain track. It's funny, because when a project takes that much time, and I've been in animation so I know, ideas come all the time. That's fine, but sometimes the ideas are scary because people want to change this and change that. That's just the nature of it, because the ideas are quicker than the process. So, I tried to keep a constant watch. Actually, I enjoyed working in this way because the project took three years, and even if I was working on other things I could make a sketch or comment on things. And as the shots got assembled, I just tried to run it through that original feeling.

I guess my main concern, was that Henry, being an artist in his own right, wouldn't do the things I wanted. I was worried about that kind of tension. But it wasn't like that. He was great. That's why it's important very early on for people to be in synch about a project. So those early meetings are almost the most important. It's like, if you were doing a book, you would try to be faithful to the material. I wanted to feel comfortable that Henry was into that, otherwise you'd be fighting all time, and that couldn't happen. I've known some people who like to fight, who like that kind of struggle on set. I don't really like that. I don't like working with actors who aren't into it. You want people that are one hundred per cent into a project, even if they don't completely get it. So, there was no better group of people to do that movie and I always felt it was a special time. The studio was incredible and I just loved going up there because that level of artistry and detail was magical, truly magical and I'd never really felt that before.

To adapt his original, three-page poem into a feature-length script, Burton originally called upon Beetlejuice writer Michael McDowell. But when the collaboration didn't pan out quite the way Burton planned, he decided to attack the project from a musical standpoint and turned to his regular partner Danny Elfman. Together, Burton and Elfman, who also provides the singing voice of Jack in the movie, fleshed out a rough storyline and two-thirds of the film's songs, which Selick and his team of animators began work on even before Caroline Thompson was brought in to incorporate them into a screenplay.

I brought Michael in at the beginning and I realized that the way I really should do it was the way Danny and I eventually did it, even though it's not the most logical way. Michael's a friend, but it just didn't work. What Danny and I had when we started was the poem that I wrote and some drawings and some storyboards, and also this story outline I did about ten years ago. I would go over to his house and we would just treat it like an operetta, not like the musicals that they did, but more like that old-fashioned kind of thing, where the songs are more engrained in the story. I would begin to tell him the story and he'd write a song; he wrote them pretty quickly, actually, at least the initial pass on them. We worked in a weird way, where there was the outline and the songs and then we worked out the script. There was a lot going on, that was what was so difficult about it. They were doing the storyboards up there, we were doing the script, all this stuff was happening at once. It's not the best way to do it, but this was a new thing we were trying to do. I had seen other stop-motion animated features, and they were either not engaging or they're just too bizarre. There was one I liked when I was a kid called *Mad Monster Party*. People thought *Nightmare* was the first stop-motion animated monster musical, but that was.

So, Danny and I would go through my little outline and I'd say Jack does this and then he does that and then he falls into Christmastown. We'd worked together so much that it didn't matter that we didn't know what we were doing; at least we knew each other. So we just took at stab at it. And again, since we had worked together before, he worked very quickly, which was good because we needed the songs so we could do the script. He wrote them fairly quickly, within a couple of months; he would play me stuff the next week, sometimes the next day. Then I brought in Caroline and she knew Danny. It was a gradual, evolving process: there's Henry, there's me, there's Danny, there's Caroline, and that's a lot to deal with. And then you add in the other incredible artists.

The Nightmare Before Christmas: sketches

While Burton and Elfman had no specific style in mind for the film's musical numbers, preferring to see where the story took them, the one sung by Oogie Boogie Man was patterned after a character found in Max Fleischer's Betty Boop cartoons, which was voiced by Cab Calloway.

I remember drawing Jack and really getting into these black holes for eyes and thinking that to be expressive, but not have any eyes, would be really incredible. Sally was a relatively new character; I was into stitching from

The Nightmare Before Christmas: Sally and Jack

the Catwoman thing, I was into that whole psychological thing of being pieced together. Again, these are all symbols for the way that you feel. The feeling of not being together and of being loosely stitched together and constantly trying to pull yourself together, so to speak, is just a strong feeling to me. So those kind of visual symbols have less to do with being based on *Frankenstein*, than with the feeling of pulling yourself together.

The Cab Calloway thing was a more specific reference, however; when Danny and I were talking about it, it had more to do with this feeling of remembering, because I remember seeing these Betty Boop cartoons, where this weird character would come out. I didn't know who it was, but it would do this weird musical number in the middle of nowhere, and it was like: 'What the hell is that?' Again, it had to do with a feeling of remembering that from when I was a child. A lot of those images come more from feelings than they do from anything specific.

It's funny, because of the movies I've done, a lot of people think that they're very much about the way they look. People don't realize that everything I've ever done has to mean something; even if it's not clear-cut to anybody else, I have to find some connection, and actually the more absurd the element, the more I have to feel that I understand something behind it. That's why we're all fascinated by the movies. They tap into your dreams and your subconscious. I guess it is different from generation to generation, but movies are truly a form of therapy and work on your subconscious in the way fairy tales were meant to. The Dog Woman and Lizard Man in those Indian tales, they're not meant to be taken literally. That's what movies do as well. I was never a scholar in any of that stuff, but I always appreciated it. It's something I've found is not ingrained in American culture, that sense of myth or folklore. The best America could do is Johnny Appleseed – kind of soft, mutated.

The Nightmare Before Christmas *marked Burton's third movie in a row to be set at Christmas.*

I think I'm off that for a while. I've exorcized my Christmas demons. Growing up in Burbank, I responded to the holidays, especially Hallowe'en and Christmas, because they were the most visual and fun in some respects. The best I can decipher from the whole thing is that when you grow up in a blank environment, any form of ritual, like a holiday, gives you a sense of place. Most other countries are rich with ritual, but I guess America is a relatively new country and a fairly Puritan one. Growing up in a suburban environment where it's pushed even further in that direction, makes you feel very floaty. So holidays, especially those two, were very much a grounding or a way to experience seasons, because in California you don't get any. So at least you could walk in the supermarket aisles and see the Hallowe'en display and the fall leaves, because you certainly couldn't experience it in the weather and the environment.

To me, Hallowe'en has always been the most fun night of the year. It's where rules are dropped and you can be anything at all. Fantasy rules. It's only scary in a funny way. Nobody's out to really scare anybody else to death. They're out to delight people with their scariness, which is what Hallowe'en is all about and what *Nightmare* is all about.

'I've exorized my Christmas demons'

The budget for Nightmare *was less than $18 million, a fraction of the cost of producing a drawn animated movie. The film was released on Hallowe'en 1993 in the US and made $51 million at the box office. Rather ironically, it was (mis)perceived as being too scary for kids.*

Which was great, which was interesting, because it's what the story is about. Here you have this story where there are no really bad characters, not even Oogie Boogie; he's not *really* bad, he's just the weird neighbour in this weird city. And you have this character, Jack, who just wants to do good; he's passionate about something, and basically he ends up being misperceived and scaring everybody. It's funny, it took on the life of what it was about in real life. It was like, 'Wait a minute. This is *exactly* what the movie is about. People are freaking out because they think it's scary, but it's not. There really isn't anything in it.' Kids are incredible. If you show it to a bunch of kids without their parents it's great, but as soon as you get the parents involved, you get: 'This is too scary.' I've seen this happen before and it's a very disturbing phenomenon. If something was too scary for me, I wouldn't watch it, I was never forced to, but when you get a parent giving you this weird vibe, it puts you on edge.

It was released as *Tim Burton's The Nightmare Before Christmas*

'Hallowe'en has always been the most fun night of the year'

because they felt it would help. But it turned into more of a brand-name thing, it turned into something else, which I'm not quite sure about. Initially, they had talked to me about what that would achieve; smaller print above the title would give it a certain kind of context which they felt would help the movie, and I went along with it. I wouldn't do that with everything. There are only a few projects that you feel so personally involved with. I felt that way about *Vincent*, and I felt that way about this. But you don't really have any control over what happens outside. I learned that on the first *Batman*, where what you read about and what actually happened were two different things.

Sometimes I'll see people wearing the *Nightmare* Burger King watch in the weirdest places. I just saw somebody wearing it who worked at Carnegie Hall, and it's incredible. People will come up and they'll have a little picture of Jack with them. It's funny because sometimes when things connect with people, maybe not a large group, but with some, it's really wonderful to me. A lot of people and critics don't get that there is an emotion underneath these weird, stupid-looking things. Some people do, and that probably means the most to me: that people get the emotional quality underneath the stupid façade.

Because of the sheer scale and length of the project, which encompassed the period he was directing Batman Returns, The Nightmare Before Christmas *represented the first time that Burton had worked on more than one film at a time.*

That was the first time where there was a lot of energy put into a couple of different things, *Batman Returns* and *Nightmare*. It was kind of heavy. I can only work on one thing at a time, unless I find the right people. A lot of it has to do with finding kindred spirits, so to speak; it really does do a lot for you, you work on a higher level that way. I find if somebody isn't going with the flow, it's not the best working relationship anyway, so it's nice to work with people who are on the same wavelength. Then they surprise you and there's less stress and it's more creative. It's better.

I have to give credit to the people in charge at Disney now because they have certainly made the place more successful; they have more of an idea about what's going on. When I was there, there was a group of people who could have done *The Little Mermaid,* and things like that, back then. They had that pool of talent, even stronger, ten, fifteen years ago; they could have ushered in that renaissance back then had they been given the opportunity. At the time most people were out of Cal Arts, or college. Disney was just opening up, hiring young people, and everybody was completely eager to go for it and make a great movie, everybody was a Disneyphile. It's not like they were wanting to bring Disney animation into the R-rated world. So there was that talent, and finally the regime that's there now recognized that talent and have obviously been very successful in bringing the studio around, and that's good for animation as a whole.

Cabin Boy and Ed Wood

Following The Nightmare Before Christmas, *Burton co-produced, with Denise Di Novi,* Cabin Boy *for Disney. The film, a camp homage to the Sinbad movies starring Chris Elliott, Ricki Lake and Russ Tamblyn, was a massive critical and box-office disaster.*

It was sort of a weird comedy, and I didn't want to direct it because I thought it would be too expensive. But it didn't meet with too much critical or financial approval. Disney didn't like it; they didn't get it, and it just fell by the wayside. It was directed by Adam Resnick, who wrote it with some people who were on *The David Letterman Show*. I just tried to pass on my expertise on certain things, but I couldn't be there all the time, and I think I've learned a bit of a lesson from that. It's like on *Nightmare*, I was working on something else, but that project was different because I loved that one, it was my thing. But with *Cabin Boy*, I didn't know what was going on. I think I've just got to get involved with something or not do it. I don't think I would do anything like that again, not unless I felt the same way as I did about *Nightmare*. People ask me, but I won't unless I feel very confident about certain things.

Burton was set to direct Mary Reilly, *for Columbia Pictures, a version of Robert Louis Stevenson's oft-filmed tale* Dr Jekyll and Mr Hyde, *told this time from the point of view of Jekyll's housekeeper, with* Beetlejuice *and* Edward Scissorhands *star Winona Ryder in the title role.*

I was into that for a while, but what happened was the studio wanted to push it. Whereas before I could take my time to decide about things, in Hollywood you get shoved into this whole commercial thing. They want the movie. I remember them coming up to me and going, 'Oh, we've got five different directors who want to do this movie.' And I remember being turned off by the process. It's like, 'Well, you know, if you've got five other people that want to do it, maybe you should have them do it.' So basically they speeded me out of the project, because they saw it in a certain way. They saw it with Julia Roberts, and now they're getting what they want. I don't know what they think. I think they've got a weird feeling about me. I don't follow their way of thinking a lot of the time.

He was replaced on Mary Reilly *by Stephen Frears, and Julia Roberts was indeed cast in the title role opposite John Malkovich. Meanwhile Burton had become interested in a project based on the life of Edward D. Wood Jr that had been brought to his attention by Larry Karaszewski and Scott Alexander, the writers of the* Problem Child *movies. Karaszewski and Alexander had toyed with the idea of writing a film about Wood, often referred to as the world's worst director, ever since they were students at the University of Southern California film school. Irritated at being thought of solely as writers of kids' movies, they wrote a ten-page treatment and pitched the idea to* Heathers' *director Michael Lehman, with whom they were at USC. He, in turn, took the project to his producer on* Heathers, *Denise Di Novi. A deal was struck with Lehman as director and Burton and Di Novi producing. When* Mary Reilly *fell through, Burton became interested in directing* Ed Wood *himself, on the understanding that it could be done quickly. With this in mind Karaszewski and Alexander delivered a 147-page screenplay in six weeks. Burton read the first draft and immediately agreed to direct it as it stood, without any changes or rewrites.*

Wood, the director of such cult classics as Glen or Glenda, Bride of the Monster *and, most infamously,* Plan 9 From Outer Space, *died in 1978, aged fifty-four, penniless and forgotten. Sadly he achieved near legendary status only posthumously, in the early eighties, thanks to publications such as Michael and Harry Medveds'* The Golden Turkey Awards, *which voted* Plan 9 *the worst film of all time. Born in Poughkeepsie, New York in 1924, Wood lived his entire life on the cusp of Hollywood, aspiring to be the next Orson Welles, but never even coming remotely close. A famed transvestite with a fondness for angora sweaters and an engaging personality, Wood surrounded himself with a bizarre coterie of admirers and wannabes, including Criswell, a showman/psychic, Tor Johnson, a Swedish wrestler, and Vampira, a TV horror show host, many of whom believed Ed was going to make them stars. In 1953, Wood met his idol Bela Lugosi, a Hungarian immigrant and the celebrated star of Universal's 1930 version of* Dracula. *In the two decades since the release of* Dracula, *Lugosi had slipped into virtual anonymity and become addict-*

ed to morphine, which he had been prescribed to relieve the pain from a war wound. Wood vowed to revitalize his career by putting him in his movies, giving him roles in both Glen or Glenda, *Wood's autobiographical tale of a transvestite (played by Wood under the name of Daniel Davis) and* Bride of the Monster, *and using the last remaining footage he shot of Lugosi as the basis for* Plan 9. *Karaszewski and Alexander's script follows Wood's life through these three movies, and focuses on the Wood/Lugosi relationship, one that both they and Burton acknowledge is not unlike the friendship between Burton and his idol, Vincent Price.*

Denise had talked about producing this movie that Larry and Scott wanted to write. I was in Poughkeepsie, in upstate New York at the time. It was after *Batman Returns* when I was working on the *Nightmare* book, and I didn't know what I wanted to do. I started thinking about the idea of *Ed Wood*, and I started making notes and stuff because I was going to produce it. And then I thought, 'You know what, I like these people, and I want to direct it.' What was odd was that Ed Wood was from Poughkeepsie, which is where I was hanging around, and I had thought, 'This is cool, this is a weird place.' I got a kind of karmic rush when I decided to do it, and then I read this book *Nightmare of Ecstasy* and realized Ed Wood was from Poughkeepsie. So there was this weird connection and I just started to get into it. I talked to Scott and Larry and they wrote a script really quickly, within a month. I've never seen a script get written so fast and it was really long too, like 150 pages. They certainly had it in them, those guys. They were fans. They were into it. I just started doing what I usually do, which is to look for the emotional connections.

There were aspects of the character and his thing with Bela Lugosi that I immediately responded to. What's great about *Ed Wood* is that it's rough, it's not like a completely hardcore realistic biopic. In doing a biopic you can't help but get inside the person's spirit a little bit, so for me, some of the film is trying to be through Ed a little bit. So it's got an overly optimistic quality to it.

I grew up loving *Plan 9*, which is a movie you see when you're a kid and it remains with you. And then later on, Wood gets acknowledged as the worst director in the world, and then starts to get a little bit more known, and then there are festivals, and they show his movies and everybody laughs at them. But the thing is, when you watch his movies, yeah, they are bad, but they're special. There's some reason why these movies remain there, and are acknowledged, beyond the fact that they're purely bad. There's a certain consistency to them, and a certain kind of weird artistry. I mean, they are unlike any other thing. He didn't let technicalities like visible wires and bad sets distract him from his story-telling. There's a twisted form of integrity to that.

Ed Wood is very much the classic Burton character: a misfit, a misunderstood, misperceived individual.

He fits that theme, yes, but I think the difference with Ed, unlike the other characters, is that there are some different elements to him. What I liked about Ed Wood is that he is so optimistic. The thing I was taken by back when I'd read interviews with Ed Wood, especially since I knew the movies and the other aspects of his life, was his extreme optimism, to the point where there was an incredible amount of denial. And there's something charming to me about that. It's like with the Catwoman or the Sally characters – the idea of pulling themselves together, the stitching. Being passionate and optimistic is great to a certain point, and then you're just in complete denial, it becomes delusional. That's what I liked about the Ed Wood character. I could relate to him that way. I think everybody is in some form of denial. Denial is an incredible thing. Most people don't go through life with an extreme awareness of every aspect of themselves.

People think it's funny that I did this movie. Because I've been so successful, why would I want to make a movie about somebody who's not successful? But the way I feel about that, and him and me, is that any of my movies could go either way, they really could, and so the line between success and failure is a very thin one. That's why I responded so much to him. I believe that and, who knows, I could become Ed Wood tomorrow. Believe me, if you asked the studio before any of the movies that I've worked on have come out, they wouldn't have predicted their success. If it's a movie like *Lethal Weapon*, then they feel more comfortable. They know it's probably going to be okay. But the films that I've worked on, there's never been that certainty or feeling of confidence. And so I respond to Ed. I love him because he's got enthusiasm, and he's flawed, and there's that delusional sort of feeling.

And there was an aspect of his relationship with Bela Lugosi that I liked. He befriended him at the end of his life, and without really knowing what that was like, I connected with it on the level that I did with Vincent Price, in terms of how I felt about him. Meeting Vincent had an incredible impact on me, the same impact Ed must have felt meeting and working

131

Tim Burton directing *Ed Wood*

'I love Ed because he's got enthusiasm.' (Johnny Depp as Ed Wood)

Bela (Martin Landau) and Ed (Johnny Depp): 'There was an aspect of Ed's relationship with Bela Lugosi that I liked.'

'There's something very appealing about people that go out on a limb.' (Jeffrey Jones, Sarah Jessica Parker, Martin Landau, Johnny Depp, George 'The Animal' Steele, Max Casella and Brent Hinkley)

with his idol. And then there was this weird group of people that hung around with Ed. I liked the people. I just liked the idea of them. I liked that they were all completely out of it and everybody thought they were doing the greatest things, but they weren't. There's something that's very appealing about people who go out on a limb, who are perceived by society to be something else. In some ways, that loosens them up just to be themselves.

There are similarities between myself and Ed. Whether or not people sense it, I always try to relate to all those characters. There are aspects of Ed Wood that I can identify with because I think you have to, because, as I said, I'm not proficient enough to wing it. It's like, even if nobody else understands it, even if the movie comes out and everybody goes, 'What the hell is this?', for me to do it I have to relate to him. I have to be on his journey with him.

One of the things I liked about Ed, and I could relate to, was being passionate about what you do to the point of it becoming like a weird drug. It's like with any movie I've ever made, you get caught up in it; you're there and you think you are doing the greatest thing in the world. You have to think that. But you thinking you're doing the greatest thing in the world maybe doesn't have anything to do with how the rest of the population perceives it. So yes, I definitely felt and feel that way. Again, that's why I admire Ed so much, and those people – he was doing *something*.

If I see something, a piece of work, a painting, a film, anything, and somebody's going out on a limb and doing it, I admire them. I don't even care if I like it, I just admire them, because they're doing something that a lot of people won't do. You meet these people who build weird sculptures out of cars in the desert. I mean, you have to admire those people more than anybody.

I remember around the time I did *Hansel and Gretel* having this feeling that there were a lot of people judging it, and saying this doesn't work, this is bad. And I'm saying to myself, 'Fuck you! You do something. You may be right, but just do something for God's sake!' I like it when people do things. But now there's a lot of people waiting in the wings, there just seems to be more media around, therefore there's more judgement, and more people *not* doing things. The world seems to be getting a lot more judgers and a lot less doers. I've always hated that. That's why *Ed Wood* has a weird tone, because Ed just goes through the movie and remains optimistic.

The film ends with him very optimistic, driving off thinking that he's made, with *Plan 9*, the greatest movie ever. In reality, his story only gets more tragic as it goes along. His life is so bad, it's so redundant, it just gets more and more negative; but we just let him be him, and it ends at that point.

All Burton's characters have a duality to them and Ed's is ostensibly his transvestism.

It's brought out. I try to be matter-of-fact about it. I don't make judgements about people, especially people who I like and don't really know. So it's there, and it's just a part of his life. The thing about transvestism in movies that I've never liked is that it's an easy joke, and I don't know why. I don't like that, so I didn't want to make it a big joke. It's just a part of his life. Some of it's funny, I think. He was a heterosexual who liked to do that. I understand it too, women's clothes *are* more comfortable. If you walk into a clothing shop the women's clothes are the best. Guys' clothes have been the same for years. But they always use the best fabrics for women's clothes. So it's not hard to understand transvestism. But that was a part of his life, and the great thing was that the people around him, for the most part, just accepted it.

There's a moment in the movie which I love, and it's not a big deal, it's something I always liked from the script. It's where he tells his wife, Kathy, and she just accepts it, without any big fanfare. It's just a simple little moment, but that's kind of a fantasy to me. I think why it chokes me up is that it's simple acceptance, which is something you rarely get in life. People rarely accept you for who you are, and when that happens, even on a simple level, it's kind of great.

One can look at Burton's films as being essentially live-action animated movies. Ed Wood, on the other hand, is a first in that it's a film about people who really existed.

It is a bit of a departure in that respect, yes. It's real people, but I always treat everybody like real people, it's part of the process for me. I have to believe everybody. These are real people, but the great thing about these real people is that they're real people in *my* sense of real people – which is that they're not. If you read *Nightmare of Ecstasy*, the great thing about these people's story is that there is no story. The book is a series of recollections from these people who have a vague remembrance of this time.

135

Somebody will say this, somebody will say that, some of it's even contradictory, which I felt is very much in the spirit of this character, but these people, these slightly delusional kind of achievers, have a kind of upbeat 'Let's put on a show' attitude. I always saw it as a weird Andy Hardy movie in a way, because that's what my take on these people was like.

These people were never perceived as real people, they weren't treated seriously. And I guess they were all so out of it that their memories are worse than mine, if you can believe that. So that allowed me the opportunity to take off. You're not dealing with the well-documented life of Orson Welles here. When Ed Wood died he didn't even have an obituary in the paper. He died in this little building on Yucca watching a football game, having a heart attack, and nobody knew who he was.

Initially Ed Wood *was in development with Columbia Pictures, but when Burton decided he wanted to shoot the film in black and white, studio head Mark Canton wouldn't agree to it unless the studio was given a first-look deal. Burton insisted on total control, and so in April 1993, a month before shooting was scheduled to start, Canton put the movie into turnaround. The decision sparked a studio frenzy, with Warners, Paramount and Fox all interested in picking up the option, but Burton decided to accept an offer from Disney, who had previously produced* The Nightmare Before Christmas. *With a budget of $18 million, low by today's standards, Disney didn't feel the movie was that much of a risk, and granted Burton total creative autonomy. He began shooting in August 1993.*

Ed Wood is the hardest movie I've ever had to get off the ground. I thought it would be the easiest movie because I didn't take a fee. I did it for scale, and the fact is it's not that outlandish a movie, either. I mean, believe me, when I read the script I found it to be very good, certainly no weirder than anything else I've done. It's certainly the cheapest movie, cheaper than anything since *Pee-Wee*, and I got most of the actors to do it for not a lot.

The decision to do it in black and white was pretty much the same thought process as with anything you do. We were at make-up artist Rick Baker's with Martin Landau, who plays Bela Lugosi, and we were doing some make-up tests, and we were saying, 'What colour were Bela's eyes?' And then I started thinking, this is bullshit, I don't want to get into this. This should be in black and white because you don't want

136

to be sitting there going, 'What colour were Bela's eyes?' You want to do what's right for the material and the movie, and this was a movie that *had* to be in black and white. Everybody should have the opportunity to say this movie would be better in colour, and then you think about colour. But if it shouldn't be in colour, well then don't make it in colour. It's the same way *Frankenweenie* should be in black and white, *Vincent* should be in black and white, *Beetlejuice* should be in colour, *Pee-Wee's Big Adventure* colour, *Batman* colour. It really should be whatever's best for the movie.

So at some point I had a meeting with Columbia and they just didn't want to go for it. My argument was it doesn't matter if a movie is in black and white or in colour, the movie has to work. I said I can't predict if this movie is going to be successful. I can't predict if any movie is going to be successful. Either it will click with people or it won't, and I'm trying to get it to a place where it has the most potential to click with people, and I feel that this material is black and white. It's not a pretentious thing. In fact, I resist doing things in black and white because I don't want to be perceived as being pretentious. I find that I don't necessarily agree with a lot of things that are done in black and white, but it shouldn't be a big deal. You just make whatever you think is right for the movie. End of story.

Columbia didn't buy it, which is fine, I don't want to be involved with people who don't understand. Who needs it?

I'm in this meeting and they're crowing about their big hit *Last Action Hero*, you know, all egotistical and stuff, and I'm thinking, I'm glad you people know so much. Egotism, that's something I can't tolerate in a field where you don't know shit, nobody knows shit. All you can do is believe in something, care about it and try to make the best movie. I've grown less and less tolerant of all that other bullshit. I'll tolerate a conversation where somebody will say, 'Do you think this is a good idea?' That's legitimate. But it's like living in this complete fantasy world – that's why I'm here in New York, that's why I've gotten out of Hollywood lately, because I don't want to fall into the fantasy world these people create for themselves. The only fantasy world I want to create is in a movie. The fact that people can sit there and spout their philosophy and be egotistical about their big summer hit and think they know what they're talking about is a joke. I was glad that I left.

My leaving opened it up, actually. I did have the relationship with Disney because of *Nightmare*, but I talked to a few people and every other studio besides Columbia was nice about it. They all seemed to get it and want to do it. Certainly it wasn't as big a risk as people thought. Every-

Ed Wood: Sketch for the Spook House

body was a little leery about the black and white, but in the end, and I firmly believe my own philosophy in this case, when I decided to do it in black and white I felt it was the best idea to help the movie be what it should be. Therefore, with that one goal in mind, which is that the movie needs to work, it doesn't matter what colour it is. Disney were the most go-ahead. They're into this thing of changing their image, which I don't think they need to work so hard at.

As with every Burton movie, Ed Wood's *casting is suitably eclectic, with* Edward Scissorhands *star Johnny Depp as Ed, Martin Landau as Lugosi, Bill Murray as Bunny Breckinridge, Ed's transvestite friend,* Beetlejuice's *Jeffrey Jones as Criswell, Lisa Marie, a former model and now Burton's girlfriend, as Vampira, wrestler George 'The Animal' Steele as Tor Johnson, Sarah Jessica Parker as Ed's girlfriend Deloris and Patricia Arquette as Wood's wife Kathy.*

I tried to get a weird mix of people. Johnny liked the material, he respond-ed to it. I feel close to Johnny because I think somewhere inside we

something with skeletons

Ed Wood: Skeleton sketch

respond to similar things, and this was a chance after working on *Edward Scissorhands* to be more open. Edward was interior, this symbol come to life; Ed is more outgoing. It was interesting for me, after working with Johnny before, to explore a more open kind of thing. He did a really great job and he found a tone which I like.

I wanted to go with some knowns and some unknowns, Lisa Marie and George 'The Animal' Steele hadn't acted before; it was like trying to get a mix of people, just like in Ed Wood's movies. I wanted it to have its own kind of weird energy. With Bill Murray I didn't want to get into a situation where it's like a bunch of cameos. But the great thing about Bill in the movie is that he is a character. It's not like: 'Here's Bill Murray.' He plays this weird character that floats in and out. It was important to me to temper it with people who hadn't acted, or maybe hadn't acted as much, just to create an odd mix.

There's something about Martin Landau. I had a feeling about him. He's a man who's been in showbusiness a long time. I don't know what there was about him that made me connect him with the Bela thing, perhaps just talking to him made me feel he was perfect for the part. He's seen a lot, probably like Bela, and been through lots of things. He's cer-

'We re-created a few scenes ...' (George 'The Animal' Steele and Lisa Marie)

tainly not tragic like Bela, but I think he has been in Hollywood long enough to understand those aspects of it. I think he could just relate to it, and had been through enough ups and downs to understand Bela Lugosi. He's got his own presence in his own right. He's done the road tour of *Dracula*. He's been in horror movies. It was a case of 'That guy looks weird, let's put him in a horror movie.' He's been through it. He's worked with Alfred Hitchcock. He's been in cheesy horror movies. It was something he could bring, that knowledge.

As Ed Wood's wife, Kathy, I wanted somebody with presence, because it's not a big role; she comes into it late. Patricia Arquette's got a gravity that I like, and that's what Kathy needed. Those things are the hardest to pull off: simply being there. You just have to have it; it's not something you can create from an outside source, so I was very happy that she did it, because this movie is a hotchpotch of things. It needs the gravity that certain people bring to it.

The funny thing about these people is that none of their lives were really documented. And I know how that feels. These people were a little out of it, they just weren't there. So, now that Ed Wood has come out of the closet, so to speak, and more has been talked about the movies and they have more festivals on him, there's all of this revisionist history. I've seen it happen in my lifetime. It's scary. I got the worst reviews on *Pee-Wee's*

'... but it was more about the shooting of them.'
(Johnny Depp and Norman Alden)

Big Adventure, and then, as the years went by, I would read things from critics saying what a great movie it is. That's why this movie does not pretend that in 1952 Ed Wood actually did this. It's not that. In some ways it's a little subjective, it's an acknowledgement that there is no hard core. I'm only taking what I think some of this stuff is, and trying to project a certain kind of spirit. The movie is dramatic, and I think there are some funny things in it, but it's treading a fine line because I never wanted it to be jokey. Never. I'm *with* them. I'm not laughing at them. I don't quite know how people will perceive the perspective and the energy that that creates because they may go, 'This isn't real.' But you know what, I hate most biopics. I find that most biopics are stodgy and really boring, because people, in my opinion, take too much of a reverential approach and it's fake.

Everytime I've seen a biopic, it just doesn't feel real. There's something about it, the sheer fact that it's a movie and that an actor is portraying someone, means there's a level of façade and fakery to it. I decided to go along with that a little bit more and not to treat these people so reverentially or in a documentary style. In some ways I'm a purist. I wasn't there with these people, I don't know them, but I have a feeling about them. So that's what I'm doing. I'm doing my feeling. I'm sure these people were more horrible than the way I'm portraying them. But these people should feel good, because they've been made fun of their whole lives and I'm certainly not doing that to them. I like them. I did as much research as I could in terms of learning what I wanted to learn about them, but again, the film is just more my idea about these people.

Kathy is still alive. She's very sweet. She loved Ed. That's the other thing, it's nice when people love each other. That's what I loved about her. She loved him, it seems.

Again Burton refrained from going back and reviewing Wood's movies, preferring mainly to go with his memory and his feelings.

We had them around. People watched them. I didn't too much. There might have been certain instances, but again I kind of watched from around a corner. I didn't want to get into too many weird re-creations. I thought, I don't want to sit here and make judgements. I treated it matter-of-factly, so we re-create some stuff, some stuff we don't. We re-created a few scenes from three of the films, but it was more about the shooting of them, the process. It has a fragmented, kind of slightly out of it tone I felt the book had. I had the art department and the people on the movie who hadn't heard of Ed Wood look at the films. I gave them copies of the movies and that Jonathan Ross documentary about Ed. I liked that documentary most because I felt it captured the true spirit of these people.

There's a sparseness to the movie. Again, I don't know how it will come across because it's an amalgam of feelings, and I don't know how they will all finally connect. But the thing I always loved about those Ed Wood movies was that they were relatively timeless. They seemed like they were ahead of their time and behind their time. There was a kind of ponderous sparseness to them that I remember. So a lot of the time I would just try to keep it sparse because that's just the way I felt about them. They were living in their own world.

Surprisingly, given his six-film relationship with Danny Elfman, Burton chose composer Howard Shore to provide the music for Ed Wood.

The situation with Danny right now, I don't know if it will stay that way or not. I don't know what to say about it because I don't know where it's going. We're taking a little vacation from each other.

Ed Wood opened in America on 7 October 1994 to rave reviews. Burton produced the third Batman movie, Batman Forever, *directed by Joel Schumacher.*

I don't think Warners wanted me to direct a third *Batman*. I even said that to them. I think what happened was I went through a lot on the last one; a lot of it was personal, a lot of it had to do with the movie, a lot of it was a desire to make the movie something different. I've always been a little at odds with them. Any time people start saying things are too dark to me I just don't get it, because I have a different perception of what dark is. To me something like *Lethal Weapon* is really dark, whereas to them it's not. They see people walking around in regular clothes shooting guns, and it makes them feel more comfortable than when people are dressed up in weird costumes. I'm disturbed by the reality of that; I find it darker when there's a light-hearted attitude to violence and it's more identifiable than when something is completely removed from reality. I've always had trouble understanding that, and I think at the end of the day, when the movie came out, it was a no-win situation. If the movie doesn't make the same amount of money or more, it's a disappointment. And they got a lot of flak from parents thinking it was too scary for their kids. So I think at the end of it all, I put them through the ringer too much.

But I feel close to that material. I certainly don't feel like dissociating myself from the material completely because I feel I gave it something.

Ed Wood won several major US Critics awards, for Martin Landau and for Stefan Czaspsky's marvellously evocative black-and-white cinematography. Yet despite the almost unanimous critical acclaim the film received, it failed to ignite the public's attention and was Burton's first box-office failure.

I guess if I was left to my own devices I wouldn't think about how much money they make – except for the fact that you are in a business, so you're forced to think that way. I felt great about *Ed Wood* – you always feel like it's your child, you feel positive about it. We had shown it at the New York Film Festival and it got a very good response. So when it didn't make any money, I felt a little like, 'Well, it just goes to show that you never really know.' I love the movie, I'm proud of it. It's just that no one came. I guess if I was like everybody else, I would just blame a bad marketing campaign. But that's too easy.

However, the film was nominated for two Oscars at the 1995 Academy Awards, and won both: Best Make-up for Rick Baker and Best Supporting Actor for Martin Landau, who also picked up a Golden Globe.

That was great. They deserved it. I never think about that stuff, but I was happy for Martin. He's had such a long and varied career, he did such a great job, and he seemed really into it. It was just nice that somebody who I think really wanted that, got it, you know?

James and the Giant Peach, Mars Attacks!, Superman Lives and The Melancholy Death of Oyster Boy

Following Ed Wood, *Burton and producer Denise Di Novi once again collaborated with* Nightmare Before Christmas *director Henry Selick, producing a live action/animated version of Roald Dahl's children's story* James and the Giant Peach. *It would be their last film together and in 1995 Burton and Di Novi dissolved their partnership.*

Although Burton's name was frequently linked to various projects (including the long-in-development Catwoman *script by Daniel Waters), in 1995 Burton began pre-production for Warner Bros on* Mars Attacks!, *an adaptation of the Topps Trading Cards first released in 1962 by Bubbles Inc. The script was written by Jonathan Gems, an English playwright and screenwriter who had done a few weeks' rewrite work on* Batman *and had subsequently written a number of unproduced scripts for Burton, including a* Beetlejuice *sequel,* Beetlejuice Goes Hawaiian, *an updating of Edgar Allen Poe's* The House of Usher *set in Burbank,* The Hawkline Monster, *a cowboy/monster movie that was to star Clint Eastwood and Jack Nicholson, and* Go Baby Go, *a beach movie in the style of Russ Meyer.*

During the summer of 1994, Gems was in a gift shop on Melrose Avenue in Hollywood when he happened upon sets of the Mars Attacks! *and* Dinosaur Attacks! *trading cards. Intrigued, Gems bought both sets and showed them to Burton, commenting that they'd make a great movie. A few months later, Burton called Gems and asked him to write a script based on the* Mars Attacks! *set.*

I remembered those cards from types of cards I had as a kid. I just liked the anarchistic spirit of them. Jonathan has sort of an anarchistic spirit himself, I think – being British and living in America and having an alien perspective of it, which I sort of have myself. And I like people – and this sometimes gets me into trouble – who write scripts differently. Usually after you read a few scripts they kind of feel the same. But he just brought a different kind of energy to it.

And I connected to the whole thematic idea of 'Things aren't what they seem'. I was feeling really strangely about things at the time, about America – everything just seemed really off-kilter to me, and I think that was a partial dynamic of what I liked about the material. I was just feeling more anarchic, and that was the energy I liked in it – I saw that in the Martians. Plus a lot of it had to do with *Ed Wood*, in the sense of how hard it was to get that movie done, and feeling good about it and then it not doing well. I know it's not just me because I hear about it all the time from other people – how hard it is to get movies made these days. It's like this *Alice in Wonderland* experience, and it seems like it takes longer and longer from movie to movie. It's kind of like being an athlete: if you start having too many false starts, it begins to unnerve you. And I just remember this one taking too long to get up and running.

Gems' original script was budgeted by Warners at $280 million: a wholly unfeasible cost. After turning in numerous drafts in an attempt to bring the budget down, Gems was replaced by Ed Wood *screenwriters Larry Karaszewski and Scott Alexander, but he later returned to the project. Gems wrote twelve drafts in all, and the film's final budget came in at $70–75 million, of which a large percentage went on the film's special effects. Yet Burton and Gems were consciously trying to ape the cheesy sci-fi movies of the 1950s rather than going for a hi-tech* Star Wars *approach.*

Yeah, those 1950s invasion movies, they were the inspiration for it, although I never thought of *Mars Attacks!* being like 'a science-fiction film' because I always feel real science fiction is, in some ways, more serious. With those 1950s films, I mean there's a lot of ones I remember being great ... I remember one I loved was *Target Earth* and then seeing it again I couldn't believe it was so bad. But the thing about *Mars Attacks!* – most of my decisions are subconscious rather than a conscious 'I'm gonna do a 1950s science-fiction film' or whatever. I do things based on a feeling. Then you go through the process of making a film and you get all tied up with those emotions and so it takes a while to actually let the picture go and see it for those kind of subconscious clues of why you did something. So that one's probably another year or so off, given my usual three-year period of discovering what the fuck I was thinking about.

Detailing the four days prior to a Martian invasion of earth followed by its aftermath, Gems' script takes in locations ranging from Washington

A Burton sketch for the Martians' whistle-stop destruction of the Taj Mahal

A fraught moment in *Earth Versus the Flying Saucers* (1956)

DC, New York, Las Vegas and Kansas, to Paris, London, Easter Island, even India (where in one of the film's funniest set pieces several Martians pose for photos in front of a burning Taj Mahal); and a battery of characters from virtually every social and political group, among them the American President and his family, scientists, members of the media, donut shop workers, former boxing champions and property developers. In terms of its structure, its locations and its vast smorgasbord of characters, Mars Attacks! owes as much to the Irwin Allen-produced disaster movies of the 1970s (such as The Poseidon Adventure, The Towering Inferno and Earthquake) as it does to Earth Versus the Flying Saucers and its ilk.

I've always liked all those Irwin Allen films – those 'Celebrities Getting Killed' movies. That's a genre in itself, where you have Charlton Heston married to Ava Gardner, and his father is Lorne Greene, who is about three years younger than his daughter Ava Gardner. You get all these weird mixes of people in those movies. So that was one aspect of it, yeah. I don't think there was one overriding thematic thing. But it seemed like a good idea just to blow away celebrities with ray-guns.

Although Gems is credited with both the screen story and screenplay of Mars Attacks!, *he dedicates his novelization of the movie to Burton, who 'co-wrote the screenplay and didn't ask for a credit'. Gems claims Burton's contribution to the script cannot be underestimated. 'He has a fantastic instinct for film structure. I come from the theatre where you tell a story through characters and dialogue, but Tim comes from animation, where you tell characters and story through pictures. A lot of the process was me writing and Tim drawing. He would say everything in terms of pictures.'*

We went through the cards picking out the ones we liked, just as a starting point, to get a feel for it – we didn't follow them literally. They're kind of funny, taken on their own – they have great captions, like 'Burning Cattle'. So we picked out our favourites. That's how you start with an animated film, too.

In H. G. Wells' novel The War of the Worlds – *to which both the Mars* Attacks! *cards and the film adaptation owe much – mankind is saved from the Martian invaders not by military strength but by the common cold: a plot point that Gems loosely co-opted in his screenplay, which called for music to be responsible for destroying the Martians. Exactly what type of music, Gems left open. It was Burton who decided upon Slim Whitman.*

That came from the dynamic of those 1950s movies. In most of them, at the end it comes down to one thing that will kill the aliens, and often I remember it being some sort of sound-wave, like in *Earth Versus the Flying Saucers* or *Target Earth*. I recall Slim Whitman's voice from when I was a child, and his voice was very sonic. It was almost like one of those sonic frequencies that might tap right into the brain and destroy. His voice seemed very science-fictiony too, almost like that instrument, the theramin.

Burton's initial instinct was to once again utilize stop-motion animation to create the Martians. A team of animators, headed by Manchester-based Ian Mackinnon and Peter Saunders, was hired, set up shop in Burbank and began work on stop-motion effects, only to be replaced by George Lucas's Industrial Light & Magic, who would eventually design and animate the Martians using CG (computer-generated) imagery.

We did some testing with stop-motion. But with the amount of characters we had, and because they all looked the same, it just didn't work. And the time factor came into it, so it made sense to go with CG. I had never worked with it before but I thought I'd just give it a try: it would be a new medium, a new thing to check out. I tried to keep it like we did on *Vincent* or *Nightmare* – to make the animated characters act, to treat them as real, because sometimes I've noticed that computer stuff can get a little floaty. CG doesn't give you that weighted feeling, like when you first saw *Jason and the Argonauts* or some Ray Harryhausen movie with three-dimensional animation. CG can be great – it's close – but on the other hand I am very interested in the tactile, just how different media create different emotions, and I think it's worth thinking about each time out. But in the end I actually appreciated the CG on *Mars Attacks!* because otherwise it would have been near impossible to shoot anamorphic screen ratio the way we did – registration problems would have been a nightmare. So in that case I don't think I missed the tactility of stop-motion as much as I would have on other things.

Something else I felt about CG at the time, and I actually still feel this

Burton imagines the Martians in sketch form

The Martian leader gleefully incinerates the US Congress

way: being able to do anything, it can kind of diminish the effect. It's funny – even with the new *Star Wars*, when you can do anything ... it's almost like humans need boundaries. It needs to be in a framework, it needs to be held in check with other elements, so that you're still feeling something that's much more present. For me, there's no such thing as unlimited resources in movies – you need boundaries.

Despite his vast budget, Burton, in common with earlier movies such as Beetlejuice, *stylistically chose to have the film's effects look as low tech and cheap as possible.*

Sometimes I actually felt like I was turning into Ed Wood. But it was definitely a movie where I threw in a bunch of different ideas. I remember feeling like I had felt when I was working at Disney in the animation department, where you just try a bunch of different stuff and throw it into the thing and see what happens. But it can cause certain things to become at odds with each other.

The film reunited Burton with Batman *star Jack Nicholson, who had been so supportive of his young director during that movie's difficult shoot. Originally Warren Beatty had been mentioned as President Dale and Nicholson as sleazy Las Vegas property developer Art Land. Ultimately Nicholson wound up playing both roles.*

He has always been so great to me. I love working with him because he gets it. He's somebody who has gone through so much, but still understands and appreciates the absurdity of the business and the fun of it. Jack is just willing to try stuff, and the idea of him as President, I thought was great, given the spirit of the film. I'd asked him to do the Las Vegas guy but I didn't think he was going to do it, so I said, 'Well, Jack, what about this part? Or this one?'. And he said, 'How about 'em all?'. For *Mars Attacks!* I don't think he tapped into his Academy Award bag of tricks; he probably delved more into his Roger Corman or *Head*-style career moves. We had to play 'Hail to the Chief' every time he walked on the set. The sound guy played it once just as a joke but then Jack got to liking it, and then it became ... necessary. He'd do a couple of laps around the set and then get into it.

Hail to the Chief! Jack Nicholson as the US President

In common with the Irwin Allen disaster movies that had so inspired Gems, the cast of Mars Attacks! *was a veritable star-studded confection that included Pierce Brosnan, Michael J. Fox, Annette Bening, Glenn Close, Natalie Portman, Pam Grier, Rod Steiger, singer Tom Jones, as well as faces familiar from past Burton films: Danny DeVito, who played the Penguin in* Batman Returns, *Sylvia Sydney, the chain-smoking after-life official in* Beetlejuice, *Sarah Jessica Parker, who starred in* Ed Wood, *and O-lan Jones, one of the nosy neighbours in* Edward Scissorhands.

I sort of sectioned off the casting into two different types of people: people who I like, and then people who I thought represented certain aspects of culture and society that were more satirical. And it was fun – it was a great way to meet people and watch different actors work together in different styles. I think I got into that on *Ed Wood*. I like the mix of great actors, method actors, A-actors, B-actors, and people who haven't really acted before. I enjoy the energy of it. And it was such a surreal thing – I remember thinking that having all these people together in the same room was funny. When you've got a 'great actor sampler platter', it's different than when you're working with individuals constantly on a movie. You get more of a quick impression. But people were really cool – they would come in and get shot with a ray-gun and then leave.

Mars Attacks! *was released in the US on 13 December 1996 to mixed reviews and indifferent box office. It was not helped by a marketing campaign that failed to grasp the film's anarchic approach and ignored its obvious appeal to kids.*

Warners in the US didn't know what to make of it, which is sort of usual; I mean, it's always been that way, and in some ways it's better off when they don't know. People kept coming up to me afterwards saying it was a bad ad campaign, but I couldn't tell. You get so close to something you don't really know. I know that when we took it to Europe it did much better. It was still Warners but it was their European arm, which seemed to have a better handle on it. I actually felt European audiences understood it much better or seemed to get it better. They didn't seem to have that American egotism of, 'You can make fun of some things, but you can't quite make fun of other things.'

Moreover, the film's thunder was stolen by the surprising success that summer of the similarly themed Independence Day.

It was just a coincidence. Nobody told me about it. Then somebody said, 'They're doing this movie, it's kind of the same thing,' and I thought, 'Oh? I've never heard of it.' Then it came out, and eventually I saw some of it on cable. I was surprised how close it was, but then it's a pretty basic genre I guess. *Independence Day* was different in tone – it was different in everything. It almost seemed like we had done kind of a *Mad* magazine version of *Independence Day*.

Providing the score was Danny Elfman, who had had a falling out with Burton prior to Ed Wood.

I think he was mad at me from *Nightmare*. *Nightmare* was hard because between Danny, Henry and Caroline we were like a bunch of kids, fighting. That's what I felt like anyway, and I think it was just one of those times when, like in any relationship, we just needed a break, and it was probably good for all of us. Danny works with many different people, so I think every now and then it's worth trying something new, and I enjoyed working with Howard.

By the time the fourth Batman movie, Batman & Robin, *came around, Burton was no longer involved with the franchise.*

I saw *Batman Forever*, but I didn't see the last one. I couldn't. I'd never been in an experience like that before, so it was kind of surreal. It's like you're involved with something and then you're not, but it's still kind of like yours. You feel like you've died and you're having an out-of-body experience. That's the best way I can describe it. I didn't feel like 'I hate this' or 'I love this', I just had a shock.

Yet having successfully reinvented one comic-book icon, Warners felt Burton was the obvious choice to direct a new movie version of another: Superman. *Although Warners had produced three* Superman *films starring Christopher Reeve (the fourth was made by Cannon Films), beginning with the Richard Donner-directed 1978 movie, the potential for another blockbusting superhero franchise was not lost on executives. Film-maker and comic-book fan Kevin Smith was employed by* Batman *producer Jon Peters to write two drafts of a screenplay based on the* Death of Superman *comic-book storyline, and Oscar-winner Nicolas Cage was signed to play the Man of Steel.*

They came to me. I wasn't necessarily attracted to *Superman* per se because I felt like it had been done – unlike *Batman*, where it had been a TV series but our approach was different. But *Superman* had already been a movie not that long ago, and a pretty successful one. So what do you do? What was presented to me was Nic Cage and doing our own version of *Superman*, and I thought, well that sounds great because I love Nic Cage. So I met with him and we thought of the idea of focusing more on the fact that he's an alien, and maybe for the first time feeling what it's like to be Superman. Part of my problem with Superman was that he's fine on a comic-book level, but on a movie level they never really addressed the fact that here's this guy with this blue suit and this funny yellow belt and all that stuff. He's actually the most two-dimensional of any comic-book character. For me, you never really get into what Superman really is, whereas with Batman I always felt he's a fucked-up guy and you can get into his head a little bit. So we were going to try to analyze it, get a bit more in-depth about what it would feel like to be somebody who's from another planet, who can't tell anybody and is completely different but has to hide it. All those comics are basically the same thing, it's duality – what's shown, what's hidden.

I was excited about working with Nic because the way we were thinking about it, it would have been the first time you would believe that nobody could recognize Clark Kent as Superman – that he could physically change his persona, so it wouldn't be as simplistic as taking off a pair of glasses. Without doing make-up or anything, Nic is the kind of actor who can pull something like that off. And we were talking to Kevin Spacey for Lex Luthor – he was perfect.

So the idea was you have a great actor and you, the audience, can understand him as a character. That's what intrigued me about it. And technically you could go to another level now – you wouldn't have to hang the guy by fucking wires. The flying was terrible in those movies. Even seeing them at the time – I wasn't in movies – I was going, 'I don't know about this ...'. You could do that better, no problem.

It was called *Superman Lives*. I was pushing for it be *Superman*. I always hated those titles like *Batman Forever*. I thought, '*Batman Forever*, that sounds like a tattoo that somebody would get when they're on drugs or something,' or something some kid would write in the yearbook to somebody else. I have high problems with some of those titles.

After a year of development, during which locations were scouted, an art department employed under the direction of long-time collaborator Rick Heinrichs, and the Smith script rewritten by a series of writers, including Wesley Strick and Dan Gilroy, Warners put the project on hold.

Warners were balking pretty much all the way. We were going to be going at this date, then that date. I was working for a year on script meetings with them, and once you go down that path the script doesn't get better, it becomes committee-ized. I don't know this for sure, but on the last *Batman* they did, I remember them thinking that it was so great, and I think they were taken aback when it got dissed so much. So, all of a sudden, Warners was getting press like they had destroyed a franchise. I think they were feeling the heat of that, since the overriding factor in Hollywood is fear – decisions are based on fear most of the time. And I think they were fearful that they were going to fuck up another franchise. The way they saw it was, 'We don't want to do this unless it's going to be right.' And I didn't want to go into it and it not be right either, because it's *Superman*. It's too much of a target.

Also, my original fear came true. I had thought, 'Okay, Jon Peters is the producer. I've dealt with Jon before on *Batman*, and it was a nightmare, but

I did it. So therefore I can probably deal with that again.' But that wasn't the case. I remember at one point saying to Warners, 'You've got three things here. You've got me, you've got Jon Peters and you've got Warner Bros. And I can imagine a situation like one of those Spaghetti Western gunfights, where three people stare at each other for twenty minutes because they've each got different ideas.' And that turned out to be the case. The truth of the matter is, if it had ever really had a chance of getting done, then Warners should have got rid of me or Jon, and then let me or Jon make the film. Jon had his own ideas, Warners had its own fears, and I had my own thoughts. And Jon, he's like a whirlwind, it's like trying to control the weather. It's a very difficult energy to deal with. And I basically wasted a year.

It was terrible because you think you're working on something and you're not, and you realize at the end of it all that it's a load of crap, because you're having all these meetings and you're kind of working in a vacuum. It's one thing to work on something to make it better, and it's another thing just to spin your wheels. It's fine if you get something done, but to go that hard and that long and not get something done is devastating, because really I'm in it to make things. I'm not in it to have these bullshit meetings. Part of the joy is 'doing', and I spent a year 'not doing'.

In 1997 Burton published The Melancholy Death of Oyster Boy & Other Stories, *a collection of twenty-three illustrated stories of varying length written in verse. The stories (whose titles include 'Stick Boy & Match Girl in Love', 'The Girl Who Turned into a Bed' and 'Melonhead') were typically Burtonesque in content and tone, and once again managed to convey the anguish and pain of the adolescent outsider in a manner that was both delightfully comic and mildly macabre, and which, in the words of the* New York Times, *was 'both childlike and sophisticated'.*

They're just little things – stories for the modern person with a short attention span. But it was fun for me. Luckily I was doing *Oyster Boy* while I was doing *Superman*, so I had a little bit of an outlet there. I've kind of been writing for a long time. In a weird way it's how I think about things, so it's a bit of a peek into how I think. And it's a little calming Zen-type of exercise that I enjoy. It helps centre me and focus my thinking a little bit because I get all over the place. There's a lot of Lisa Marie in there, too, in different ways. She gives me a lot.

sometimes I know it bothers him
that he can't run or swim or fly,
and because of his only power,
his dry cleaning bills' too high.

for christmas stain boy
got a new uniform.
it was clean and well pressed,
comfy and warm.

but in a few short minutes,
(no longer than ten)

those wet, greasy stains
started forming again.

The hapless Stain Boy, symbol of Burton's *Superman* woes

Two stories featured the exploits of Stain Boy, a child superhero whose 'gift' is to leave a nasty stain behind him wherever he goes, and who, with a cape and figure 'S' emblazoned on his chest, is indicative of another, better known superhero character.

Stain Boy is one of my favourite characters, and in a way he's probably the perfect symbol of that whole *Superman* experience, that year – truthfully that's pretty much how I felt. If anybody wants to know what that year was like, then just read that, that's the best description of it.

In addition to being an accomplished painter and illustrator, Burton's interests also extend to photography. He works in a number of different formats, from regular 35mm to 3D cameras and extra-large Polaroid cameras.

It's just a way I like to work and think of different ideas. I like working out things visually because it taps into your subconscious and therefore, for me, it's a more real emotion than if I intellectualize it in my mind. I like just trying something either in a drawing, or a photo with Lisa Marie; it's a visual concept, as opposed to thinking.

The majority of Burton's photographic work features his girlfriend of eight years, Lisa Marie.

I felt a connection when I met her that I'd never felt before and I guess that's chemistry. It's how we have fun, you know. We go on road trips and take pictures and be as bohemian as we can possibly be in this world. There's some photos in which we made up some weird plants and animals, but most of them are her. It's just nice to have somebody that you love around, as opposed to spending my whole life doing things on my own.

Burton's muse, Lisa Marie has appeared as Vampira in Ed Wood, *as the mute, gum-chewing Martian with the massive beehive who inveigles her way into the White House in* Mars Attacks!, *and as Ichabod Crane's mother in* Sleepy Hollow.

Fooling around: Burton photographs Lisa Marie ...

... and Poppy, canine star of *Mars Attacks!*

Since we're together we can kind of fool around together. That's not something that I can do with other actors, because it's more spontaneous. On a weekend we just fool around with costumes and make-up. I remember we fooled around one day when we were in New York, bought a little cheap wig, went to Washington and took some Polaroids and did kind of inspirational work for *Mars Attacks!*

Lisa Marie's performance in Mars Attacks! *is one of the film's standout moments. Poured into a red-and-white dress that was designed by Burton, she glides wordlessly into the White House, in a manner that's eerie, unnerving and hysterically funny, intending to assassinate the President and the First Lady.*

That was a fun challenge, and I think she did a good job. It's hard stuff to do, to move and not speak. We spent a lot of time working on things for her to wear, and we did a couple of things technically so that her walk was like a combination of her own movement, juxtaposed with technique. It's almost like choreography, where you do movements to create an optical illusion of another type of movement. We worked with a movement guy called Dan Kamen, who had worked on *Chaplin*, and I learned a lot from him.

Trivia fans should also note that the chihuahua belonging to Sarah Jessica Parker's character, onto which her head is grafted, belongs to Burton and Lisa Marie, the latter having found it on the street in Japan.

We were in Tokyo in a car talking to two other people, in this sleazy night-club area, and it's really crowded, with all these lights, like Las Vegas, and Lisa goes, 'Stop the car.' I don't know how she saw this dog like fifty yards away in a little cage on the street. So yeah, we got that dog in Tokyo. Poppy, she did good.

In 1998 Burton directed his first television commercial for a French chewing gum called Hollywood Gum. The thirty-second spot features a garden gnome who escapes from his back-garden home and, hitching a ride on a garbage truck, ends up bathing in a pool in an enchanted forest glade, with a young woman who looks like Lisa Marie (but isn't).

An early sketch by Burton of That Dress

Martin Short as Jerry Ross and Lisa Marie as the pneumatic Martian assassin

It's okay. I'm not sure I would rush out and do a bunch of commercials. It came along just at the time when I hadn't worked for a while, and it was pretty simple and a fair amount of money, and I thought I'd just try it. Part of my problem is, no matter what I do, I treat everything like it's a movie. People have told me, 'When you do a commercial, just do it and make a little money, but don't let it bother you.' But I can't not let things bother me. You know what? Dealing with clients, it's like dealing with a studio. I just get sick of it.

Sleepy Hollow

In 1994, Kevin Yagher, a make-up effects designer who had turned to directing with HBO's Tales from the Crypt *(for which he had designed and built the show's ghoulish host, The Crypt-Keeper), had the notion to adapt Washington Irving's short story* The Legend of Sleepy Hollow *into a feature film. Through his agent, Yagher was introduced to Andrew Kevin Walker, a young writer whose 'spec' screenplay* Seven, *though favourably received in Hollywood circles, had yet to be produced. Yagher and Walker teamed up and spent a few months working on a treatment which they subsequently pitched around town, finally securing a deal with producer Scott Rudin, who sold the project to Paramount. The deal called for Yagher to direct, with Walker scripting; the pair would share a story credit. For a variety of reasons, the project, like so many in Hollywood, became mired in the development process and looked pretty much dead until the summer of 1998 when Burton, fresh off* Superman, *was approached by Rudin and his producing partner Adam Schroeder with a view to directing Walker's script.*

After *Superman* I didn't know what to do. Then they sent me this script and I really liked it, it was very strong. I had never really done something that was more of a horror film, and it's funny, because those are the kind of movies that I like probably more than any other genre. The script had images in it that I liked – the windmill, the Tree of the Dead – although I'm not a big horse fan. And it's a fascinating story, a story that a lot of people know about but that nobody's really read. Everybody thinks they've read the book, including myself. But actually I only read it not that long ago. The story's basically about a guy looking for food, and it's pretty short. In a way it's much better in your mind than it is in reality. It's one of the few real early American horror stories, even though its roots are based in other myths. Somebody said that Washington Irving ripped it off from a German folk tale, which seems appropriate because it has that Germanic feel to it. But it's kind of nice that it is an early American horror story, because there aren't that many of them. And I think that's why people know it – because it's got the kind of symbolism that good fairy tales or horror stories have.

Burton's rendering of the Hessian Horseman

First published in The Sketch-book of Geoffrey Crayon, Gent. (1819–20), *Washington Irving's* The Legend of Sleepy Hollow *relates the adventures of gangly, superstitious schoolteacher Ichabod Crane who, whilst attempting to win the affections of Katrina Van Tassel from rival Brom Bones, is said to have encountered the spectre of a headless horseman, though the pumpkin found at the scene indicates that forces other than supernatural were at play. Walker's script (given a production polish by Tom Stoppard) transforms Crane into a New York City police constable whose belief in new investigative techniques and scientific procedures is resented by his superiors, who dispatch him north to the Hudson Valley and the small town of Sleepy Hollow to put his theories to the test in a series of murders in which the victims heads have been removed. There Crane discovers that the Horseman is a real, albeit supernatural entity, rather than a practical joke. Irving's tale has been filmed on a number of occasions, most notably a 1949 Disney animated short,* The Adventures of Ichabod and Mr Toad, *narrated by Bing Crosby, and a 1980 TV movie starring Jeff Goldblum as Ichabod Crane.*

A production sketch by Burton ...

... reveals the inspiration for Ichabod Crane's remarkable face-furniture

I hadn't seen the TV version. I guess I know it better for the Disney cartoon more than anything else; I remember always liking that. I remember getting excited by the chase sequence – I still get excited by it. Actually, when I went to Cal Arts, one of my teachers had worked on it as one of the layout artists on the chase, and he brought in some layouts from it, so that was exciting. It was one of the things that maybe shaped what I like to do – one of the reasons why I wanted to work at Disney. The layout and the colour and the design were so beautiful. It had a great energy all the way through it, and it captured the upstate New York feeling well, for a cartoon. It had a very good mixture of humour and scariness – a sort of fun, energetic, visceral kind of scariness. So the script had those kind of elements. But it's funny, sometimes part of what you like about a script is the thing that's dangerous about it – like those kind of real groaner lines you get in bad horror movies. The girl sees her father being decapitated and the doctor says, 'It must have been a terrible jolt to the system.' Those kind of lines – we've worked on that a little bit. But it has good imagery. And also the names are good – Ichabod Crane, Van Tassel ...

The majority of Burton's previous films have been fuelled by his strong sense of identification with his lead characters, and his identification in Sleepy Hollow *is just as personal, if less obvious.*

I think I've always responded to characters who have conflicts of interest within themselves, and Ichabod's a character who's pretty fucked up, in the sense that he's smart but sometimes there's a kind of tunnel vision. If you think too much, sometimes you can think yourself into a corner. Reading the script, what I liked about Ichabod, which is different from the cartoon, is that he was written very much as somebody who's just living too much up here – inside of his own head – and not relating to what's happening in the rest of the world. And that, juxtaposed against a character with no head, was a really good dynamic.

Ichabod Crane (as played by Johnny Depp) can be seen as an outsider to both the town of Sleepy Hollow and his profession.

There's a certain thing I've always loved about horror movie actors, like Vincent Price or Peter Cushing. There's a separateness about them. They're just doing their own thing. They're the lead in the movie, but they're like, 'I can't be bothered, I have to go do my work, my research.' You see that they're intelligent, but you don't really know what's going on with them. There's some mystery to who they really are. You feel their aloneness, you feel like they don't socialize much, that they're having some problems, are somewhat tormented, are somewhat living inside their own head. That's why you relate to them. And that's what *Sleepy Hollow* had, it was inherent in the material, and it was one of the strongest elements that I gravitated towards. And Johnny's really good, because he really gets all that stuff, the Price–Cushing thing, in his own way.

Burton acknowledges his own feelings of separateness, and of living in his own head.

You go through phases where you try to open up more, and you go through phases where you feel you're becoming more reclusive. I'm going more reclusive, I think. Not to become a crazy recluse, but it's like all you really want to do is *do* things, and that's what's been great about this movie – an opportunity to do something. I just feel happy to be making something and focusing on that. That's what gives you the energy and makes you happy. Lately I haven't paid any attention to what's going on in the movie business or the States. It's best not to look at it, and to just keep trying to do what you want to do. It's all so temporary, this whole business – one second they want you, the next they don't, then they do again. It somehow seemed easier at the beginning when people really didn't know you. You just kind of did it and were flying below the radar, so to speak. Now you get marked for certain things: 'Oh, he likes weird things' or 'He spends too much money' – whatever rap they want to pin on you. That's the thing in Hollywood – they like to label everybody. The labels can change, but they stick with you until you're re-labelled.

For Burton, Sleepy Hollow's *setting is as important as his identification with Ichabod Crane.*

The other side of it was spending some time in upstate New York over the last seven or so years. I've been trying to get out of LA pretty much my whole life. There's something about getting out of LA that just opens me up. If I spend a little too much time there I close myself off. I was spending time in New York and renting a house upstate – I have friends there – and

I was staying near Poughkeepsie, the home of Ed Wood, in a little farm-house. I had a little studio to do artwork and I'd sort of wander out into apple orchards. It was a very good time to think. I felt like I did when I first came to London on *Batman*. I like seasons, I like the fall, and there's just something about the Hudson Valley that's very compelling. You drive through it and you see little towns and churches. There's something very strong about it, and this story really represents that to me. It's also one of the few places I've been in America that feels haunted. I mean, you can go to lots of places in Europe and feel haunted, but the Hudson Valley's got a very strong feeling of that, too.

The original intention had been to shoot Sleepy Hollow *predominantly on location, and towns were scouted throughout upstate New York and the Hudson Valley – including Tarrytown itself – and as far afield as Sterbridge, Massachusetts. The film-makers even considered using a number of Dutch colonial villages and period town recreations. But when no suitable existing location could be found, coupled with a lack of readily available studio space in the New York area needed to house the production's large number of sets, they were forced to look further afield, and it was Rudin who suggested England. 'We came to England figuring we would find a perfect little town,' recalls producer Adam Schroeder, 'and then we had to build it anyway.' Filming began on 20 November 1998 and ran through to April 1999, including a month-long location shoot at Lime Tree Valley on the Hambleden Estate near Marlow, Buckingham-shire, where the town of Sleepy Hollow was constructed around a small duck pond in a style production designer Rick Heinrichs terms 'colonial expressionism' by way of Dr Seuss.*

The story, the placement of it, is so important, and that's why it's so fun-ny and strange to be here in Britain. But the Lime Tree Valley where we shot and built the town reminded me of the Hudson Valley, which was great. And the forest that we built on the stage, that reminds me of upstate too, even though I kept thinking, 'Is it because I like it up there and I'm sort of projecting, or does it really feel like that?' We made a model of the town a long time ago, and when we went out on location it looked strangely the same as the model. It's wonderful to be able to make a loca-tion look like a stage, pumping a lot of smoke into the atmosphere. Hammer films did that quite a lot – trying to make the exteriors look like a stage and the stage look like an exterior. All those great Hammer horror films had such a beautiful atmosphere – that was another of the reasons why I wanted to do this film.

Although Hammer Films started out as a distribution company in the 1930s, it remains best known for its reinterpretations of such classic horror characters as Dracula, Frankenstein, the Wolfman and the Mummy, beginning with The Curse of Frankenstein *(1957). Gory, full of nubile female flesh and barely repressed sexual tension, Hammer's period horrors earned a small fortune at the box office around the world and made household names out of stars Peter Cushing and Christopher Lee, the latter most famously remembered for his portrayal of Dracula.*

They're very lurid, and very gutsy. There's a certain emotional simplicity to them which is great. And a certain joy. When I watched them I got joy out of them, and I tried to inject the joy that I got from them into this. The funny thing is when you look at Hammer films now, they're all over the place. It's like Disney movies – in your memory they are more intense than when you look at them. They all have great moments, and the feeling of a certain kind of lurid beauty – that kind of gore and the colour of the blood.

Another major stylistic influence on Sleepy Hollow *was Mario Bava's* Black Sunday: *as with the Hammer horrors, Burton was drawn to the otherworldly quality it evoked as a result of being filmed primarily on soundstages. Responsible for* Sleepy Hollow's *look was Rick Heinrichs, who had been production designer on* Superman *as well as the Coen Brothers'* Fargo *and* The Big Lebowski. *While the production team was always going to build a substantial number of sets, the decision was taken early on that to fulfil Burton's vision best would necessitate shooting the movie in a totally controlled environment, which meant that all the interiors and virtually all of the exteriors – other than those shot on location at Lime Tree and one or two other brief scenes – would be shot on stages at Leavesden, with some studio work also taking place at Shepperton, where the massive Tree of the Dead set was built. In all, Heinrichs estimates that 99 per cent of the movie was filmed on sets. 'You don't see them doing lots of exteriors on stage any more because it doesn't really fit the overall naturalism that films tend to gravitate towards. But we're not going for naturalism, we're going for a kind of natural expressionism.'*

'Lurid beauty': Christopher Lee in *Dracula Has Risen from the Grave* (1967)

Barbara Steele, poised to get the point in Mario Bava's *Black Sunday* (1963)

Lisa Marie, photographed by Burton *en hommage à* Barbara Steele

There's a different vibe on location and a different vibe on the set. Stylistically they're two different things, and it's a question of how to marry those two together. In the Hammers there's often a combination, and I remember thinking *Dracula Has Risen from the Grave* (1967) was a pretty good one. Sometimes the transitions from location to set are pretty jarring, but they're also part of the energy of it, in a way, so I felt that was fairly successful. *Black Sunday* is one of those movies – and this happens mainly when you're a child – that leaves an impression on you, and you don't necessarily know why. You just know there's a clarity of the image, of the design, that helps to create a feeling in you. Those kinds of movies made me realize that movies can work on lots of different levels. You don't have to have this great linear story to get a feeling out of a film, and *Black Sunday* is a good example of that.

I know the way forward seems to be the digital backdrop, as in the new *Star Wars*, and I know it's amazing – it has a place, for sure. But in films like *Black Sunday*, what's important to me is you definitely feel like you're there – that definite feeling of being stage-bound or earth-bound, being in a world that's very present. There are certain shots in *Sleepy Hollow* that people might think are models, like the one looking down on the town. It doesn't look real but it is, and that's the wonderful thing about it.

Applying to Sleepy Hollow *many of the techniques they had used in stop-motion animation – such as false-perspective sets – Burton and Heinrichs were able to create a set-bound world quite unlike anything today's audiences have seen.*

We had space but we didn't have a lot, so our forced perspective was pretty forced. You need a little bit more depth to help sell that, but it's also good because it gives the film a graphic quality, and it is kind of reminiscent of those Hammers, where they used sets and all the effects were more alive as opposed to being added later. Working with those limitations can sometimes be fun. I remember one day we wanted a shot of a figure going through the apple orchard. So we had somebody get a doll and the wardrobe department, in fifteen minutes, made up a little cape for the figure and we wired the little figure through the apple orchard. We did that stuff kind of on the cuff every now and then, and it makes you feel like you're really making something as opposed to just punching it in. For me it helps keep that energy alive of why you like making movies to begin with – making stuff.

Ichabod Crane (Johnny Depp) examines the grisly handiwork
of the Headless Horseman

'There's a different vibe on location': the *Sleepy Hollow* crew

'Like agony captured in wood sculpture': Burton inspects the Tree of the Dead

The feeling one had walking around Sleepy Hollow's *sets, and in particular the town at Lime Tree, was almost as if you were walking around the inside of Burton's head.*

That's what I always felt about the expressionist movement: it is like the inside of somebody's head, like an internal state externalized. I like all different types of painters and paintings, but I like a lot of impressionists and expressionists, I guess. If I look at certain Van Gogh paintings, they're not 'real' but they capture such an energy that makes it real, and that to me is what's exciting about movies.

I hope the film ultimately has its own believability. I felt pretty good about the quality of the photography: I feel like we got a good dream-like quality. I also felt good when I was in some of those sets – even though this is much more stylized, it felt good, it felt like that haunted feeling I get when I go upstate in New York. You're obviously dealing with sets, but you want to do something stylized that doesn't look too phoney. If it starts looking phoney then it doesn't have any impact to an audience.

Responsible for Sleepy Hollow's *highly stylized photography was*

175

Emmanuel Lunezki, the gifted Mexican cinematographer who previously shot A Little Princess, Great Expectations *and* Meet Joe Black.

It wasn't one particular film that made me want to work with him. I just love his work. *A Little Princess* was beautiful, but everything he's done has been different in a certain way. He seems to have exactly the same process as me, in terms of it being intuitive – he thinks things up. The lighting schemes for the stages were thought out for several months, but on set he's very intuitive. I feel very in synch with him and it's the most fun I've had working with somebody in a long time. He's like another character in the movie.

Initially, he and Burton contemplated shooting the film in black and white and in the old square 'Academy' ratio. When that proved unfeasible, they opted for an almost monochromatic effect which would enhance the fantasy aspect and make the 'unreal believable'.

The saturated look I'm going for is not that big a deal. It's just a binding together of the sets and the locations. It's not as extreme as black and white, which you can do anything with because it melts together in one strong thing. This is different to that, but it certainly helps when we go from the stage to the set work. It's not sepia, it's not monochromatic, it's just a colour filter with a slightly muted quality.

In the lead role of Ichabod Crane, Burton again cast Johnny Depp. As was the case with Edward Scissorhands, *while Depp was his first choice for the part, Burton was still required to examine other options before casting him.*

You kind of go through this little song and dance with the studio. Not that they don't like Johnny. But as soon as it's going to cost a certain amount, they go, 'What about ...?', and you go through the list that everybody goes through. It's not that there's anybody else specifically, it's normal Hollywood procedure – 'What's Mel Gibson doing?'.

When you work with somebody more than once there's a sense of trust. It's great, because you don't have to verbalize, you don't have to talk about every single thing. That's what I love about working in England. A lot of people on *Sleepy Hollow* worked on *Batman*. Craftsmen in England are excellent. I love the painters here because they very quickly give you the story without you needing to know it. You work with a scenic painter and they paint a beautiful sky, and it gives me something. Same thing with an actor – you have a feeling about something, and they do something that's their own thing, and it fits in with everything. It's very exciting, it creates a positive momentum.

Johnny also understands the visuals. He understands how to move, he understands how to hit a mark, which sounds kind of boring but it's very important, and it makes it very easy on a film like this. In a way, we've been kicking and dragging him around for months, and I don't think he particularly enjoys it, but at the same time he's good at it and keeps that good energy going.

Depp plays Ichabod as a cross between Angela Lansbury and Roddy MacDowell with a pinch of Basil Rathbone. Typically of the actor, he's not your standard action-movie hero.

He hits like a girl, he throws like a girl, and he acts – as far as I can tell – like a thirteen-year-old. It's good because I'm not the greatest action director in the world, and he's not the greatest action star, so what we're trying to do is something that hopefully satisfies on that level but comes at it from a slightly different angle. Johnny probably sees it differently from how I do, but again the best example I would use is Peter Cushing, who's not an action star – but you put someone like that in a role where they're running around and doing stuff and it's sort of great. And even though we changed the Ichabod character from the original story, there was a certain spirit of this sort of prissy, wimpy guy. He lives in his head but then he's forced to open up and become physical, not because he wants to but because he has to. The idea was to try and find an elegance in action of the kind that Christopher Lee or Peter Cushing or Vincent Price had. Again, this goes back to the Disney cartoon, to try to find a beauty and an elegance to action and movement. Johnny's really good at it. He strikes poses without striking poses, and he finds an elegance without being Lord of the Dance.

Depp says he appropriated Hammer's style of acting: 'It is acting in a style that wouldn't normally be accepted in a regular movie; it's a fine line that we're walking here. It's sort of got that style that's almost bad acting. Certainly I'm trying to stay with the idea that it could be bad, and if it is a little bad, it's good, you know?' But Burton, as always, is reluctant to comment on the film's tone.

I can't say just yet. I don't think it's 'bad', because it was actually important to me. I wanted to make sure that it feels like it's a real story, that it's serious. Nobody's being campy. There's humour in it, I think. Anytime you do something that's period or horror, there's something kind of absurd about it, isn't there? It seems to be somewhat in the nature of it, I don't know why. Again, I go back to the cartoon, wanting to try to get that mixture of things. We're not joking it up or anything because we wanted to keep the spirit of a horror movie, but also to have fun with it, in a sense, to try and find a balance. The original script had a really serious nature which we didn't go against, but I think between us we ... I wouldn't say 'lightened it up', but we didn't make it like a Merchant-Ivory horror film. We tried to give some life to it.

Many have commented on Depp's role as Burton's on-screen alter-ego, among them Sleepy Hollow *producer Scott Rudin, who said, 'Basically Johnny Depp is playing Tim Burton in all his movies.'*

Vice and versa? Burton directs Johnny Depp

I don't think that way and I prefer not to. That categorizes it in a way that I don't like, and it undermines a working relationship, because part of the charm of making a movie is that there are still some unspoken things. You try to find any bit of mysterious joy left in it. It's nice if an actor sees something I'm interested in, and they try to get into it, because you're all making one thing in a way. I can see similarities in the characters Johnny's played, yet they're all different in other ways. And I like chameleons, I like people who like to change and do different things. I enjoy working with Johnny because he's very open to ideas. You spend months going over the script with the studio, trying to analyze and think about every single element when, in fact, it's a movie and you can't figure out everything. There's a journey that happens and you try to think enough about it so that you go in with an idea, but if you go in with too much of an idea, you'll be wrong about it. You see certain Fellini films and you see he understood that in a way. You get the magic. You see the lights and you see the set, and behind the set which creates the total environment of it, it's a magical thing which is … it's like trying to control the weather, you can't do it.

If Edward Scissorhands *represented Burton's inability to communicate as a teenager, and* Ed Wood *reflected his relationship with Vincent Price, Depp proposes that Ichabod reflects Burton's battle with the Hollywood studio system, even the world.*

It's funny that he said that. It's probably true in a simple sort of way. In fact, at one point Scott Rudin said to me, 'You've made the horseman into Jon Peters!', and I was like, 'Wait a minute,' and then I thought, 'Well, you know what? In a way he's right, that's kind of true.' As I've said, I find that I feel much more secure doing things from a subconscious point of view as much as I can, without thinking about it, but not going too far because I find I spin myself into a hole pretty quick. That whole year of not working after *Mars Attacks!* affected me deeply, deeply. I don't think I've ever been quite affected that way and that's why I put a lot of misplaced energy, trauma, from that into this.

To support Depp, Burton again amassed a truly eclectic collage of on-screen talents, ranging from British character actors – Michael Gambon and Miranda Richardson as Lord and Lady Van Tassel, Richard Griffith as the town magistrate Phillipse, Ian McDiarmid as Dr Lancaster – to

Rogues' gallery: Michael Gambon, Jeffrey Jones, Michael Gough, Ian McDiarmid, Miranda Richardson, Christina Ricci

those returning to the Burton fold: Jeffrey Jones (from Beetlejuice *and* Ed Wood*) as Reverend Steenwyck, Christopher Walken (*Batman Returns*) as the Hessian Horseman, Martin Landau in a cameo role, and Hammer veteran Michael Gough (Alfred in the* Batman *movies), whom Burton tempted out of retirement to play the notary Hardenbrook; plus relative newcomers such as Casper Van Dien who plays Brom Van Brunt.*

Again, we wanted to have a good mix. With these fairy tales you try and build the cast in an interesting way. All those Brits together in one room is incredible, just seeing their faces – amazing to work with.

In the pivotal role of Katrina Van Tassel, Burton cast Christina Ricci, an actress who excelled as the ghoulishly deadpan Wednesday in the Addams Family *movies, and who always seemed destined to appear in a Burton film.*

She reminds me of Peter Lorre's daughter, you know? It's like if Peter Lorre and Bette Davis had a child, it would be like Christina. She's just got a mysterious quality – you look at her and you don't quite know what's going on. She's like a silent-movie actor, and I like people like that.

The daughter Peter Lorre never had: Christina Ricci as Katrina Van Tassel

The Hammer influence was further confirmed by the casting of Christopher Lee in a small cameo.

When I first met him we were sitting there for two hours, and it's like you're looking at Dracula, even now. He's talking to you and you're like hypnotized. If I was an actor, that's the kind of actor I'd want to be.

In part a reaction to the computer-generated effects in Mars Attacks!, *Burton adopted an almost back-to-basics approach to film-making for* Sleepy Hollow, *choosing to utilize as little post-production jiggery-pokery as possible.*

I wanted to get back to making a movie where you're building sets and dealing with actors and doing things that are less manufactured, less computerized – just making an old-fashioned movie that way. It's the hardest time, but my favourite time is being on the set, which is where you're making this stuff. There's just such a good atmosphere. It's nice if you can create as much of it there and then add as little as possible, because it makes it a more immediate experience. I enjoy doing things on the spot, because you're there on set and that's the only time in those circumstances, with everyone in costume, and the smoke and the lights. It suggests things. It's hard on this sort of movie because you need so many elements pre-planned. But it's also hard to look at a storyboard now and go, 'That's it!', because things suggest themselves when you're on set that really make a difference. I did start out storyboarding every single thing and now I can barely look at them. When you're in the town, looking at the bridge, and you walk through it with the lens, you feel something that a storyboard wouldn't give you. You get a sense of movement and space. But I have to use storyboards for certain things, especially when you are dealing with all these actors. It's nice to let them know what they're supposed to be doing.

Although Burton has acted as his own producer since Batman Returns, Sleepy Hollow's *production duties were handled by Scott Rudin and Adam Schroeder.*

Scott's smart. I met him when I brought *Edward Scissorhands* to Fox. He gets good stuff done, he's intelligent and eccentric, and you sense that he cares about the movie and wants it to be good. A good, strong producer can come in handy if they have clout, and are good at selling a movie. That's where you get at odds with yourself a little bit. You spend all this time working on it, and then I'm not so sure myself that I'm the best at knowing how to sell it properly. It requires somebody outside of it a little bit, who can just be tough. I didn't have that on *Mars Attacks!* – we were kind of doing it ourselves – and I kind of felt that on *Ed Wood*, too.

One of Sleepy Hollow's *executive producers is* Godfather *director Francis Ford Coppola. Burton only became aware of his involvement during the editing process when he was sent a copy of the film's trailer and saw Coppola's name on it.*

I went, 'What the fuck! Wait a minute, Chris [Lebenzan, editor], play that back.' As my editor said, Coppola probably made a phone call back in the 1970s. It often happens that way. I remember on *Batman*, I never even met the executive producers. You spend a year or two working on something, and then the main credits come up and you go, 'Who the fuck is that guy?'.

A preliminary sketch by Burton of the sinister scarecrow

Sleepy Hollow *opened in the US on 19 November 1999 to some of the best reviews of Burton's career.*

Planet of the Apes

In March 2000 Burton went to Prague to shoot two commercials for Timex I-Control watches. Produced by LA-based commercials company A Band Apart, the two ads were Matrix-like in tone, with fight sequences choreographed by Andy Armstrong. The first, 'Kung Fu', featured a man in a suit pursued by patent-leather-clad villains well versed in kung fu. It premiered in cinemas in the US with Mission: Impossible II in May 2000, before being shown on television. The second, 'Mannequin', starred Lisa Marie in a skin-tight black cat-suit pursued through cobblestone streets by a man in a stitched-together mask and dark glasses. At one point she tries to evade her pursuer by diving into a puddle, before finally hiding out in a warehouse filled with mannequins. The commercial aired in the autumn of 2000.

It made me realise that it's best if I don't do commercials, I felt. I don't find it easy. People say, 'Try commercials, it's fun, it's quick!' But I didn't find it that quick, and I found it quite difficult – it's as if a studio were hanging over you at every second. You have a client, and you're basically serving whatever product it is. I worked with A Band Apart as a production company and it was a concept they had, though there was nothing about the look of the characters, so that's where I tried to have a bit more input. It was fun to do it, though – it was interesting to go to Prague, and to make those kinds of costumes. But I haven't done one since, put it *that* way . . .

In October 2000, the first of six animated episodes of Stainboy appeared on www.shockwave.com. Based on characters from his Melancholy Death Of Oyster Boy And Other Stories, each three-minute long episode was written and directed by Burton and created by Santa Monica-based Flinch Studio using Burton's watercolour drawings as guides. The music for the series was composed by Danny Elfman and Lisa Marie and Glenn Shadix provided some of the voices. The final episode, 'The Birth Of Stainboy'

A sketch by Burton for his Timex I-Control commercials.

featured a host of new characters, including Brie Boy and The Boy With Nails in His Eyes, who later appeared alongside Stainboy, Toxic Boy and Match Girl as part of the range of Tragic Toys created by Burton in conjunction with Dark Horse.

It was right at the beginning of that dot-com boom and it was an interesting time, like the gold rush – people were made billionaires in a couple of days, and the next year it all comes crashing down. But it was interesting because at the time I didn't really work a lot with computers, and all these companies were asking me to do something. So I just got the opportunity to try something in a different medium – that was about the only real reason to do it. In reality, what I would have loved to have done with those characters was make it more stop-motion – that's what I would do now, because those characters seem to lend themselves more to that kind of form. So I don't think it was necessarily the right medium for those characters, but it was fun to try and to play around with them, and worth exploring. It was pretty simple, very minimalist animation. Flinch Studio did the actual production of the animation, and I did some storyboards and some key-frame kinds of things. But I'd rather – and I maybe will, at some point – try to do those characters in stop-motion.

Based on a novel by Bridge On The River Kwai *author Pierre Boulle and adapted for the screen by Michael Wilson and Rod Serling,* Planet of the Apes *was released in 1968. Directed by Franklin J Schaffner, who went on to helm the Oscar-winning* Patton, Planet of the Apes *told of four American astronauts – Taylor (Charlton Heston), Landon (Robert Gunner), Dodge (Jeff Burton) and Stewart (Dianne Stanley) – whose spacecraft enters a time warp, is propelled years into the future, and crash-lands on an unnamed planet on which man is the primitive, mute, and physically inferior species ruled over by intellectually superior talking apes. After their ship goes down in a lake, Taylor, Landon and Dodge (Stewart died in space) trek across a desert wilderness looking for food, and come across humans scavenging a cornfield, whereupon a group of gun-toting gorillas on horseback charge from the woods, hunting them down. While Dodge is killed, Landon – who's later lobotomized – and Taylor – who's shot in the throat, rendering him speechless – are captured and taken to an ape city. Eventually, Taylor is befriended by a pair of sympathetic chimpanzees, scientist Zira (Kim Hunter) and her archaeologist husband Cornelius (Roddy McDowell) who, intrigued by Taylor's speech and ability to reason, posit that he could be the missing link between man and higher primates, although their theory is dismissed by the ruling ape council who consider him a threat and schedule him for cranial surgery. With the aid of Zira and Cornelius, Taylor and a female companion, Nova (Linda Harrison), escape and together they set off for the Forbidden Zone – an*

Planet of the Apes (1968): Zira (Kim Hunter) and Cornelius (Roddy McDowell) reason with Taylor (Charlton Heston)

uncharted area of land where apes are prohibited – in an attempt to prove that intelligent man existed before simian-kind. There they discover a secret that has earth-shattering implications for them all.

Long considered a cinematic milestone and a classic of the sci-fi genre, Apes also proved to be culturally significant as well, tapping into the social and political climate of the time (notably Vietnam, the civil rights movement, racism, the Cold War, and the nuclear threat) and went on to spawn four sequels, a television spin-off that ran for two seasons, and an animated TV series.

The idea of resurrecting the franchise and returning to the planet of the apes had been floating around Twentieth Century Fox for almost a decade before Burton became involved. Several filmmakers, among them Oliver Stone, James Cameron, Chris Columbus, and the Hughes Brothers, had at one time flirted with the project, while various screenwriters, including Terry Hayes (Dead Calm) and Sam Hamm (Batman), tried unsuccessfully to crack the script. But it wasn't until Apollo 13 co-writer William Broyles Jr picked up the challenge in 1999 that the project finally found its momentum. In an attempt to differentiate it from what had gone before,

Broyles decided not to set his story on Earth, 'to remove the thought that this is a repetition of the first', and also jettisoned the original's cynical human protagonist who, so embittered and disenchanted with mankind, hurls himself out into space, in search of something better than man. Instead, Broyles' hero was not only written to be much younger than before but would also be on a journey of self-discovery.

When Burton responded to Broyles' draft (which had the working title 'The Visitor') and signed on to direct in 2000, Fox's president of production Tom Rothman put the film on the fast track for a summer 2001 release. 'To inaugurate a franchise like this and to re-energise an idea there's a familiarity with, you need a unique, individualistic, iconoclastic filmmaker,' Rothman told me. 'Tim has that uncanny ability to walk the line between making very commercial films and yet very individualistic and distinctive films.' Fox were keen not to term Burton's take a sequel or a remake, but rather a 're-imagining'.

It was another one of those situations where a project's been floating around for years and they want to do it, they want to do it, they want to do it . . . and finally they give it to me. I'd probably say that it's the first project I've been involved with where I knew it was . . . not a mistake, as such, but that it was the most dangerous, because it's based on a movie I loved growing up. And it's a classic, and that's like the first rule of thumb – 'Don't try to remake a classic. If you're going to remake something, pick something that was bad, so you can make it better.' At the same time, I had an affection for the material and I had that thing that I sometimes get on a project, which is a perverse fascination of attempting something you probably shouldn't do. But that's part of my personality, I guess. I often feel that way . . .

Obviously, you do something based on something else and that's your immediate target comparison. There was a pressure on this that was probably even worse than *Batman*, in that it's a known thing where people have expectations. But any movie is a risk, and any movie I do I always try to treat it like it's new to me, somehow. If I thought it wasn't, then I don't think I would be interested.

I saw *Planet of the Apes* as a kid and loved it. It had a lot of impact. And I saw pretty much all the sequels. So I was a fan, but at the same time one of the things that made me feel it was okay to do another version was that it wasn't a remake – because you can't remake that film. If people like it so much, like I do, then you just go back and watch it – that's *that* movie. And I feel in a certain way you can't really beat it. But knowing that this wasn't necessarily a remake was helpful – because then you just focus on the material. And there is something very strange about talking apes . . .

What was intriguing to me about it was the simplicity of the idea – the reversal. I've done a lot of stuff with masks and makeup, but there was something about the ape/human thing that was primal. And it was intriguing to see these great actors sort of being apes – it's kind of absurd but there's also something kind of classical about it, it kind of goes back to an older style, before films, of mask-acting. And makeup sometimes has a tendency to take the person away, but in this case, with apes, you could still feel the person in there somehow . . .

Although Burton signed on to direct Broyles' script – which was very science fiction oriented and featured three huge battle sequences – Fox declared it prohibitively costly. And so in August 2000, two months before shooting began, screenwriters Lawrence Konner and Mark Rosenthal, who had penned The Jewel of the Nile *(1986) and the remake of* Mighty Joe Young *(1998), were hired to do a page-one rewrite. Sets were being built even as the script was being retooled.*

The other problem with a project like this is that's been around for so long that it gets into a kind of weird state of 'Okay, we want the project, and we want it out at *this* specific time, and *this* is the script that we want to do.' You're like, 'Oh, okay.' And then you get involved and you get it budgeted and it's something like $800 million and you go, "Wait a minute, of *course* it's too much . . .' But it was one of those projects that got into that unfortunate Hollywood spin cycle where there's a release date and a script that the studio likes but it's too much, and so you spend months and months not really working on a project but trying to cut a budget. You hear of it happening all the time in Hollywood – why I don't learn my lesson I don't know. I hope I have now, finally. And it only seems to happen on big budgeted movies – it happened on *Batman*.

In analysing it, I think I was more intrigued by the idea of it than I was by the thing in itself. And if I searched deep down in my soul, if I had to start all over, I would probably do a completely different kind of movie with it. If somebody came to me and said 'Do you wanna do a version of *Planet of the Apes*?' and I'd started the whole thing from scratch, it would have been a completely different movie with completely different types of characters. Maybe. I don't know . . .

Again it's a Hollywood thing. There's a momentum going, and it's so hard to get projects going that you get caught up in the groundswell of it. And then I started to get into a kind of angry-mode, because the studio would say, 'Just cut the budget' and I kept saying to them, 'You guys are a movie studio, you have a huge production team, I know you do your own budgets, you know how much a movie is roughly gonna cost.' So there was a lot of that going on which, again, was counter-productive to making the movie. It started to turn into something else, it kind of mutated in a way.

We were supposed to shoot in November and I don't think we got the green light until the week before. So it's extremely frustrating. You give your best, but it's my own fault for going down that route. I guess that I felt – and it's not necessarily a positive thing – that I'd done it before with *Batman*. But it's really not a good way to work and you don't end up saving money, plus you end up aging and wasting time and energy and your health declines, so it was tough that way. I felt like I was spending so much time fighting these conflicting forces that by the time I was doing it, I was just 'doing it', in a way. Which isn't to say that every day I didn't try to find something in it for me, because otherwise I couldn't do it. But by that point you feel like an athlete that gets the shit beaten out of you before a race, and then you're expected to go win.

I wanted to keep it serious, but you couldn't do that. The point is not to make it the same. There was room for other explorations of ape manner-isms, while still trying to keep it kind of serious, not jokey. And you need it to be serious to some degree, because it's somewhat absurd anyway – talking apes. I remember seeing production photographs from when they were filming the first movie, an ape sitting at a chair reading *Variety*, that kind of thing. We did a few twists on lines from the original, which you might consider to be jokey. But it probably had more to do with casting people like Paul Giamatti, who are naturally funny – even if he's doing a dramatic thing he has humour about him. Same with Tim Roth, there's a certain kind of intensity. Not that they're trying to be funny, it's just that there's something inherent in those people.

The intention was never for it to be jokey-jokey. But that's maybe me. My love of 50s horror movies turned out like *Mars Attacks!* – it didn't turn out like *Independence Day*. So there's a certain retro thing inside me, and why it comes out in a certain way, I'm not sure.

The producer of Planet of the Apes *was Richard D. Zanuck whose father, Daryl F. Zanuck, had founded 20th Century Fox. As president of pro-duction at Fox in the 1960s, Zanuck Jr. had given the green-light to the*

A sketch by Burton for the character of Limbo, incarnated on screen by actor Paul Giamatti

original Planet of the Apes *(and was married to Heston's co-star Linda Harrison at the time.) Later fired from Fox by his own father, Zanuck continued as an independent Oscar-winning producer, often in conjunction with his long-time partner David Brown. His credits include* Jaws, The Sting, Cocoon, Driving Miss Daisy, *and* The Road To Perdition. *He and Burton connected immediately, and Zanuck remains his producer of choice.*

I love Richard – he's fantastic. The other night I was watching a biography on his father and it was like, 'Jeez . . .' I'm surprised nobody has done the biography on that whole story, because it's like one of those Harold Robbins novels for real.

He amazes me. For somebody who's done and seen so much, he's not jaded and I admire that. I'm a lot more jaded than he is, and if I'd been through what *he* has I don't know if I could still do it. But he still maintains a certain innocence when something stupid happens, which I find amazing, and which is probably one of the things that keeps him able to keep doing it. This guy was hired by his father, then fired by his father, and he's got a sense of humour about it, he's *hilarious* about it. His observations about things are quite amazing. You can learn so much from these people. When I met Vincent Price I was so grateful to see somebody who'd been around and to see that they're nice, they're interested in lots of things, they're not jaded – and you learn from that, and you should always keep learning, and I feel grateful for that. I see the way of certain studio executives, they don't even know who people are. But Richard has got a wealth of information, is fascinating, has seen it all, and people are missing out on something when they don't delve into that a little bit.

When I first met Richard I was actually kind of scared of him, because this guy is very intense. But he's extremely funny when you get to talk to him, and extremely knowledgeable. He's incredibly wise and he's got the most incredible stories. They're like those tell-all books in which people are being really bitchy and mean about people. Well, he can do that without being mean. They'll be great stories but without one mean bone in his body, and there's something really amazing about that.

And the idea that he ran the studio, then he comes back to the studio to do a movie and they don't even know who he is . . . it's surreal. But he's seen it all and therefore he's somebody who has what I think is lacking these days – he's completely supportive of the filmmaker. He's there every day but not in-your-face. He understands the process, and because it's such a business it's just such a pleasure to be around somebody who knows what the process is and has respect for it. To grow up with a father who was one of the people who started the whole business, to be the head of the studio, then get canned, then become a successful producer and kind of span generations – he's really seen it all.

Despite his initial reservations, Burton was drawn to film's theme of reversal, of the topsy-turvy world, of the outsider thrust into an alien landscape – familiar motifs that echo throughout his world. In this case, however, it's not just Mark Wahlberg's astronaut Captain Leo Davidson arriving on an alien planet, but also Helena Bonham Carter's liberal chimpanzee Ari – who, with her sympathetic tendencies, calls for humans to be released from subjugation and slavery – who can both be seen as outsiders.

I think that's what I liked about it – you see reversals on so many different levels. But I haven't looked at the film recently. Usually it takes me a few years to process, and I'm still not at that stage. This one's taking me a little longer, maybe it's still a little too painful, so I'm still in the zone. But there were a few things I liked – there was the juxtaposition of the ape-outsider and the human-outsider. But I also wanted to explore a bit more of the ape-like aspects of it, and their movement.

While the central premise of an astronaut crash-landing on an upside-down world where apes enslave humans remained essentially the same as before – although the ape planet definitely isn't Earth; the script refers to it as Ashlar – Burton was adamant that his apes should be substantially more animal-like than the shuffling men in makeup present in Schaffner's film. Burton's apes would fly through trees, climb walls, swing out of windows, and even go ape-shit when angry. The concept was 80 per cent ape, 20 per cent human, and so his actors were schooled how to move and behave like apes for two to three days a week over two months at a special Ape School.

I like people who act like animals or visa versa. Pee-Wee acts like an animal, Beetlejuice, Penguin, the Catwoman . . . Batman is an animal. I like animal people somehow. I don't know if it's an emotional response to things versus an intellectual response, but there is something about it I feel is important or is something I relate to somehow. It's just that primal, internal, animal instinct of people and I did enjoy that with the Penguin character and the Bat. So this was a juxtaposition of that, along with the flip-flopping of my brain that doesn't necessarily have a conscious or verbal reasoning.

There were also some technical things that I was interested in exploring: just doing a little bit of ape research and trying to give them a bit more of a weird mixture of ape mannerisms, and weave that into the reversal. You start to think not just what that reversal would be like, but how we are with apes, how we anthropomorphise them and make them kind of cute in a certain way, when, in fact, they're quite scary – especially chimps. Although most people would consider gorillas more frightening, chimps have a very hidden quality – they're very open on some levels, but they're much more evil in a certain way, and to me, much more scary. They'll rip you to shreds. But I'm fascinated by them. One of the first things we talked about was the unnerving quality that chimps have, because it was originally written that Thade was a gorilla and we changed his character to a chimpanzee.

When we were shooting some of the spaceship scenes there was a chimp there and one day all it wanted to do was hump me – my foot, my leg, my arm, my face, my back. And the next day it was spitting on me, and you just don't know. And it's because as humans we've treated them as cute, performing monkeys, and at the same time they can kill you. So I find that disturbing. Tim Roth really captured part of the weird energy that chimps have, he really tapped into that scary quality.

Although there was talk initially of the apes being created using CGI, Burton insisted on using actors and make-up under the supervision of Rick Baker, a multiple Oscar-winner widely considered to be the king of cinematic apes having created the realistic primates in Greystoke *(1984),* Gorillas in the Mist *(1988) and* Mighty Joe Young *(1998) among others, as well as having transformed Martin Landau into Bela Lugosi for* Ed Wood. *Because of his reputation, Burton found there was no shortage of actors willing to endure up to six hours a day in the make-up chair, with Tim Roth, Helena Bonham Carter, Paul Giamatti, and Michael Clarke Duncan among those who would arrive at the studios between two and three in the morning to begin the process, and then often working until nine at night.*

There was an early thought that they should be CG because that's the modern way of thinking. But Richard and I felt very strongly that part of the energy of this material is the good actors behind it. You get good actors,

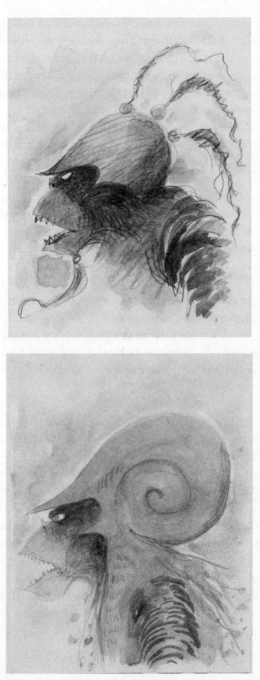

'They'll rip you to shreds' – sketches by Burton for the more warlike ape characters

kind of hidden, but *doing* this stuff. When I first saw the first one I didn't know who Roddy McDowell was, but you got the vibe from him, his performance gave it a gravity that it wouldn't have had otherwise.

I have to hand it to these actors, they didn't have it easy. I mean, it was like being buried alive every day. I tried as best as I could beforehand to tell if people could take it, because it's like torture, and some people flourish under that stuff and some people hate it. Imagine waking up at 2 a.m. and having three people poking and prodding you, it's like a nightmare, it's like going to the fucking dentist at two in the morning.

In the Charlton Heston role, Burton cast Mark Wahlberg, formerly known as Marky Mark, a rap star turned actor whose breakout performance in Paul Thomas Anderson's Boogie Nights *was followed by roles in* Three Kings, The Perfect Storm *and* Rock Star.

I found him to be just very impressive, really solid, in the films I'd seen him in, and what this needed when you've got talking apes was somebody who's solid . . . I don't know how to describe it, it's a certain kind of acting which is very hard to do, just a simple, solid 'What-the-fuck-is-going-on?' quality, to ground it against all this other weird shit . . .

Unlike Heston in the original, Wahlberg's astronaut barely reacts to what's going on around him. His headlong charge through the film in search of an escape from his predicament seems to reflects Burton's own feelings about the production period.

It's possible . . . Let's put it this way, I wouldn't say no. Because it is something I talked to Mark about the character. As I've said before, I do work from the subconscious, and as I go on and look back at the films, I do see myself more in things than maybe I thought. But I certainly did talk to Mark and asked him to play it real straight and 'Get-me-the-fuck-out-of-here.' And he did play it with that Steve McQueen straightness, kind of barrelling his way through. That's what we were going for. And that is perhaps my psychological problem . . .

Burton cast Charlton Heston in a small cameo role as an elderly ape, the father of Tim Roth's chimp Thade who, on his deathbed, tells Thade a dark

Captain Leo Davidson (Mark Wahlberg) and Daena (Estella Warren)

secret: that in the 'time before time', apes were slaves to man. When Thade refuses to believe his words, his father has him break open a vase, inside of which lies the proof of man's power and technology – a gun. It was both a deeply iconic and highly ironic piece of casting, since Heston is president of the National Rifle Association (NRA).

Richard and I talked about having him play a role, but it wasn't until we thought of the right thing that it dropped into place. He scared the living daylights out of me as a kid and I loved him for that, because I was of the era of *Soylent Green* and *The Omega Man*. He had an intensity about him, and I guess when you're smaller the screen seems bigger, so he seemed bigger and scarier than real life. I've always been fascinated by him because he has a gift that's very rare, to make that kind of stuff work, and he did and was so compelling and sort of scarily believable, in a weird way. And he had that thing that I have always liked in some actors, like Vincent Price – that tortured quality, that quiet sort of internal pain. These people are amazing because you really do soak up an energy and a feel of people that have been through this forever, that they are kind of beyond human. I felt it with Christopher Lee too. They've been in it a long time and they're still cool and doing stuff.

197

Not everyone was so enamoured: particularly Tim Roth who was neither a fan of Heston nor of his politics.

With 90 per cent of people, I don't necessarily agree with their politics, but for me that's the thing about making a movie or any artistic thing. Part of its joy is its purity. I won't work with convicted murderers . . . but I like to find the good in whatever. For me this person had a lot of impact so that's what I focused on. And I think it gave the scene a real energy.

Filming began on November 6, 2000 and although the production was based in Los Angeles, using soundstages on both the Sony lot in Culver City and the LA Centre Studios in downtown LA, Apes also shot on the black lava fields in Hawaii, as well as Trona Pinnacles at Ridgecrest in the Californian desert, and at Lake Powell, a man-made lake on the border of Utah and Arizona where parts of the 1968 film had been shot. Due to the complexity of the production, the tightness of the filming schedule – 17 weeks shooting, 16 weeks post-production – and an immovable release date, Burton often shot with several units at once and had a mobile editing suite on location with him.

In some ways I'd rather have not much time. Or you should be able to take a month off and look at it again, because there seems to be sort of a middle-ground process where you almost fuck it up even more, where you get a little bit too much time to think but still not enough time overall. So, in some ways, doing it quickly is not such a bad thing. Because these things take years, so any kind of quickness is almost good on that level – at least it's momentum, it's movement. In fact, the quicker these things are, the better it is, because people have been in make-up since 2 in the morning, and on these kind of films where it takes an hour-and-a-half between set-ups, you crash and the energy dissipates. That's where the quickness of energy is probably more helpful than hurtful. So I never felt any compromise in that way. It's just more of the overlapping nature of all the stuff surrounding it. I remember the same on *Batman*, but that's why I was happy to be in England – because it was a little removed. Even though I have a pretty strong shell and can kind of not let that stuff bother me when I'm doing it, I noticed it then. And I know that aspect of the film world has gotten more intense that way.

During filming, Burton broke a rib.

It was in the last week in Trona. I was showing somebody how to hit the ground and I showed them exactly the right way, except for the part where I broke a rib . . . I'm lucky that's the only thing that happened, because I don't really focus where I'm walking, climbing up rocks or walking off a platform. You try and keep those moments to a minimum on any film. It's amazing more things don't happen sometimes.

At the same time I got a cold, and I thought I had pneumonia because my chest hurt so bad, but I had to keep going anyway. You have to do that, you can't take time off to go get better. There's nothing you can do about it anyway: you're going to feel excruciating pain for six weeks and then it'll go away.

Burton was not the only one hurt. Wahlberg was hit by a fireball during a stunt, while Michael Clarke Duncan, who played the gorilla Attar, injured himself falling while running.

Running in an ape suit covered in armour, and being a big guy . . . I wish I'd gone to the hospital with him, because seeing them wheeling him in, as an

Michael Clarke Duncan as Colonel Attar

ape, was maybe the best thing about the film. We should have been shooting that. For a while after, we had to move him around on set in a chair in full makeup, rather than having him stand.

The ending of the original Planet of the Apes *– Heston and Harrison on horseback on the beach, coming upon the half-buried remains of the Statue Of Liberty revealing that this is indeed the planet Earth – presented Burton with a tough act to follow.*

It's one of the strongest endings ever. In some ways people know that ending more than they know *Planet of the Apes*. And people are looking for you to either top it or do the same thing. But you can't do the same thing. And you can't top it, that's the thing you realise. So if you do something else, in the audience's minds it's not doing what they want you to do.

So we just went back to the overall mythology of *Planet of the Apes*, of the book, even the other movies. For me the whole thing has got a sort of circular structure to it, it goes around on itself somehow – parallel universes, time travel, man/ape, evolution, religion. Where do we come from? Where are we going? Do we just keep re-evolving? There was a feeling of wanting to do something where it was a parallel world but it was all apes, and there was something about that I liked – I had this image of a weird twisted parallel universe. I thought about in a big picture – even though I couldn't give a shit about sequels, but if you do something like this you think about a bigger picture of the material. So there was the idea of going back in a sort of twisting of time, and again going through this juxta-position of human/animal, and coming back into a world where you think it's normal but something has happened. The original series of movies always did that in some way, shape or form, though they had the luxury of going through several movies to map that out. At the time, I wasn't ready to have a three-hour discussion on the art of time travel . . .

Throughout the shooting of Burton's film, the crew's scripts didn't include an ending in an attempt to preserve the secrecy of his climax. As such the ending became the subject of much speculation on the Internet, with rumours that Burton had filmed several different versions.

Our original idea was that we wanted to do the same thing as we eventually did but at Yankee Stadium, and it would all be apes – and I don't know if it would have been better. There were different talks about different ways of doing it but again it was lot of budget bullshit. But we didn't shoot five different endings – we may have *talked* about different types of things, but we didn't *shoot* five different things.

Burton's Planet of the Apes *was released in the US on 3,500 screens at the end of July 2001. While the critical reaction was less than enthusiastic, the film went to number one at the box office in its first weekend, grossing more than $68 million, eventually taking $180 million in the US and almost $360 million worldwide. Nevertheless, the perception remains that* Apes *was a box office flop.*

It fell off but it still kept going, and it made a lot of money. To be honest, if you look at the box office of the movies I've made, it's up there, it's probably one of the higher ones. The reviews – as always, I don't really look at them, I just assume they were like every review of every movie I've ever done, some okay and some really bad: you know, 'It's a crass remake of a classic movie, a big Hollywood mindless summer movie. Don't monkey with the classics . . .'

I haven't seen it in a while but I bet when I do watch it in a couple of years there will be some things that I'll get very attached to and find interesting. If I go emotionally back to it, I can analyse feeling as intense as you do on *anything* that you do. Shooting the scene with Tim Roth and Charlton Heston was a weird, amazing experience for me. I did enjoy it, because it's a really perverse scene – having Charlton Heston and the weird juxtaposition of him as an ape, with the whole gun issue . . . that was a surreal day and an amazing day. So I had some moments. It was a hard movie to make, but just seeing apes standing around talking, or apes in the desert . . . you'd find things in it that kind of keep you going throughout the whole thing. And it's the first time I'd worked with Richard and Katterli [Frauenfelder] who has worked as my first AD since, and has probably been the only person to keep me on time and budget in my entire career, so that's been kind of a good thing. All the actors, too. There's always something positive, no matter what.

I didn't particularly enjoy the studio experience. After doing it a couple of times in a row you get kind of tired of it. You're sitting there working on the movie and there are posters and trailers and people talking about it like it's done and out, and it's just an uneasy feeling, like an out-of-body or after-death experience. Part of the thing I enjoy about the process is that moment of doing it, the *unknown* of doing it – and that kind of gets zapped out of it somehow. In this kind of quick schedule, you never completely finish something before all this other stuff starts. I understand that, but there's a real pre-emptive nature to it, it's a feeling that I don't like. I don't pretend to know what's best to sell something all the time, but as the world gets more corporate I guess you just want to protect that artistic feeling as much as you can. I don't want to create a Me-versus-Them, because that's not what it's about. I actually take it to heart. It's a large operation, it's a lot of people, it's a lot of money, so I take that seriously and I try to work with people that way. I feel like I'm in the army sometimes – it's kind of scary.

I think the real problem with the film was that the script that they wanted to do, I couldn't do, and I don't know anybody who could have done for the budget that we had to do the film for. So that's where the deconstruction begins. You have a release date and you are deconstructing the script for mainly budget reasons, and very quickly the whole *thing* deconstructs. I don't know how better to say it.

A few months after Apes' *release, Burton broke up with long-term girl-friend Lisa Marie and moved to England.*

I've always liked it. When I first came here to do *Batman* I loved living here and when I did *Sleepy Hollow* I loved it. I do feel more at home, I can't explain it. I don't think I came over with the idea of 'I'm moving', because I'm semi-nomadic – I had a place in New York, didn't have a place in LA anymore. But England has always been a place I've gravitated towards and loved being here.

Soon afterwards he began dating Helena Bonham Carter, which gave rise to many tabloid stories.

It was a tough time, and that was the other thing that made me have bad feelings about the *Apes* experience, because I was sort of in the midst of some personal issues at the time. And then after *Apes* came out there were all these news stories that I'd had an affair with Helena on the set, which was complete fabrication. So that made it unpleasant. It really tainted that experience for me in that way, because it was not fair to anybody. It didn't have anything to do with the movie, just with the other stuff surrounding it.

Big Fish

Burton's father Bill had passed away while he was in pre-production on Planet of the Apes *in October 2000, and his mother, Jean, died in March 2002. Although he was never close to his parents – moving out of the family home when he was very young – their deaths affected him deeply. Professionally, Burton wanted to get back to making something smaller and more personal, especially after the studio shenanigans involved with* Superman *and* Planet of the Apes. *Together with Zanuck, he began working on 'another script, more personal, that takes place in Paris, sort of a weird period thing.'*

But Burton put that idea on hold when he was sent the script for Big Fish *by producers Dan Jinks and Bruce Cohen, who had picked up the Best Picture Oscar for Sam Mendes'* American Beauty. *Based on a book by Daniel Wallace entitled* Big Fish: A Novel of Mythic Proportions, *the script had been adapted by screenwriter John August who had read it in manuscript form in 1999, when, hot off the success of his script for* Go, *he was given a deal at Columbia and had the studio option Wallace's book on his behalf. August's script initially attracted the interest of Steven Spielberg, who had him write a couple of drafts with Jack Nicholson in mind for Edward Bloom Sr. A year later, with Spielberg no closer to committing, August put together a 'Best Of' draft from the many that he'd done, removing much of what Spielberg had overseen, before Jinks and Cohen sent it out to Burton, who found in the material the personal connection he had been looking for.*

Big Fish *revolves around the exaggerated adventures of Alabama travelling salesman Edward Bloom, a gregarious, romantic and prodigious teller of exceedingly tall tales, now in the twilight of his life and estranged from his only son, Will (Billy Crudup), a journalist living in France, soon to be a parent himself. When Will returns home in the hope of reconnecting with his dying father (beautifully played by Albert Finney) and attempts some kind of reconciliation with the real person he believes is beneath the persona, the film then cuts back between the time-present drama and a fantasy version of Edward (with Ewan McGregor as the younger Bloom) through whose eyes we see events. And it's through these mythical tales that William eventually comes to a better understanding of his father, learning lessons about acceptance, tolerance, and unconditional love.*

I was ready for something like this. And reading the script just surprised me. It was also nice to do something that wasn't a known entity – probably not since *Beetlejuice* have I done something completely off the radar, so to speak, and it was nice to work like that again, where you don't have a release date before a script, where you don't have a brand name, or something that everybody knows and compares it to. It was nice too, after a few years of doing this other kind of stuff, to connect with something again on a certain level.

My father had recently died and, although I wasn't really close to him, it was a heavy time, and it made me start thinking and going back to the past. It was something that was very difficult for me to discuss, but then this script came along and it actually dealt with those same issues, and so it was an amazing catharsis to do this film – because you're able to work through those feelings without having to talk to a therapist about it. For me, that kind of stuff is always quite uncomfortable and sappy and hard to put words to. That's what I liked about the script – it kind of put images to the things that I couldn't say. And when you start to analyse your relationship with your parents, it's so bizarre and complicated, and yet so simple at the same time. Why, if a parent is like a hippie, are the children little straight-arrows? And why, if the parents are two boring accountants, then the children are wild? You realise it's the strangest relationship you can have.

> My dad was a professional baseball player early in his life, before I was born. He played for the Cardinals, it was a Triple-A team, I think, and I think he got injured. Then he worked for the Park and Recreation Centre in Burbank, he was city employee, but he stayed in sports. He was very well liked, he had a very outgoing personality, because he had to deal with kids' baseball teams, girls' and men's softball teams, all the different sports, because Burbank had a good city sports program. And then he became a part-time travel agent, so he would travel a lot.

I don't know if there's any real reason why I didn't get on with my parents. It had more to do with the fact that when I was living there, I felt old for my age. I didn't get along with my mother so much, and my father was away a lot, and they were having whatever their problems were, and I was just always remote. That was my personality, it seemed – and even when I went to live with my grandmother, it wasn't a big deal, I just sort of did it. And then I got my first apartment when I was 15, so I always felt older. I had to make my way. To go to Cal Arts, I had to get a job. My parents didn't pay for my college, but I never felt really angry about that with them. I actually felt it was probably good, because I was the one who had to go do it, and I did it. In a kind of perverse way, that teaches you to be independent, and I *always* felt independent. And ultimately I feel that in some ways I was lucky that I was allowed that independence.

When my dad was ill . . . you start to prepare yourself. As I say, I didn't have the closest relationship with them, but as he got ill I tried to kind of re-connect a little bit. I didn't get to the point where Billy's character does at the end of *Big Fish*, although it wasn't as bad in the first place. I made some headway. But I did start thinking too about how the relationship starts out quite magical and then it sort of turns south, kind of similar to this film in some ways. And the thing I realised was – no matter how old you are, the relationship is still parent/son, it's not human beings together. And I never really treated my parents like human beings. They're your parents, then you grow up, and even if you're not close you kind of realise later on that they have a whole other life going on. And you can be 45 years old but still feel inarticulate and cut off with your parents. And they kind of go full-circle, they go from children to parents and then back into children, and you go full circle in your life too. So it's a very unique and powerful relationship.

Making anything should be cathartic. And with my dad, thinking about the relationship, it wasn't something I could talk to a therapist about. I've had therapy but I've never discussed my parents. But in reading this script I thought, 'This is it exactly, this puts an image to the uncommunicable.' So I liked that very much. I wouldn't normally do something like that except it hit me on that level. It's like having a baby – you can't really prepare for your real emotions. It just hits you very strongly and in a primal way. I wasn't looking for that kind of catharsis, even though I had been thinking about my parents. So, in a way, I felt it was good to be kind of surprised . . .

Wallace's book is more a collection of short stories about the adventures of Edward Bloom than a singular narrative, and John August, who had recently lost his own father when he first read it in manuscript form, first had to find a way of adapting the episodic book into a cohesive script. Part of his trick was to have several different narrators – including Edward and Will – to tell his story, so that this piece about storytelling becomes as much about the telling as the story.

It's not quite like *Rashomon*, but it had a certain quality, a freedom, and that's what I loved about it. It's a different thing, but there's a similarity to *Ed Wood* – that wasn't a biography in the classic sense, because everybody has a slightly different take on things. That was what I loved about the book, *The Nightmare of Ecstasy*, one person says one thing, another person contradicts that, and that creates a sense of reality. You see it a lot in England, historians on TV saying, 'Henry VIII did this, and that', and I think, 'How the fuck do *you* know?'

I didn't read the book *Big Fish* until well after getting the script, and if I had then I don't know if I would have said 'Yes' to it. It's got lots of ideas and yet it lacked a certain shape, but I think that probably allowed John to feel like he wasn't dealing with the Bible here. You've got a little bit of license to take the themes and work them into something else – and you're putting it into another medium anyway. I think John did a really good job of taking things from the book and giving it more structure. It's a strange structure to me, because it's like a mosaic – one thing affects another, and first it's overly complicated and then kind of overly simple. And I just felt like that was very much like the way things are in terms of those kind of relationships. So I felt John gave it a lot more than what was there in the book, in some ways.

Usually, with a studio, you have to be able to describe a movie in one sentence or else you're not able to do it – that's really the studio way. So it was really nice to have a script that I liked, and that they liked, and that nobody really wanted to change – because it was such a tricky one, going in and out of reality, you've got one person playing an idealised version of an older person, and the dual casting of Albert and Ewan and Jessica and Alison, shot all out of sequence. Everything was like a weird little piece of the puzzle. And a studio was willing to do it – this was amazing to me, because it didn't have one star to sell it. It was such a pleasurable experience, to have a script that wasn't deconstructed as we went along. I said to them before we even started shooting, 'This is going to be a tough one to market, because anything you say about it could be misleading. And there's not going to be an image in this that you're going to be able to sell' – because there have been giants and witches in other movies, done on a grander bigger scale. But then part of its problem for them was also part of its charm to me.

There are always little things that you have to do to a script, often for budget reasons – the birth scene was a late addition, because we had a whole big scene on a hill with hundreds of extras, and then we added the bathtub scene late because we wanted something between Albert and

Jessica that was just the two of them for a moment. Also the little karate fight in the dark with Ewan was a last-minute addition because it was cheap. Then there were little elements we added, like the Handi-Matic, because in the script Edward was selling screwdrivers, but we wanted to come up with something that was a bit more in his sort of world. Some of this new stuff was done on the day, some was a few days ahead of time, but it kind of freaked the prop department out – 'Let's do this, and we're shooting it in three days.' But I think people kind of enjoy that, because you get to be a bit more spontaneously creative as opposed to planning for months and months . . .

The production was based in Montgomery, Alabama, and shot from January to May 2003. Apart from a week's filming in Paris, the entire film was shot in the state of Alabama.

It's a different place, and you feel like you're in a different *country*, but then I feel that way anywhere – you can feel that way in Los Angeles, especially now, with Governor Schwarzenegger.

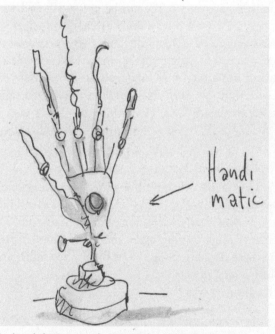

A sketch by Burton for Big Fish's 'Handi-Matic' device

There were a lot of nice people, but there's another side to it too – a sort of overly friendly thing that seems to be masking some sort of seething hostility . . . But people are very friendly – and I'm just not used to that, you know. I get kind of nervous, but that's my problem really, it's not theirs. And it infuses you with the vibe of it, I think it actually helps the movie.

The good side of it is you're in the place where the story is taking place, so for the actors – because they've got to do accents – just being in the environment is helpful to them. It's not the kind of movie you'd like to shoot on a soundstage in Los Angeles. For me, for the actors, for the crew, for the vibe of it, you just have to be there – and it's weird to go to a place that you would never go. Then when it comes to the extras, those smaller parts, you just get the local people to play them, and that's great and you meet interesting people, very different to LA extras, like the guy who gives Edward the job for the Handi-Matic.

But there were a lot of strange factors involved in being down there, because the stories jumped around, and there were never major locations, just a series of set-piece locations. Because of the nature of the story, and the duality of the casting, and the fact we were shooting completely out of order, and very quickly, we were shooting maybe two or three different locations in one day, so there was a lot of moving around.

I kind of looked at myself in the mirror every day and would go, 'Why did I end up here?' I remember I picked up the local paper one day and it said there was going to be a Klan rally, and that took me aback a little bit. It's a strange place, but again that's what makes it great to be there. Wouldn't have it any other way. And you don't get many visitors, that's the other good thing – it's not like people are going to saunter down to Alabama for the weekend.

It was probably the most extreme weather I've ever experienced. We were in the circus tent one day and it literally started to blow away. It was like *The Wizard of Oz*, everybody had to evacuate. Tornados, the river rising. Our whole circus set got wiped out. We shot one scene with Danny DeVito and the next day everything was about several feet underwater. It was really extreme. And we had some of the biggest insects I've ever seen. During night shoots it sounded like a war zone. You'd hear these dive-bombing things hitting the lights and frying, and the smell of burning insects . . .

Other than that, it was fine.

For Burton, part of the appeal of Big Fish *was its combination of a deeply emotional core with the larger-than-life, slightly exaggerated fantasy element of Edward Bloom's tall tales. What makes the film so affecting is the balance Burton achieves between the fantasy and reality elements. A consistency of tone extends from the script to the production design to the casting and to the acting. Burton allows the real world to be 'real' but never gritty – there's a movie-sheen to the real world which makes it comforting and approachable – while in the fantasy elements everything is heightened, while at the same time retaining human and lifelike proportions.*

It was like shooting two movies, in a way. I certainly felt comfortable in fantasy, but I was also interested in doing something that I hadn't done before – and that was the other stuff. But it needed both sides, because the one would just be like an episode of *ER* and the other would have been similar territory to before for me. So its appeal was the juxtaposition of the elements.

What I liked about the structure was that it kind of snuck up on you, and that was what I was hoping for in making the movie. You get to the end and you get very emotional, and you kind of know why and yet you don't – it hits you from underneath as opposed to seeing exactly where it's coming from. I couldn't tell how it played when I was finishing the film, because I didn't really show the movie to anybody, and I couldn't tell if I was just in an overly emotional mood. But I was hopeful that was the way it was coming across.

As much as Burton related to the character of Will trying to repair his relationship with his terminally ill father, he also identified with Edward Bloom, because what Edward does is what Burton does – he tells stories.

That's one of the reasons why I wanted to do it, because although I definitely understood the Will character, the whole point was to show both sides. You had to understand it and love it, and I felt very close to Edward. That was what was fun for me, because I knew I had that from the very beginning – loving that character, and also understanding the other character, and the juxtaposition of that. But if I didn't feel strongly about Ed Bloom I don't think I could have done the film or even wanted to do it, really.

To play Edward, Burton initially talked with Jack Nicholson, whom he had worked with twice before, on Batman *and* Mars Attacks! *The idea was that Nicholson would play the older Edward and would have his appear-ance digitally altered for the scenes of him as a young man.*

We discussed it – kind of a loose discussion, about how to make a younger version of him somehow, probably digitally. That was a funny discussion but it didn't really go anywhere. It was a concept that we didn't really know if we could pull off, necessarily. I think it was one of those 'Get-excited-about' conversations, kind of 'That's interesting. Is that really pos-sible?' But it would have been different. And it was fun not to have to deal with that for a change, and deal with two actors instead.

Burton then cast around for the two actors in question. The same dual casting applied to the role of Bloom's wife, Sandra, who would eventually be played by Jessica Lange and Alison Lohman. It was Jinks and Cohen – who at the time were producing Down With Love *with Ewan McGregor – who suggested the combination of McGregor and Albert Finney.*

What was hard about casting Ed Bloom was that you could never think about just the one actor. You might come up with a perfect choice for one, but unless you found a nice counterpoint, it wouldn't work. And it was a house-of-cards a little bit where we had to get them both, because what if you got one but couldn't get the other, what are you going to do? You can't hire Albert Finney and then have Ben Affleck thrown in there. It was the same with getting Jessica and Alison. Actually, I might have taken kind of a risk on that one and tried to go for Jessica without knowing yet quite who the other one would be. We were just so lucky with Jessica, and I love her.

Ewan's great, he's like Johnny. I love him because he's really talented and he's not afraid. I love actors who are willing to do anything and don't have an ego in the sense of 'How am I going to look in this?' They just go for it and there's a freedom to that which I appreciate. Interestingly, meet-ing Ewan and Albert separately, I don't know if I was looking to connect them – and they're completely different people – but there's a certain spirit about them that was very connective somehow. It wasn't so much about them really looking alike, but even when they're performing there's that similar spirit.

With Ewan it was like every day was a different movie – it was very, very enjoyable, because we had a very quick schedule, and I think if I'd had one of those 'Now, shouldn't we be over *here*?' actors then we would still be shooting. In the scene with Ewan rescuing the dog, he really impressed me.

Albert Finney, well cast as Edward Bloom (senior) in *Big Fish*

He was having to deal with this St. Bernard that didn't want to be in a burning building – nor did Ewan – it was smoking in there, the dog was freaked out, the steps were icy, we tried to make them as safe as possible, but the house was actually starting to burn down. And he was having to manage this thing, and it was one of the most amazing acting jobs I've ever seen.

Part of what I love about certain types of actors, of whom Ewan is one, is that he's not a mimic. It's character acting, it's becoming somebody else. Johnny's able to do it, but there are not many people who can do that kind of mixture of things, where you're sort of heightened and yet you're still real, and be funny and physical as well. And because he's a sort of romanticised version of himself, of Ed Bloom, there is a certain kind of slightly larger 'Aren't I wonderful?' kind of a thing which could potentially get on your nerves but which I thought Ewan got the balance of really, really well.

Albert's amazing too. I'd never met him before, but looking at him in something like *Tom Jones*, there was a spirit about him and a certain charisma that he has that very much felt like Ewan. After we thought of that casting, someone sent me a *People* magazine from a few years ago where they had contemporary stars and their counterparts, a separated-at-birth kind of a thing, and there was a picture of Albert and a picture of

Ewan together. And it was like, 'Of course! It's perfect.' Albert's got that real passion for life, very much like the character, and he brought a lot of himself to his role, while Ewan captured that heightened reality and open-heartedness – it's beautiful when actors can be open-hearted. He's done it before, he sings, he dances, but again it stays really real.

Same with Alison – she just stands there like a silent movie actress. One of the first things she did was she had to stand and hold still for two minutes, that's all she had to do and it was emotional and beautiful. Jessica too was always able to find the simple truth to something. And because nobody had a really big part, it was like a puzzle and nobody really knew how one person was going to affect the other, but that was the beauty of it for me, I always felt that Jessica was going to help Alison's performance and Alison was going to help Jessica, Ewan's going to help Albert and vice versa, unknown to them in a certain way, but that was amazing for me to see.

Although McGregor was on set from the very beginning of filming, Burton chose to shoot all Albert Finney's scenes first.

The stuff with Albert was so intense, and then we did the Ewan stuff which had a completely different energy. Ewan still came at the beginning but we didn't shoot much, but he came by. He was a quiet observer at times. We discussed things, and Albert and Ewan spent a little time together, and we had a couple of dinners. With Ewan, I sense he thinks a lot and does his own quiet study and research, and then he doesn't want to talk about it too much but he'll go for it. I sense that with him, I always sensed he was ready to start shooting. I could see him watching Albert and quietly soaking it in.

In the role of William, Edward Bloom's son, Burton cast Billy Crudup, widely considered to be one of the finest actors of his generation, who had starred in Cameron Crowe's Almost Famous *and Robert Towne's* Without Limits.

Will is a very literal person searching for literal answers, but some things in life aren't literal, they're not just black and white. There are things that can be real and unreal at the same time. Billy had the most difficult role of the movie and I thought he did really, really well because it's a tricky balance to capture. I always really felt for him and I don't know if it's because I felt

Ewan McGregor as Ed Bloom (junior)

similar to that character and had that kind of relationship with my father. But there's a certain rigidity to the character, an internal conflict, that I find very emotional, very sad, and very real. There's just something quite touching about those characters. Again it's that dynamic of parent/child, and it doesn't matter how old you are, you don't get over it. I thought that Billy did that really well. It's kind of the emotional core of the film, it's the simplest and the hardest one to get in a way. It's a complicated part. We always talked about it because it treads that line. I certainly questioned, 'Why am I acting this way? My dad's a great guy, everybody loves him, why do I have such a problem with him?' But it's just the yin and yang of life.

It was very intense doing the hospital and bedside scenes. I never went through that with my father, so it wasn't like I was replicating something. I was in Hawaii scouting locations for *Apes* when I got the news that he had died. The final few times I saw my father, he looked ill, but he wasn't bed-ridden. The only side of it was the emotional side that I had gone through.

The actors were really good. They are all very internal, emotional actors, very thoughtful, and while you've got your usual rushing around with the crew we tried to keep that to a minimum because the actors were into their space there. And it was intense. The scenes that were intense in the movie were intense to shoot, and amazing to watch. Both Albert and Billy – I felt really good that it was the right choice of people. It's a hard thing to do, that kind of emotional repression, and Billy and I talked about it and it was something we were concerned about, that fine line. But by keeping it the way he did, and then going where he does at the end, that was good.

In supporting roles there were a number of Burton regulars including Danny DeVito as the circus ringmaster Amos Calloway who also happens to be a werewolf. The part required nudity.

Talk about scary . . . The great thing about Danny is you don't have to convince him – he's game, that's why he's so great, he just does it. And I was probably more worried than he was. Mosquitoes and all . . . but he went for it.

Burton's new partner Helena Bonham Carter was given three parts to play: Edward Bloom's friend Jenny, in both young and senior guises, as well as the one-eyed witch whose glass eye holds mystic powers and which fore-tells how one will die if one dares to look into it. Casting Bonham Carter had been Zanuck's idea.

Starting this movie, I only saw one challenge and that was the tandem casting of Albert/Ewan and Jessica/Alison. And once that was set, I still had difficulty kind of dealing with the Jenny character, because again there was a little bit of age involved in that. Rather than getting two people to play her, Richard brought up the idea of Helena, and I'm glad he did because I think I could see it in a clearer perspective. You always feel a little awkward suggesting her, even though she's a great actress. So that made it easy for me to deal with. I think originally he mentioned her in connection with playing Jenny, but it just seemed appropriate for her to play the witch too. What's working with me without some heavy make-up?

Among the newcomers to Burton territory were Steve Buscemi as "poet" Norther Winslow whom Edward initially meets in the town of Spectre and later inadvertently helps commit a bank robbery, and the seven-foot eight-inch Matthew McGrory who played Karl The Giant, whom Edward first meets terrorising his home town of Ashton, and who then becomes his travelling companion. McGrory died of natural causes in August 2005. He was thirty-two.

Burton's sketch for the one-eyed witch

Matthew is in the Guinness Book of Records: he's got the biggest feet in the world. You feel for him. Here's a guy who, everything he does, people are looking at him. We all feel weird but here's a guy who obviously is getting the way we all felt in spades, he's getting it to the hundredth degree. He's really smart, and he just has a real gravity to him that I really liked. And Steve, he's so great, all you gotta do is look at him and you get excited. He's like Barney Fife's bad brother.

Tonally Big Fish *marked a sea change for Burton. Certainly it's his most romantic and sentimental film to date, but not in any mawkish, schmaltzy sense.*

It was always interesting to me to be emotional but without being overly schmaltzy. I tried to watch the bullshit-meter and just be real with it and see what happened – otherwise it's an episode of *Days Of Our Lives*. That's why I liked that there was humour in it, so it's all thrown in together. And I had a good cast that way too. I like to pick people who can do all of it at once – be funny, be real, be dramatic, hit an emotional core. It's hard, especially with this kind of tandem casting, it's gimmicky by nature, so I felt quite lucky that the people we got understood all that.

I liked the romantic nature of it as well, because although it's about a father and son, it also shows that this guy had another life and there's a connection between a man and woman. It doesn't overcomplicate that, but it was another layer that I liked about it. As a child you don't think of your parents as having their own lives, especially when you're younger, though of course they do. So I liked the romantic simplicity of that.

As for reflecting any increased happiness of my own – I don't think I could ever really be content. I don't think anybody who tries to work in the arts is ever really content – the minute you are is the minute it probably stops. I think there's always a longing, there's a desire, somewhat of a fantasy, to want to be that romantic – a longing that's probably different from a reality of happiness, if you know what I mean. It's more about wishing you could be that demonstrative and that grand and clear and simple about your feelings.

For Burton, another part of the appeal of Big Fish *was its variety of elements and time periods.*

Every day was like a new movie and so I felt like it was a little sampler-platter, you get to try everything. I actually hadn't felt that way since *Pee-Wee's Big Adventure*, where you get to try a lot of little genres all in one movie – and it's not like you're spending six months on things, it's like one day's work. 'Okay, today we're going to shoot the heist movie.' 'Today? We got wolves.' 'Now we're going to go to Korea.' So that was great.

Having shot a lot of the realistic scenes first, we then got to the fantasy side, which was kind of unleashing and unloading. And it was fun, especially after having the heaviness and the emotional simplicity and the hermetically sealed quality of the other stuff – it was nice to just open up. There was never a dull moment, and while it was strange to be in the South – fucking weird – I really enjoyed it. You know much how much sitting around there can be making movies, so it was a real pleasure to be working that quickly. And it creates an energy and a fun that is sometimes lacking when a guy's getting into a rubber suit for an hour-and-a-half – if you're lucky . . .

The Korean War stuff was a late addition. The scene was that Ewan just sort of lands there and meets two girls, but it didn't really have any purpose to it. And so we just started joking one day about giving him a mission, but we didn't have any money or time, and I just thought of a lame karate fight in the dark to throw in a little mission for him. Ewan wanted to fight a couple of guys. What it was based on, *he* said, was that he always wanted to do this in a war movie, where he kind of wipes his nose – I don't know what movie it was a nod to . . .

I love people who look for historical accuracy in the film, and I got a lot of that from some journalists while publicising the movie – why, in the Korean War, were there Chinese lettering and American songs? And I say to myself, 'They call *me* weird . . . ?' It's not an accurate portrayal of the Korean War, nor would I say it's an accurate portrayal of *anything* – that was the point.

Which is why in a movie set, in part, before the end of enforced segregation in the southern United States, the young Edward Bloom plays with black children, while baby Will is delivered by a black doctor at a time when no such physicians were permitted to deal with white patients.

That's why I took everything from Edward Bloom's perspective and made my own kind of character-profile of him. And, to me, he wasn't a racist. He was a guy who wouldn't have those boundaries. And since everything was tinged by his perception of things, it didn't matter what the time-frame was – he wasn't a racist, he didn't see things that way. When we were down there shooting the circus scene, a couple of extras came over to me – a couple of scary guys – and one said, 'You know there wouldn't be any black people here, don't you?' and I said, 'Jeez, well, in this movie there are . . .'

Big Fish exhibits a beautiful balance between the intense reality of the hospital scenes concerning Edward Bloom's illness, and the Burton fantasy sequences shot nevertheless in a very real way.

That was for many reasons. Reason One was that, because of the material in the stories, we didn't want to over rely on CG. We've all gotten CG-lazy in this film world. One time we were all standing out in a field looking at a tree for the sequence where Edward's car ends up in it, and someone said, 'Can't we just CG the car in the tree?' And I was like, 'No, we've got to hang the car in the tree.' Or 'Can't we CG the flowers in?' 'No, we're going to plant all those flowers out in that field and have Ewan standing in them, not in front of a fucking blue screen.' So it was always important that the handmade human quality come through, because of the themes of what's real and not real. Obviously there are more realistic scenes, but even with that we never wanted them to be the clichéd Southern kind of thing, but rather take the more poetic Southern Gothic stream-of-consciousness approach.

Big Fish deals in fables and fairy tales, myths and folk stories, featuring many archetypal elements – the witch, the mermaid, the giant, the were-wolf, the circus, the romanticised small town – all of which are twisted through Burton's unique interpretation. Ironically, the Burtonesque trees that come to life to prevent Edward from leaving the town of Spectre were actually Spielberg's addition to the script.

We did go off on classic images – it's kind of like *Jason And The Argonauts* in the sense that it's got those kinds of mythological symbols. But it was fun because, again, in each culture and each generation the symbols do get mutated and adapted. That's why you could see the Beauty and the Beast theme done a hundred different ways and each time it can feel different, because it's universal. But myths and folktales I've always been fascinated by. Again it's the thing that changes when people become adults, they forget the fact that these stories, even witches and werewolves, are based in a certain reality of psychology and feelings. To me they're the most natural way of having it all, of exploring real feelings in a heightened way, and it always surprised me that as people got older they would forget that stuff.

I went back to thinking about my father and, as bad a relationship as I had with him, early on it was quite magical. I mean, he had false teeth, two of which were sharp, so he would pretend that when the moon was full he would turn into a werewolf – and he could actually move his false teeth and it used to drive us all crazy, we loved it. So you realise he was quite a magical character – but you can lose that too, and it's important to remember. I lost it, I forgot that for too long, in a certain way. As much as I was self-sufficient and got out, those early experiences do have an impact on you, probably quite a good impact, and those moments were quite surreal and magical and strong and powerful.

The one motif that interested me the most – why, I can't figure out – is the circus motif, because I've always hated the circus, to this *day* I hate it. But here, it was fun, because this was like old fashioned circus-people, like the old Mud Shows that still exist, especially down in northern Florida. And there was something about it that reminded me of that sort of weird family of filmmaking, where you're out there in the sticks with a bunch of people making something, so there was that connection to it. Those were pleasurable scenes to shoot because you're in Alabama, you got all these circus people around you, and movie people are like circus people, and circus people are like . . . circus people.

My favourite was the suicidal cat – an actual suicidal cat, and he did several takes. I think we shot it twice and both times it was different. When I first saw that in a circus in Florida I said, 'We gotta get this guy with his cat.' He was Russian, I think, and he goes out there and gets the cat to jump from a great height and makes a fortune. If I wasn't a director I would probably try to get that job, because he works for maybe twenty seconds a day. I was very impressed because it's not an act I think it would do on its own, it's not natural – but I have to say that was my favourite act of the day.

Several moments in Big Fish *seem to echo others in past Burton films, not least the brief sequence with Edward Bloom presiding over his Ashton gardening business. The suburban lawns which his company tends feel remarkably similar to the landscape of* Edward Scissorhands.

A sketch by Burton for the characters of Amos Calloway and the 'suicidal cat'

I honestly can say that, as I'm doing it, I can see similarities, but I don't start out thinking that way. For instance, for the landscaping scene I was thinking more of certain ads from when I was growing up, particularly one called 'Mike Diamond Plumbing', as well as certain images out of the 1950s from, say, *Look* magazine, for that precision lawn-mowing. But it has more to do with the way I like to frame things. So those connections are the things that I can see, but I don't make the connection that early.

The film ends with a song called 'Man Of The Hour', written by Eddie Vedder of Pearl Jam. It was the first time Burton had utilised an original musical number – other than score and Elfman's Nightmare *numbers – since Prince provided songs for* Batman.

Eddie Vedder saw the movie and he liked it and said he'd like to try something. And he was really cool about it. There was no pressure, that was the cool thing, he made it very easy. 'If you don't want it, don't worry about it.' Because if I work with musicians who I respect and they do something and I don't like it, it could be tricky. But I thought his song was really beautiful, and I was kind of honoured. I thought it was very much in the spirit of the movie, and I think he's got a great voice.

Shortly before the release of Big Fish, *Burton became a father for the first time, with Helena Bonham Carter giving birth to Billy Burton on October 4, 2003. (Ironically, one of* Big Fish's *funniest moments remains the birth of Edward Bloom, a slippery delivery scene that replaced a more elaborate birth sequence due to budgetary cuts.) Burton was present at the birth of his son.*

In terms of surreal 'shock and awe', to use the American term, I found the one in *Big Fish* strangely prophetic and strangely accurate in some ways. In fact, the real birth is stranger than even that, if you put it on the Strange Meter . . .

Big Fish *opened in the US in November 2003 to generally extremely positive reviews. While many found the film truly heartfelt, some critics believed the film to be too sentimental. There were others, however, who*

Burton and Helena Bonham Carter take a moment together on the set of *Big Fish*

hailed it as a massive departure for Burton, despite the evidence of his earlier films which contain their own share of emotion and pathos, be it Martin Landau's heartbreaking performance in Ed Wood or Johnny Depp's in Edward Scissorhands.

That's why it always makes me laugh a bit to myself. 'He's a dark person, but this is a real departure, a much lighter film, blah blah blah . . .' But I don't really think too much about that. That's what the movie's about – how people perceive things, reality, what is and what's not. I think *Nightmare Before Christmas* has sad, emotional moments. But you would think I just made these dark tone poems . . .

Charlie and the Chocolate Factory

Published in 1964, Charlie and the Chocolate Factory, the second substantive children's book from Welsh-born author Roald Dahl, told of one Charlie Bucket, a boy from an impoverished home, who wins a golden opportunity for a tour inside the factory of reclusive master confectioner Willy Wonka. There he is joined by his Grandpa Joe and fellow chaperoned competition winners Mike Teavee, Veruca Salt, Violet Beauregarde, and Augustus Gloop. But once within the factory's walls, the children are subjected to Wonka's determined strangeness, not to mention his distinctive moral sense. Burton, who first dabbled in Dahl's world when he produced James and the Giant Peach for Henry Selick, was a fan of the book from childhood.

It was one of those books that was read to us in school. Dr Seuss came a little earlier for me, but Roald Dahl was probably the second layer of connecting to a writer who gets the idea of the modern fable – and the mixture of light and darkness, and not speaking down to kids, and the kind of politically incorrect humour that kids get. I've always liked that, and it's shaped everything I've felt that I've done.

Dahl's book was first filmed in 1971 as Willy Wonka and the Chocolate Factory. *Directed by Mel Stuart, produced by David L. Wolper, and adapted by the author himself, it was part-financed by the Quaker Oats Company and shot in Munich, Germany. While the picture was not a box-office success, it has since developed an authentic cult following – a tribute, perhaps, to the performance of Gene Wilder in the role of Willy Wonka, but more probably due to Dahl's distinctive vision.*

I wasn't really a huge fan of the first film, it didn't capture me the way it's captured lots of people – that's the best way I can say it. It's a strange movie; it has the oddest tone. I found it to be quite disturbing. With that weird acid flashback when they're on the boat. And Willy Wonka turns nice at the end, out of the blue. I know a lot of people love it. It's one where you might have a real strong memory of it but then if you went back . . . I wonder if people who have voted it an 'all-time classic' have watched it recently. I certainly don't feel the same way about the first Willy Wonka movie as I do about *Planet of the Apes*. That one I knew I was walking into an ambush. With this one, I didn't feel that personal pressure, just because I didn't feel that way about the original movie.

After Dahl's death in 1990 the rights to the property in the US reverted to the Dahl estate, and Warner Bros began pursuing a new version. Roald's widow, Felicity 'Liccy' Dahl, who runs the estate's affairs, was, she says, reluctant at first, but was eventually persuaded by the promise of approval, alongside Warner Bros, of screenplay, director and main actor. First to try

Willy Wonka and the Chocolate Factory (1971): Wonka (Gene Wilder) observes the fate of Augustus Gloop

adapting the book was Scott Frank, screenwriter of Out Of Sight *and* Get Shorty.

Warner Bros called and asked me about it. They had three or four drafts over the past years, and I read a bunch of them and felt that I could see the process. I've seen it happen before – it was a bit like the situation on the first *Batman*. The studio had had the project for a long time, you could see all the different stabs at it, but I think what happens to anybody when you're working on something for so long is that the wheels start to get spun a little bit. I felt that Scott Frank's version was the best, probably the clearest, and the most interesting, but they had abandoned that, and it had got caught up in that 'developmental hell' circle.

What's deceptive about it is that it's so simple. A book is a different medium, and there are things that can be simple and fable-like in a book that you can't really do in a movie without it being overly simplistic. Somehow you feel you need to do a little bit more in a movie, otherwise you're kind of plodding along, a series of characters going from this to that – and you know, they're bad kids, but who is this Willy Wonka? Some eccentric candy-maker?

I could see, in different scripts, the thought process, the modern thinking of, 'Okay, there are all these bad kids, but Charlie's just boring from a movie point of view, he doesn't do anything.' Well, Charlie is like ninety per cent of us, kids in school who disappear into the background. But in earlier drafts they were always trying to make him do something, be a whiz-kid. 'You gotta make Charlie more proactive, and we've got to take out the father because Willy Wonka's the father-figure.' You could see all the story meetings right there: this idea of Willy Wonka as the ultimate father-figure. I said, 'No, he's not! In some ways, he's more screwed up than some of the kids.' So we got rid of that.

The idea for me was to put that aside, take a step back, and say, 'Why are we doing this? Because of the book, basically. So why is the book so good? Why do we remember it?' I wanted to get a feeling of the essence of the book, and try to hit that as best and as purely as we could – not try to overcomplicate it and try to make it 'Charlie's race against time', or whatever.

I had Pamela Pettler, who had done a draft of *Corpse Bride*, take a crack at it, and then had John August, who did *Big Fish*, take a crack at it. And with John I thought he had good takes on things and made it fresh, going to the roots of the book but adding a little bit of psychological foundation, so that Willy Wonka's not just 'this guy' . . .

It's about having those textural things. In simplistic terms, Charlie's family – they don't eat a lot so make the family look under-nourished, make Charlie thin, not some blond-haired rosy-cheeked guy who looks like he's just had a nice lunch. His grandparents – they're old, so make them look old, like they can't get out of bed. In the original movie, Jack Albertson who played Grandpa Joe – if he was still alive he'd be about the right age to play him now. It needed to feel like that for it to have its own weird reality.

I had to feel comfortable with what I feel is Dahl's sensibility, but I feel it's close to my own. We added new elements that aren't in the book, but I always felt comfortable that everything was in the spirit of his work. Also, it's an interpretation, and there's an anarchic spirit there, so you kind of take it a few different ways.

During pre-production Burton visited Dahl's former home in the Buckinghamshire village of Great Missenden. Liccy Dahl remembers Burton entering Dahl's famed writing shed and saying, 'This is the Bucket house!', and thinking to herself, 'Thank God, somebody gets it.'

Well, it's nice to see the roots. I always get a little leery because there's this person and his life, so you want to be respectful but not too entrenched. It was interesting to see where he wrote, and how he wrote, and just the eccentricity of the man.

Liccy showed me his original handwritten manuscripts and they were incredible. Because he wrote everything longhand. He was even more politically incorrect than what ended up in the book, you know – he had all this stuff in there. Originally he had five other kids, he had a kid named Herpes in it.

It's difficult because you're in the middle of making the film so it only helps you on an emotional level to confirm what you already know – that the guy was interesting, eccentric and creative. And that's why you like the stories. He is what he wrote, there's a reason why the books are what they are. And it shows you the power when somebody's writing from the heart of what they are, it comes through.

The idea of Burton tackling Dahl's world was a marriage made in creative heaven – two idiosyncratic, creative minds with a similarly dark and macabre attitude to children. Helena Bonham Carter recalls watching a documentary on Dahl and being surprised at the similarities between the two. 'A lot of things Dahl said, Tim could have said, in fact, he had said to me. The lack of PC-ness and his black, black humour couldn't be more Dahl. Another thing Dahl said which is so Tim, is that [kids are] little savages. I think Tim is often understood best by kids or at least adults who have big kids inside them.'

It's not so much that it was politically incorrect but it's when you're a kid you like things that are dangerous and scary. That's part of what sparks your growth and creativity and points of view and development process. Some kids are great, but we've all been in school, so we all know that nobody can be more horrible to each other than kids. That's why I think Dahl was good – I don't really know how he felt about kids, but it didn't really matter if he liked or disliked them, he was certainly able to speak on their level. He certainly didn't talk down to them, he connected. There's a reason why kids like that book, why it's a classic – it speaks to them, there's a connection.

And in common with all his films, Burton again found several personal connections in Dahl's book.

Thematically it's not dissimilar to what I found in Batman, or Edward Scissorhands, or Ed Wood. It has to do with a character who is semi-anti-social, has difficulty communicating or relating, slightly out of touch, living in his own head, rooted in early family problems – all those things I could relate to in the Wonka character. There's also an Edward Scissorhands fear of human contact and interaction, in a way, not tactile.

I think the thing that I respond to in the character of Charlie is that feeling of when you were in school, of feeling in the background, if people thought back they wouldn't really remember you. He's not affected, there's an openness and a simplicity to him that I responded to. So Charlie's the positive side of oneself, and Willy's the more complicated and probably more accurate side . . .

It's tempting to see a correlation between Willy Wonka the candy visionary and Burton the filmmaker. The former allows his imagination to run riot in creating elaborate confectionary worlds inside his factory while Burton conjures up rich, detailed fantasy worlds on film.

Yeah, and sometimes in a seemingly quite meaningless and abstract way. Certainly, as the years have gone on, I have been accused of mindlessly doing things for no apparent reason. So I can relate to that as well . . .

There's a childlike enthusiasm to Willy Wonka too, and the sense that he hasn't grown up – much like Ed Wood in fact.

Yeah, I think of Willy as sort of the Citizen Kane or Howard Hughes of candy – somebody who was brilliant but then was traumatised and then retreats into their own world. I think there are probably a lot of creative people to whom that happens. They have their own sense of enthusiasm, whether anybody else goes along with it or not.

In adapting Dahl's book, John August's script gave Wonka a psychological motivation for his eccentricities. It's a familiar one, centring his fractious relationship with his father who, in Burton's version, is a dentist played by Christopher Lee.

Yeah, that's the one thing that we added that's not in the book, a little bit of his back-story. Well, the parents have always got to figure into it somewhere, haven't they? We're all a product of that in some way, shape or form, your parents and social upbringing, everything helps create, especially if it's traumatic. I guess that's the fear now, in becoming a parent: 'What trauma are you going to unwittingly inflict upon them?'

Wonka's a complicated character, he has to be, and that's why we tried to give him a little context. There's none in the book, it's a fable . . . but in this day and age you have to, because if you don't show any of that or feel any of that, he's just a weird guy. You can't just have a funny guy in a bow tie who's whimsical. I don't know how as a director or an actor you'd latch on to it unless you found some psychological foundation for the character.

He's got arrested development, I would say. I remember talking to John about it, and he was always very good at picking up things to help personalise the thing for me. We wanted to give Wonka a profile, we started talking about psychological profile, and I remember talking to him about braces and dentistry.

I had every type of brace imaginable. And it was such a painful, isolating experience, because I had one of the big braces that wrapped around your head. I remember getting them tightened was like somebody turning

Burton's sketch depicting the orthodontic sufferings of the boy Wonka

screws in your head. And this throbbing pain, like a headache in your mouth. It was really symbolic, when you have this ugly-looking thing on your head and you already feel like an outsider, you don't have lots of friends and can't really communicate. It all kind of becomes one thing.

That brace was really a symbol of the lack of being able to connect with people – or even my own bed. I remember trying to lie down on my bed wearing this huge thing, and not being able to touch the mattress – just lying there three inches from the mattress, drooling, in pain. So I remember the trauma of that, and the trauma of going to the dentist. And if you put that and parents together, you've got a real dangerous combo . . .

Johnny Depp was Burton's only choice to play Wonka, marking the fourth time they've worked together. In contrast to both Edward Scissorhands *and* Sleepy Hollow, *on which Burton had to battle studio executives to cast him, Depp was, courtesy of his Oscar-nominated performance in* Pirates Of The Caribbean, *everyone's ideal choice.*

I didn't really think about anybody else, didn't have to – for the first time. It was the first time where I didn't have any trouble from the studio about casting Johnny. I think it was even Alan Horn [Warner Bros President and COO] who mentioned it right away. Usually you have to go through more, even though everybody knows he's a great actor and blah-blah-blah. But it was like, 'Yeah!' So that was nice, finally. There didn't have to be that kind of struggle.

I think of Johnny a lot just because he always wants to try different things, and you need someone who's willing to do that. And you know he's capable of it. It's always risky, you never know if it's going to fully work or whatever, but I like that, it's kind of what's exciting about it to me. I don't think he, as an actor, ever wants to feel like, 'Well, I'm going to do this, or that.' He's basically a great character actor.

Our relationship over the years, I think, has always been kind of the same, in a way, and that's what's been so good about it, for me. Working with Johnny, it's an organic process. We talk about things, inspirations, but we never try to land on anything specific. Whether he's using a reference or I'm using a reference, it's never 'Oh, go do this' – it just somewhat gets created organically, and he feels it out. A lot of it is his sense of things, so for me it feels like an organic process – it's exciting because you're not quite sure what it is, ever. Part of the fun of it is an exploration of things.

It's interesting. Your memories of the book as a child are vivid, then you go back and look at it and it's somewhat enigmatic, open for interpretation in terms of what the character was. We started discussing memories of certain children's show hosts when we were kids. Every town, every city, at least in America, had its local TV channel and they all had these weird kids' show hosts – Mr Wishbone, The Pancake Man, Captain Kangaroo and his sidekick Mr Green Jeans, Baby Daphne, this weird witch. Even when you were a child, they were weird. You almost think it might have been a dream or a nightmare because they were so strange. I used to watch a guy with a sheriff's hat, or a guy who wore a weird leisure suit, or Captain Kangaroo, this guy had a weird haircut and a moustache and sideburns. And you think back and go, 'What the fuck was that?' But they left a strong impression on you. So a lot of it had to do with that, I think, in a certain way, a kind of strange amalgamation of those weird characters.

And yet there is an expectation now that comes with a Tim Burton film, especially one starring Johnny Depp.

Burton and Johnny Depp confer on the *Charlie* set

That's not so good . . . That's a problem. Early on in your career you struggle to get things done, but at the same time there's the amazing freedom that comes with lack of expectation. And it's always nice to surprise people. It's harder to surprise people when they have certain expectations. And the thing you realise as you go on is that everybody's different and so are their expectations; they come at it from their respective sets of those. So there's a certain heaviness that comes with that, but you can't really pinpoint it.

Although Wonka is essentially child-like, there's something a little bit terrifying about him too.

Again, it's that visceral feeling of certain children's shows. I remember having a birthday party, I can't remember what age I was, but with Chucko The Clown . . . and it's like, 'Fuuuuccccckkk . . .' It's engrained in your consciousness.

While Burton typically sketches out his characters to help devise a look for them, his Wonka took longer than most.

This one was the most . . . I'd say I had the most trouble, in a certain way, conceptualising early on. It's interesting when you read the book because it sort of describes the character but it's actually hard to see that coming to life in the way that it's written. It's sort of abstract, leaves room for interpretation too. It's funny, when most people think of Batman, generally he looks like Batman – you can put nipples on him or make him all black, but it's still an iconic image. So I kept thinking, 'If you went out into the street and polled people, would they go, 'Willy Wonka, who's that?' Or would they go, 'Oh yeah, he wears a top hat and a purple coat and beige pants, has a big bow tie.' Like the Gene Wilder movie. Do they really care about that to a degree?

But there's a certain kind of elegance to the character that's described and that you kind of want to retain. I did have a feel for the darker purple colours with a slight sixties-psychedelic feel, there's a little bit of paisley in there. You mix it up but still keep something of the classic figure. He is someone like a Phantom of the Opera, he hides, closes down, lives in his own world so he's not necessarily completely contemporary, not hip to the jive, you know. We gave him a certain language, kind of out-of-date verbiage – somebody who's trying to be hip to the kids but isn't, somebody who's a bit out of it that way.

So while Depp's Wonka retains the purple coat and top hat of Wilder's version, Burton added in a weird Beatles wig, perfect teeth, bug-eyed glasses and latex gloves.

I took the tack that people who are considered geniuses or leaders of their field, they're usually kind of crazy. They have certain spots that make them brilliant and certain spots that are giant blind spots. It's often the case that you see or meet people who I consider really creative in certain areas, and they have really big deficiencies in other areas. And when you spend all of your time alone with a bunch of Oompa Loompas, you know, it can make you even stranger.

We always thought that Wonka as the Citizen Kane of candy became mythic then kind of went underground and became a recluse. He's hidden, he's out of touch. His hair has probably to do with those earlier kids' show inspirations – if you look at a picture of Captain Kangaroo or I think the Boy in Crackerjack Box, or The Pancake Man. As for the glasses and so on, there's a certain hidden quality to the character. That's why we gave him the gloves, his trouble relating to people. That's his connection to his father too.

To play Charlie Bucket, Burton cast Freddie Highmore, who'd acted alongside Johnny Depp in Finding Neverland.

I hadn't seen *Finding Neverland*. I must have asked Johnny about him, but I don't remember. But in just meeting him both Susie Figgis the casting director and I thought he was great, there was just no question he was the right one. The reason I wanted him was for the very reason that Warners was worried about what the character was. It needed somebody with gravity. The whole point of the character is a person who like ninety per cent of us in school people don't remember, the non memorable kid. But it's not something you can tell an actor to do, they either have that or they don't. And Freddie just has an intelligence and a simplicity in his acting, he doesn't really have false moments because he's not a false person. He's one of the most well adjusted actors I've ever worked with, young or old. Just because he . . . it sounds kind of ridiculous to say, but he's interested in

233

other things, so it's not like 'I'm an actor and that's it', which I think is always healthy for anybody. Charlie's not a type like the other kids, all of whom are a bit more defined in a simple, fable manner. He just needs to have it, and that was very clear from just meeting him for the first time.

When you see a lot of kids, it's brutal. There's something about it that makes you feel kind of weird, it's different from any other kind of casting. It's like finding what is the right type. I tried to find kids who had something of the character in them, so that they could be that character as opposed to them having to do something. I just find it's easier with kids, it feels a bit more real, even if you're doing a fantasy. But with all the kids we cast, both the casting director and I felt, 'Yeah, these are the ones.' Mike Teavee was the hardest, that took the longest, I don't know why . . .

There was only a brief moment when the issue of whether Charlie should be English or American was raised.

We worked with the kids and actually tested them doing a more Americanised accent, and what became very clear to me – even though

The prize-winners – including Charlie (Freddie Highmore, bottom row, left) and Grandpa Joe (David Kelly, top row, left) – share a spectacle with Wonka (Depp)

some of them did it very well, Freddie did it very well – was that the American accent was just lacking simplicity. And because of the mix of elements, the way we were doing it, I just felt English was better, it was more pure, it kept it consistent and more real, it had more emotional resonance.

As Grandpa Joe, Burton cast the veteran Irish actor David Kelly, who has played many distinguished roles in Irish theatre but is better known to British audiences from the TV comedy series Robin's Nest *and the film* Waking Ned.

He wasn't somebody I knew, then Susie Figgis showed me a picture of him and I go, 'This guy looks great.' Then I met him, and he's such an amazing man. From my point of view he looks like exactly like Grandpa Joe – rail-thin and old, like he wouldn't get out of bed for twelve years. He actually looks older than he is – this guy walks in and I thought, 'Oh geez, better sit down . . .' But he went through a six-month shoot.

In the small but pivotal role of Charlie's mother, Burton again called upon Helena Bonham Carter, pairing her with Noah Taylor, the chameleon-like actor from Shine *and* Almost Famous, *to play his father.*

As I said, in previous drafts you could see the thinking of 'Let's get rid of the father, he's a boring character', and that makes Willy the father-figure. But then after John got involved, we felt, 'You know what? The father is part of the book.' It was lucky that Noah wanted to do it because he brings, both of them just bring something to it. When you read the book you kind of do question the father. But you look at her and you look at him and you look at Charlie and you look at the grandparents and it does look like a weird family. There is something about it that's very connective to me about them.

In the 1971 film version, for which Dahl wrote the script, the father was excised.

Well maybe he didn't like the dad, I don't know, but you're right . . . maybe they cut it out after he wrote it. I'd be curious to know.

Charlie and the Chocolate Factory *began production in June 2004 at Pinewood Studios, England, where Burton had filmed* Batman *in 1988, with the Wonka factory exterior built on the same backlot that Anton Furst had used for Gotham City.*

I like working in England, and I've done two other films here, therefore I know a lot of people. And also I wanted it to be more art-based, in the sets, and here there are great sculptors, painters, everything. So it made sense on all levels. And Pinewood, it's the one studio I feel kind of romantic about, because it's still the same. It *feels* like a movie studio. There's something really nice about how they have all the movie posters up in the hallways, all the *Carry On* posters, and every day you walk by and look at every one.

Despite Hollywood's increasing use of blue/green screen technology and computer-generated backgrounds, a technique employed in the Star Wars *prequels,* Sky Captain And The World of Tomorrow *and* Sin City, *Burton prefers the more traditional approach: building real sets and avoiding digital effects as much as possible, even resorting to such old school techniques as forced perspective, oversized props and miniatures. Bringing Wonka's imaginative world to life was production designer Alex McDowell whose credits include* Fight Club, Minority Report *and* The Terminal *as well as Burton's* Corpse Bride.

I'd heard good things about Alex – he's done a lot of good work, lots of different types of things. With a designer you're often going by just an emotional instinct – it's not like I study somebody's work, but you meet somebody and you feel like you connect and you like them. But especially with a new relationship, you never know until you go through it. But Alex is very good. And this was a real interesting challenge, because we had the luxury of building sets as opposed to blue screen all the time. But still there were a lot of weird things that we were trying to accomplish where you couldn't base it on anything else.

If we looked at anything, it was that we went back to the illustrations in the original book where the boat was more like a Viking boat. But not much else. Beyond that it was open to interpretation. One good thing that Alex did, a first for me and that I'd do again, was that all the rooms we pretty much built 360. There's always this argument of, 'Build half. The Nut Room is round, so just build half of it.' But the nightmare of that . . . I think it was John Boorman who said he could only build half of the Round

236

Table for *Excalibur* and it took them about five times as long to shoot because it's weirder than it seems than if you build the whole set. But most of our sets were completely enclosed, which was great, because first of all it got rid of visitors on the set, and second you were in a complete environment. It's not like you're looking out at the crew. And that just helps – especially when it's not a real environment, it helps make it real. If we had built half, we'd still be shooting . . .

Dahl's book is vague in terms of when or even where it's set. Is it America or is it England? In translating the material, Burton and McDowell took a similarly ambiguous approach to the film's design, opting for a mid Atlantic setting – industrial America combined with northern England – melding fifties and seventies visuals with a futuristic sensibility that seems straight out of a sixties' sense of the future.

Alex and I looked at photographs of northern England, and he actually scouted up there. But it also reminded us of Pittsburgh, Pennsylvania. So it was a mixture of elements, trying to make it its own place and not necessarily say, 'This is England' or 'This is America.' For Wonka's factory we kind of wanted a building with a kind of Hoover Dam-like optimism and strength, but then once it gets dark it looks slightly foreboding . . .

And Fascist.

Well, it's that Citizen Kane or Howard Hughes of Candy. Obsessives, there's something sad and slightly sinister about them. But not bad. There are many different sides to that. But it just seemed like a nice look for the factory, especially with all the intricacy and busyness of the candy. Also I kind of relate to that, because as a film director you tend towards those fascist movements – somehow you relate on a personal level. Or something . . .

Charlie's biggest interior set was the Chocolate River Set which filled Pinewood's cavernous 007 Stage. With its undulating grass, chocolate bunkers and brightly coloured foliage, the set looked very much like a giant crazy-golf course. It's a locale that harks back to the climax of Frankenweenie.

I'm a huge fan of those. We had them in Burbank when I was growing up and I have a book of old miniature golf courses from around the world. The idea was that it's a place that's organic and it's mined and used and cut out and scooped out, and basically made out of chocolate with some extra added bits. And so that gave it the shapes that it ended up with. Alex and I didn't set out to make a candy miniature golf course . . .

It was funny to build a set like that on the Bond Stage, because it's usually submarines and the lair of the evil genius. And a couple of people came by and thought we were making a James Bond/villain movie and thought, 'What the fuck is this? Is this a megalomaniac who owes a golf course?' But it was fun to do . . .

You don't really have anything to go on, there's nothing to base that on necessarily, you couldn't say, 'Make it look like this'. But the more real elements you have as opposed to blue screen is good, especially with the kids, a lot of whom hadn't really done anything before, so it just helps to be in an environment as opposed to a blue screen.

The important thing for me was that we wanted to give the chocolate river a really chocolatey feel, give it a weight, not just brown water. That's why we tried to use a real chocolate substitute, to give it movement

A sketch by Burton for the décor of the chocolate river set

A sketch by Burton depicting the hi-tech siphoning of Augustus Gloop from
the chocolate river

and texture. And we wanted to make the chocolate waterfall real as
opposed to CGI, so with Alex and Joss Williams, the effects guy, we spent a
lot of time experimenting with different consistencies and thicknesses.

Then there's choosing the right kind of fake grass, because there's fake
grass and really fake grass. And wanting the plants to look somewhat
organic, not completely phoney – we tried to use real plants sometimes, or
painted them, so it was real juxtaposition of when it started to look too
phoney and when it started to look too real. We had to try and find a weird
balance in there, a middle ground of something that was both real and
unreal.

*As visual reference for a number of the factory's internal spaces – namely
the TV room, Nut Room, and Inventing Room – Burton had McDowell
watch Mario Bava's live action comic strip* Danger: Diabolik.

Just because I like that movie – but it's worth watching anyway. Each room
took on its own persona. We tried to keep the spirit of the book in terms of
what the rooms were and what they did, but then in terms of the look of it,
it could be anything. The TV Room you can most clearly link to something

Danger Diabolik (1968): John Phillip Law and Marissa Mell canoodle amid an archetypal sixties set

like *2001* or *THX-1138*, those 'white' movies. The layout of the Nut Room we arrived at fairly quickly, though the colour scheme we played around with for a long time, for different reasons. The Inventing Room was just finding shapes, taking things we had but also using found objects. There were a lot of piecemeal, weird parts of machines that we found. So there was a lot of, 'Oh, we found this weird mixer, maybe we can make something out of it.'

In line with his keep-it-real approach, Burton opted to train forty squirrels for five months to perform in the Nut Room sequence – shelling nuts and attacking Veruca and her odious father – rather than rely on CGI. Ultimately, the scene was supplemented by CGI and animatronic squirrels, but for the close-ups and main action, they're the real thing.

It just felt like in the age of *Lord of the Rings* and those kinds of grand hi-tech movies . . . this isn't that kind of a movie, it's an expensive movie, but it's not an action movie, it doesn't really satisfy on that level. So it just didn't feel right to over-rely on the technology. And I just felt that, in conjunction with the kids, I wanted to have something about being in the environment that would be helpful to the process, something that made it easier and quicker to shoot. I know when a real squirrel jumped on me the first time, it was really creepy and amazing. And for Julia Winter, playing Violet, it just makes it that much easier to respond in a proper manner. Even experienced actors like James Fox who have done every kind of thing, I think they appreciated the fact that there were real elements in real environments, it just helped them bring it to a certain place. And if you count the cost for a certain amount of CG shots next to the time it takes to train a squirrel to kick a guy in the ass, you're kind of saving money, a little.

The animal trainer Mike Alexander thought it was possible, although I don't think they'd done much squirrel work before. But I'd worked with him and he's a good person, he cares. You can argue whether animals should be used at all in a movie, but I found Mike very sensitive and thoughtful about the whole thing. And he was always very realistic. He never said, 'Oh yeah we can do this', he always had that certain look of, 'Er, maybe . . .' But he said, 'I think we can get them to do this, but I don't think they'll do that. But we can maybe link up these two things in one action.'

Burton's sketch for the alarming squirrels of the Wonka factory

The Charlie *shoot lasted six months, June to December, a consequence of British Equity rules which state children can only work for four and a half hours a day.*

We tried to schedule it so there was always something to do, but we weren't shooting eighteen-hour days, just full working days, for the most part. Luckily I found all the kids weren't jaded by showbiz – because a few of them hadn't done anything before, I found that actually turned out to be a benefit in a certain way.

The shoot actually went fast, we finished slightly ahead. We tried to shoot as quickly as we could, it wasn't like it was six months of waiting around – that's the killer. Sometimes we had three different units going, we'd have an Oompa-Loompa unit going. And there was a lot of jumping around and looking at lots of different things and trying to move quickly. So that helped it, to some degree, not to feel like six months.

To play the Oompa-Loompas, the tiny inhabitants of Wonka's factory who in the Wilder version were played by dwarves in green wigs and orange face paint, and who in book and both films provide a musical accompaniment (and moral message) to each child's demise, Burton's solution was to take four-feet four-inch Deep Roy, who'd featured in Planet of the Apes *and* Big Fish, *and have him play all of them.*

A quartet of Oompa-Loompas as envisaged in an early Burton sketch

That was an interesting challenge. One thing we spent a lot of time looking at was the right height for the Oompas. I think in the book they're knee-height. I didn't want them to be regular little people, like they were in the other movie, munchkins or whatever – that didn't feel right to me. And I didn't want CG, I wanted people. There's a human quality that they needed to have, at least in my interpretation. So we did a lot of size comparisons and rough sculptures too, because I wanted to try to find the right height, kind of weird, not tiny-little, like The Borrowers, but not little people – so somewhere in between.

I had worked with Deep before and I've always felt he's an interesting-looking person, you can't really tell where he's from, and he's got an ageless quality, and a strange nobility that I felt was right for the Oompa-Loompas. And since he is little, we could actually do shots with him just using the right lenses and things, not all special effects. So it was both an interesting way and more fun, because he could be on the set for a lot of it.

At the end of Charlie, *Wonka is reconciled with his father and embraced into the Bucket family. Neither plot-point is in Dahl's book, although the theme is familiar, and shared, of course, with* Big Fish.

I can't speak for John, but obviously it's something that must be important for him as well on a certain level. As I've said before, we're all affected by our parents. I remember at a certain point trying to reconcile with my own parents but it didn't quite work out, and then when I went to the next level it was kind of too late. But I think all artistic endeavours are a way to resolve things, a form of therapy, a fantasy resolving of something. That's why I choose to resolve it that way.

I remember the studio saying, 'Shouldn't you have the father there at the end?' I thought, 'No, it's not that cute, it's not that simplistic.' Both John and I felt, 'No, we're not going to have Christopher Lee sitting at the table. "Pass the turkey" . . .' But it is some resolution, with the sense that nothing is ever really resolved but that you have layers of resolving things. That's why it was important to do it. It felt natural, it felt right.

I remember talking about it with Helena and she actually mentioned the kind of thing that I was thinking about, which was when we went to visit my mom before she died. I didn't have a great relationship with her, but we went to her little house in Lake Tahoe and she had posters of stuff of mine. And it was quite horrifically touching in a way – we couldn't really connect but at the same time she was certainly following what I was doing. Anything like that that's real makes it easier for you to do, in a way.

Burton's vision on paper for an Oompa-Loompa assigned to the factory's 'TV Room'

Although Burton has often run foul of both ratings boards and studios in regard to what is dark and what isn't, he says there were never any concerns from Warner Bros about Charlie's *tone, nor was Depp's performance considered too weird or too creepy for a PG rated movie.*

Most of the discussions came before shooting, concerns about this and that. There weren't any real issues. I remember one line where Wonka says, 'The least horrible child wins.' And they were worried that it's not necessarily politically correct, even though that's the point of the book, in a way. Just little things like that. But nothing during, nothing at all. They were just very supportive. It remains to be seen what people find creepy or not creepy. I remember on *Batman Returns* there was an equal percentage, 50:50, of people who thought the movie was lighter than the first one and people who thought it was darker. I thought that was very strange. It says more about where people's minds are than what you're actually doing.

We've not done anything that's not in the book: it's maybe more suggestive and worse in the book. Maybe someone will say the squirrel scene's too intense. But you know what? The squirrel scene in our movie is the squirrel scene in the book – even looking at the original drawings, where you see squirrels dumping her down a hole.

I always have trouble with the ratings . . . It seems like there's a kind of a double standard with the ratings board. You can cut somebody's head off in certain movies and you can't in others, you know what I'm saying? And I usually seem to be on the short end of that standard. I always felt, from *Frankenweenie* on, it's like they think I'm doing something, so they put a lot into the kind of 'Worried' category: 'He's not really doing something, but he might be doing something . . .'

Corpse Bride

Ever since The Nightmare Before Christmas *Burton had been actively seeking another project that could utilise the medium of stop-motion animation. But in the intervening years the film-animation landscape had changed vastly, not least in terms of the sophistication of computer-generated imagery. At the forefront of this technology was Pixar Animation Studios, co-founded in 1986 by John Lasseter, Steve Jobs and Dr. Ed Catmull whose first six films –* Toy Story, A Bug's Life *and* Toy Story 2, *all directed by Lasseter,* Monsters Inc, Finding Nemo, *and Brad Bird's Oscar-winning* The Incredibles *– would not only gross more than $3 billion at the worldwide box office but also shift Hollywood's emphasis even further from traditional cell animation.*

It's funny, people talk about computers, but it's really based on Pixar – they're the ones. And basically it's because they make good movies. I don't think it's just the medium, it's not computers per se, it's because Pixar make great movies that people want to see. I went to school with a lot of those guys, John (Lasseter) and Brad (Bird). They're artists, and they've kept on trying to be innovative and to do something slightly different. And I think they do it better. I'm not a big fan of most computer animation because I find a lot of it unappealing-looking. At least with Pixar they know how to be charming, and their character design is a bit more appealing than some of the other companies. But that's just personal taste.

It's unfortunate, I don't know who it was – Katzenberg or Disney – who declared cell animation dead. I find that horrific, because sometime somebody will come along and make a great cell animated movie again. *The Iron Giant* (directed by Brad Bird in 1999) was a case of good movie, bad marketing – or no marketing. But if that had been a giant success you wouldn't have heard about the death of cell animation . . .

The Nightmare Before Christmas *had taken its inspiration from a poem Burton wrote after making* Vincent. *The germ for* Corpse Bride, *however, came from an outside source: Joe Ranft, a gifted story-developer and storyboard artist for animation, who also developed an uncommon side-line in voice artistry (from the candlestick of* Beauty and the Beast *to Igor in* The Nightmare Before Christmas *to Wheezy the Penguin in* Toy Story 2.) *In the late seventies Ranft studied at Cal Arts (where he met Burton and John Lasseter) then went to Disney. In due course he was credited with story on Disney's* Beauty and the Beast *(1991) and* The Lion King *(1994) and was storyboard supervisor on both* The Nightmare Before Christmas *and* James and the Giant Peach, *before finding his niche at Pixar. Ranft died tragically in a car crash in 2005, aged forty-five.*

Back at the time of Nightmare *Ranft had come across a 19th century European folktale concerning a young man who travels home in order to wed his fiancée. His wedding ring winds up on the rotted finger of a murdered girl, who then returns from the grave to insist that she is now the man's lawfully wedded wife. Thus he must journey to the underworld to set things right, while his fiancée remains among the living, pining for his return.*

Joe is one of the great, great story people, and he's a large part of why Pixar is so successful. Joe had heard a little story, like a paragraph, which was an

The love triangle of *Corpse Bride*, sketched in preliminary form by Burton

excerpt from an old fable – I don't even know from what country it came, my recollection is that it didn't have a specific place of origin. And Joe just thought I would like it – he said, 'This sounds like something you might really capture.'

This was around the time of *Nightmare* and I was looking for something in the same vein, using stop-motion – picking the material for the medium – and the minute Joe mentioned it to me, it just felt like stop-motion, it went right into that vein.

One of the things I enjoyed in *Nightmare* was the emotional quality that the Sally character had: there was something there that I liked. It's nice to get emotion in animation. And also I was thinking about expanding my female characters. So thinking about *Corpse Bride* was trying to do something with that emotional quality to it.

I held out to do it stop-motion for those very reasons. Because when I pictured the characters drawn or computer-generated, it just didn't feel the same to me. There's something about stop-motion that I find is an emotional medium – I don't know why, I guess it's just the tactile thing of people moving the models with their hands. It's like Ray Harryhausen – you always remember in his work there was a weird emotional quality to the monsters, even though they were just monsters, and he was able to get that. It's not that you can't get it in cell animation or computer animation, but there is a more visceral, deep-rooted emotional quality to the stop-motion, if the animation is right.

Anyhow, I did some drawings for *Corpse Bride*, but then I let it ruminate for a long time . . .

That 'long time' was the best part of ten years, with efforts to develop the project during the period of James and the Giant Peach *and* Mars Attacks! *Though Disney had released* The Nightmare Before Christmas, Corpse Bride *would find its home at Warner Bros.*

As with *Nightmare*, I don't know why things take so long to gestate, but they do seem to take ten years stewing before they move.

It's like what happened with *Nightmare* and Disney: I developed *Corpse Bride* when I had a deal at Warners, so that's the kind of thing that keeps it stuck at a place. That's why I don't have a deal anymore, because you can look at it as a positive or a negative in a certain way. With *Nightmare* I actually felt that it wasn't right for Disney, and I wished that they didn't want to do it, but once you try to get something away from somebody, that

The corpse bride has risen from the grave in these Burton sketches

makes them want to do it. Not because they like it, but because they think, 'Maybe . . . just in case.' But that's no reason to make something.

It wasn't possible to keep that group who did *Nightmare* together, I don't think, because I don't think it was seen as a success. When I was with Warner Bros and we were doing *Mars Attacks!* and wanted to do stop-motion – I don't think any of these studios ever saw anything in that. They didn't see it as a viable money-making form of animation.

And what happens in the animation world is that people disperse and get eaten up into the computer and other things . . . so unless you strike while the iron's hot it doesn't happen.

Corpse Bride was green-lit a bit before *Charlie*, and they green-lit it without a script – without anything. In getting started I sort of used *Nightmare* as the model. And it's not a good model . . . *Nightmare* was developed almost like the old days at Disney, developed by the story process – they knew they were going to do *Snow White* but they didn't have a screenplay, so they worked it the story way. It's not necessarily the best way of doing something but sometimes you have to go with the momentum of them saying 'Yes' and try to just put it along that way.

I had scripts written, there were lots of people who worked on them. Carole Thompson wrote a version, but then we had kind of an argument, she didn't agree with me and I didn't agree with her, but that was fine. And then Pamela Pettler and John August came onboard. Pamela was really helpful because she helped bring it into a certain focus that had been missing for years. And then John, I liked what he did on *Big Fish* and I like working with him, he can surprise you every now and then. And he brought it into final focus, I thought.

But it was very difficult to find the right kind of balance for it – the right balance of the emotional and the humour, but also because it's a triangle, sometimes with that triangular thing, one character or another suffers. So it became more the Corpse Bride's story, or more Victor's, or it became more Victoria's, and the balancing act never felt quite right. The thing that was important was to get all three points of view. You never wanted Victor to come across like an asshole, or the girls to come across as total bitches. It took all the way up until the end to get something, but finally I feel we've got the right kind of balance to it. You get everybody's feelings, you sort of feel for everybody involved in the triangle. You feel bad for Victoria, you feel equally bad for Victor, and there's manipulation on both sides, but you understand it.

Mike Johnson had worked as an animator on The Nightmare Before Christmas *and* James and the Giant Peach, *before directing his own short* The Devil Went Down to Georgia *(1996) and an episode of the Eddie Murphy-voiced TV series* The P.J.s *(1999). On the strength of this work Burton would enlist him as co-director of* Corpse Bride.

There was only a small group of people who could have done it. And I think you have to know that world – you can't come in out of the blue, you have to have done it. I didn't really know Mike, but he was recommended by a couple of people. I had seen a few of his little pieces of animation, and he had directed, he had done the TV show, and he had shown he could kind of get it done. All of these things are just kind of hunches, but he seemed very into it and had done enough so that he wasn't completely untested.

Will Vinton's Vinton Studios, pioneers of the Claymation technique and hugely successful in the advertising field, had produced The P.J.s *using a new technique of their invention called Foamation. At one point Vinton Studios were attached to* Corpse Bride *with the notion that production should take place at their HQ in Portland, Oregon. But the collaboration was not built to last.*

It just wasn't working out. A lot of things are chemistry and it just wasn't a good chemistry, it wasn't going the right way. Nothing against them, they do great work, there are great people there – it's funny, some people you connect with, and some you don't.

So I sort of ended that and was lucky then to find Allison Abbate, who actually worked on *Nightmare* too, and she was one of the producers on *The Iron Giant*. So she's done animation, she's dealt with a studio.

Burton made his own drawings for the characters and passed them on to Spanish character designer Carlos Grangel, a favoured associate of DreamWorks, whose work had first been widely noted on The Prince of Egypt *(1995) and was especially acclaimed on* Shark Tale *(2004). In terms of the style of the characters as eventually realised, keen viewers of the Burton oeuvre might detect that* Corpse Bride's *male lead Victor somewhat resembles* Vincent *grown up.*

That's not lost on me. I definitely felt the same thing, and said as much to myself after the fact. Any project you try to make personal. And that then was the seed of what to do with the human characters in the film. I did the initial sketches of Victor and the second one I hit was Victoria's parents, Finnis and Maudeline. Once we got past those first few then it kind of became clear. Carlos took my drawings and fleshed them out, but what was great about him was he was always very respectful to the spirit of it. He just got it right away, he was a bridge from me to fleshing it out to the guys who made the puppets – McKinnon and Saunders, who built all the puppets up in Manchester. I'd worked with them before, they did some of the puppets on *Mars Attacks!*, and they do beautiful work on a par with *Nightmare*. It's all about finding the right people, especially in this medium, just because not many people do it any more.

Another internal reference, returning to the world of Frankenweenie, *might be seen in the look of the character of the Corpse Bride herself, a distant cousin to Elsa Lanchester's Bride of Frankenstein.*

That was inspirational on two levels – on a character level, slightly, but also inspirational in terms of the medium – so it goes even deeper than that. The great thing about stop-motion is that it's very tied to *Frankenstein*, which is to say that you're sort of making something inanimate come to life. So it's almost thematic for the whole process. You try to analyse why you like things, what draws you to one medium as opposed to others, perhaps. You take a little model and make your stop-motion movies. And I realise that one of the reasons is that, as a child, the Frankenstein myth-ology is such a primal thing. And it's really why you like stop-motion, it's tied to loving that theme.

Corpse Bride *is classic Burton in that it proposes dual worlds of the living and the dead, and yet, contra to convention, the austere, grey land of the living by no means diminishes or overshadows the more colourful land of the dead.*

That thematic thing of the living world being much more 'dead' than the dead world, playing with those juxtapositions and those feelings – I remember having that from very early on. It goes back to childhood: I just remember that feeling that what people call 'normal' is not normal and

Finis and Maudeline

what people call 'abnormal' isn't abnormal. And that's why I always responded to characters and monsters, and cultures like Mexico and its Day of The Dead, because I always felt there was more life there . . . I came from a sort of puritanical suburban existence where death was looked upon as dark and negative. But it happens to everybody, and I always responded to cultures that made death feel more a part of life.

Burton was able to assemble an outstanding cast of voices to bring Corpse Bride to life: among them Johnny Depp as Victor Van Dort, Emily Watson as Victor's fiancée Victoria, Helena Bonham Carter as the Corpse Bride, and Albert Finney and Joanna Lumley as Victoria's parents, as well as Christopher Lee, Richard E. Grant, Jane Horrocks, and Paul Whitehouse, the latter known mainly to UK audiences for his comedy series The Fast Show, of which Johnny Depp is a self-proclaimed fan.

I normal leg

I skeleton leg

The demure and somewhat alarming charm of the corpse bride as seen in sketch-form

I was very lucky, because this is not a high-profile, hugely budgeted project, so it was nice that people did it just to do it – and I really do appreciate that, because it kind of gets you back into the situation of just doing things as opposed to a huge payday. It becomes a project as opposed to a business, and so I felt really great about that. And I didn't choose the actors just because I knew them, I tried to find ones who were right for it. I mean, Albert's voice with that character is great. Joanna Lumley, great, Emily has

The onscreen realisation of Victor Van Dort, as voiced by Johnny Depp

a great quality. And Paul Whitehouse, he's so talented, it's amazing. He's almost too good.

I've got great voices in this, and none of them were doing shtick, yet they do really good performances. We did put an unobtrusive little camera in there while they were recording, so we filmed them – it can be a help, some people can be more demonstrative. And if it was any benefit to the animators, so be it.

While The Nightmare Before Christmas *was a quintessentially American tale,* Corpse Bride *is more rooted in a European sensibility, with affinities to the Gothic tradition and the mores of Victorian-era England.*

I definitely didn't want to root it in a specific place, and wasn't really interested in what the real ethnic origins of the tale were, because the thing that got me was the fable aspect of it. But it does have a somewhat Victorian feel, because in terms of the living world it sort of represents that kind of Victorian repression. I could understand it. Burbank wasn't Victorian, but you had that kind of rigid structure of society where people are categorised and put into certain boxes, the same thing you identify with Victorian rigidity and society. *Corpse Bride* probably has even more of a flavour of that too because we did it in Britain with a large British cast – although I was trying to watch that, using voices that aren't British too, so it mixes it up a bit and doesn't make it quite so place- and time-specific. Johnny does a little bit of an English accent for Victor, but that's to kind of fit into some of the secondary characters.

Although Burton extols the relatively lo-fi medium of stop-motion for its organic qualities, certain technological improvements since Nightmare *– notably using digital still cameras rather than film cameras and more sophisticated puppets – have been a boon for the filmmaker's imagination.*

Technology has its pluses and minuses, but it is what it is. We're trying to keep the technology to a minimum and keep the stop-motion as pure as possible. The one thing that's different from *Nightmare* is that we used a lot of replacement heads on *Nightmare*. This one, there's a greater range of subtlety. There was beautiful animation in *Nightmare*, I think really the only difference for me is the subtlety and complexity of the heads. But that causes its own problems too, because replacement heads can be clearer in some ways. That was one of the challenges on this for me – with the subtleties there can be more problems. The thing that made *Nightmare* easier is they were all weird-looking characters, whereas doing humans in stop-motion is, I think, really difficult. The supporting characters are a bit easier to fit into the stop-motion world, but usually when you see stop human characters it's weird. It's always a fine line about what's working and what's not working. But you don't want to get to the point where you're questioning why you're doing it stop-motion. So once we found the right design for the human characters, once we nailed that, I felt quite good about it.

Background characters are great because you can just look at them and get a sense of character, which is nice. Maggot is basically Peter Lorre. I always loved those few old Warner Bros cartoons where it was him, it was a caricature of him. I never knew who he was, I hadn't seen Peter Lorre movies, but then you'd see this weird little character and go, 'I like that character.' That's what we were trying to do, even with those characters who are there for only a couple of scenes. They register as such a type – even if you don't get a chance to know the character, you get a bit more information. So it does help create a character just by nailing what the designs are.

The Corpse Bride in all her glory, as voiced by Helena Bonham Carter

One such character is Victor's deceased dog Scraps – now a skeletal mutt in the Land Of The Dead. This, like so much else, can be seen as a reference to Burton's childhood.

I had several dogs when I was a kid. That's always an important relationship. I think for most kids that's kind of your first relationship. And it's usually the best, it's the purest in a way. With dogs, it's pure love and pure emotion. And it's always important to try to remember that in your human relations. Pepe was my first real dog, I was two or three, I think. He was just a kind of a mutt, he had a disease called distemper, and he wasn't supposed to live past a few years. He had a limp after a while, but he lasted quite a long time. Great big eyes, the whole emotional thing. Pure . . .

Again, practised Burton watchers may see in Corpse Bride *elements of theme and style that bear on previous works. Where* Nightmare *referenced Cab Calloway,* Corpse Bride *has a small homage to Sammy Davis Jr in the character of Bone Jangles. Neither Victor nor Victoria get on with their parents. While the film's setting, tone and love triangle shares some similarities to* Sleepy Hollow *and Disney's animated cartoon version that was among Burton's early loves.*

Certain things leave you in your life and certain things stay with you. And that's why we're all interested in movies – those ones that make you *feel*, you still think about. Because it gave you such an emotional response, it's actually part of your emotional make-up, in a way. Even though I wasn't consciously doing that, the energy of that is in there: because that was one of the first cartoons I saw that had a mixture of humour and darkness and visceral energy, and music.

The Sammy Davis thing, well, there's something about skeletons and that kind of music that seems to work in a way. That was definitely an inspiration for that character.

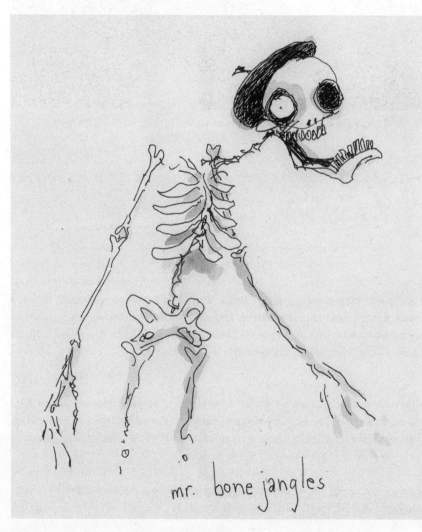

mr. bone jangles

Burton's sketches for the character of Bone Jangles, *en hommage à*
Sammy Davis, Jr

Not getting on with your parents, well, that's a fairly common thing, I think ninety per cent of children feel that way, you know. And also that juxtaposition of what is perceived as normal and what's perceived as light or dark, that theme has always stayed real heavy in me.

One distinctive feature of Pixar is that they, mostly, eschew songs and musical numbers, unlike their more conventional counterpoints at Disney. Corpse Bride, like Nightmare, has Danny Elfman songs, suggesting a lingering fondness for the old Disney model.

This is not quite the same as *Nightmare*. *Nightmare* was more operatic. This has music in it, but I wouldn't call it 'a musical'. Music just felt organic to this. With this type of story and what Danny does, it's part of the character of it. And it just felt appropriate. I'm not a fan of sticking songs in there for the sake of it – I mean, if that's the way it feels, it's not good. So I try to be wary of that, because that's when you start to smell something. We have songs, but they're not sung by Celine Dion . . .

*   *   *

2005 found Burton at a very interesting career juncture, with two movies on release reflecting on past preoccupations and pointing to the future, albeit opaquely. In the meantime his personal circumstances had been changed by parenthood, but he is leery of the obvious questions about whether the experience of child-rearing will have an effect on his work.

At this moment I don't feel like fatherhood has affected me at all, other than just physically. Some people ask the question more simplistically. 'Now that you're a father, is this why you made *Charlie*? Are you going to make films for children?' And the feeling I have now is, 'Absolutely not.' I feel more inclined to make a horror movie or a porno movie . . . Obviously, becoming a parent is an emotional experience, and an amazing experience, so it affects your life that way and it takes up some mental and physical time. But I don't foresee it changing in any way, shape or form the kind of movies I'd want to make. In fact, they might get harsher, in some ways . . .

It's so funny, every movie I've made has been with a studio, and I keep going through these nightmare-type things. And each time I go 'Why?' It's the world I know, but it's not a world I'm particularly fond of. There's no reason why I shouldn't or couldn't do a real horror movie. I would love to. But because I haven't done it yet, it would be like learning a new language, in a funny way – even though it sounds like it should be easy.

The thing I've learned is you've almost got to go out and do it without telling anybody. I've actually tried to do that in a certain way, twice. I remember on *Ed Wood* and *Edward Scissorhands*, trying to do it lower budget, and I almost felt like to do that I would have to not say it was me – I'd have to change my name and just go out and do it. There are so many obstacles because of the way you are perceived. People think you've got money, you're this big Hollywood filmmaker, so if you're not paying somebody you're ripping them off, or whatever. So it's weirdly harder to do.

But I'm going to take some time, take a deep breath, because I don't want to get into the same situation again. The machine aspect of this whole thing, I just can't . . . I think those days are over, definitely, definitely, for many different reasons. I'm not going to do this again, at least not right away. There is something that I need to do. I'm not sure which one it is, or how, but I know there's something I need to do. And in terms of how something is done next time, that's going to be of crucial importance to me. It's almost like I'm a weird drug addict. I've got to stop what I've been doing, and kind of reassess things a bit.

Filmography

1982
Vincent
Producer: Tim Burton
Director: Tim Burton
Screenplay: Tim Burton
Cinematography (black and white): Victor Abdalov
Cast: Vincent Price (narrator)
5 mins. 16 mm

Seven-year-old Vincent Malloy fantasizes about being Vincent Price.

Hansel and Gretel
Executive producer: Julie Hickson
Director: Tim Burton
Screenplay: Julie Hickson
Cast: Michael Yama, Jim Ishida
45 mins. 16 mm

A variation on the Grimms' fairy tale with an all-Asian cast.

Frankenweenie
Production company: Walt Disney
Producer: Julie Hickson
Director: Tim Burton
Screenplay: Lenny Ripp, based on an original idea by Tim Burton
Cinematography (black and white): Thomas Ackerman
Editor: Ernest Milano, A.C.E.
Music: Michael Convertino, David Newman
Art director: John B. Mansbridge
Cast includes: Shelley Duvall (Susan Frankenstein), Daniel Stern (Ben

Frankenstein), Barrett Oliver (Victor Frankenstein), Joseph Maher (Mr Chambers), Roz Braverman (Mrs Epstein), Paul Bartel (Mr Walsh), Domino (Ann Chambers), Jason Hervey (Frank Dale), Paul C. Scott (Mike Anderson), Helen Bell (Mrs Curtis)
25 mins. 35 mm

Victor Frankenstein's dog, Sparky, chases a ball into the road and is hit by a car and killed. When Victor's teacher, Mr Walsh, shows his science class how electricity can be used to give life to a dead frog, Victor digs up his beloved pet from the local pet cemetery. He reanimates Sparky and keeps him out of sight in the attic. But Sparky sneaks out and terrifies the neighbours. When Mr Frankenstein discovers his son's secret he decides to invite everyone from the neighbourhood to the house to reintroduce them to Sparky. The evening descends into chaos and Sparky runs off to the local miniature golf course. Victor follows him there, along with an angry mob of neighbours. Sparky is killed saving Victor from a flaming windmill. The neighbours rally round and bring him back to life using jump leads attached to their car batteries. Revived, he finds romance with a poodle.

1984
Aladdin and his Wonderful Lamp

Production company: A Platypus Production in association with Lion's Gate Films
Executive producer: Shelley Duvall
Producers: Bridget Terry, Fredric S. Fuchs
Director: Tim Burton
Screenplay: Mark Curtiss, Rod Ash
Music: David Newman, Michael Convertino
Production designer: Michael Erler
Cast: Valerie Bertinelli (Princess Sabrina), Robert Carradine (Aladdin), James Earl Jones (Genie of the Lamp and Genie of the Ring), Leonard Nimoy (Evil Magician), Ray Sharkey (Grand Vizier), Rae Allen (Aladdin's Mother), Joseph Maher (Sultan), Jay Abramowitz (Habibe), Martha Velez (Lady Servant), Bonnie Jefferies, Sandy Lenz and Marcia Gobel (the Three Green Women), John Salazar (Servant)
47 mins. Colour video

Version of the classic tale shot for Shelley Duvall's *Faerie Tale Theatre* TV series.

1985

Pee-Wee's Big Adventure

Production company: Aspen Film Society-Shapiro/Warner Bros
Executive producer: William E. McEuen
Producers: Robert Shapiro, Richard Gilbert Abramson
Director: Tim Burton
Screenplay: Phil Hartman, Paul Reubens, Michael Varhol
Cinematography (colour): Victor J. Kemper, A.S.C.
Editor: Billy Webber
Music: Danny Elfman
Production designer: David L. Snyder
Cast includes: Pee-Wee Herman (Himself), Elizabeth Daily (Dottie), Mark Holton (Francis), Diane Salinger (Simone), Judd Omen (Mickey), Irving Hellman (Neighbour), Monte Landis (Mario), Damon Martin (Chip), David Glasser, Gregory Brown, Mark Everett (BMX Kids), Daryl Roach (Chuck), Bill Cable, Peter Looney (Policemen), James Brolin (PW), Morgan Fairchild (Dottie)
90 mins. 35 mm

One day after breakfast, Pee-Wee Herman takes out his beloved red and white bicycle to admire it. Later, rich kid Francis offers to buy it from Pee-Wee, who refuses and rides into town to visit the local joke shop and pick up a new horn for his bike. When he returns to where he padlocked it, he discovers the bike has been stolen. The police can't help, so he consults a fortune-teller who (wrongly) informs him that his bike is in the basement at the Alamo.

Setting off to find his bike he hitches a ride with, firstly, an escaped convict and then Large Marge, a ghostly trucker, who died a year previously. She drops him off at a roadside diner where he is befriended by Simone, a waitress who dreams of visiting Paris. Pee-Wee encourages her to go and after being chased by Simone's jealous boyfriend eventually he makes it to the Alamo where he is horrified to discover there is no basement. Later, after riding a wild bull and wooing over a bar-room full of bikers with a dazzling version of 'Tequila', Pee-Wee has an accident and winds up in hospital where he sees his bike on TV being presented to a child-star for use in a forthcoming film. Rushing to the studio, Pee-Wee sneaks on to the lot, steals back his bicycle and is chased through various soundstages.

Having escaped, he spies a pet shop on fire and stops to rescue the animals from the blaze. Passing out in front of the store he is arrested.

However, a studio executive is convinced Pee-Wee's story will make a great movie and turns his tale into a James Bond-style adventure with Pee-Wee cameoing as a hotel bell-hop. Later, everyone who Pee-Wee encountered during his quest turns up for the film's world premiere at the local drive-in.

The Jar
Director: Tim Burton
Screenplay: Michael McDowell from Ray Bradbury's original teleplay
Music: Danny Elfman
Cast: Griffin Dunne, Paul Bartel
23 mins.

Episode of the *Alfred Hitchcock Presents* TV series.

Family Dog
Cartoon TV series produced by Amblin for which Burton acted as executive producer as well as design consultant.

1988
Beetlejuice
Production company: The Geffen Company
Producers: Michael Bender, Larry Wilson, Richard Hashimoto
Director: Tim Burton
Screenplay: Michael McDowell, Warren Skaaren, story by Michael McDowell, Larry Wilson
Cinematography (colour): Thomas Ackerman
Editor: Jane Kurson
Music: Danny Elfman
Production designer: Bo Welch
Cast includes: Alec Baldwin (Adam Maitland), Geena Davis (Barbara Maitland), Jeffrey Jones (Charles Deetz), Catherine O'Hara (Delia Deetz), Winona Ryder (Lydia Deetz), Sylvia Sidney (Juno), Robert Goulet (Maxie Dean), Glenn Shadix (Otho), Dick Cavett (Bernard), Annie McEnroe (Jane), Michael Keaton (Betelgeuse), Patricia Martinez (Receptionist), Simmy Bow (Janitor), Maurice Page (Ernie)
92 mins. 35 mm

Happily-married couple Adam and Barbara Maitland decide to spend their holiday decorating their idyllic New England home. Returning from a trip to town, Adam swerves to avoid hitting a dog. Their car dives off of a bridge into the river and they are killed. The couple arrive back at their house where a book entitled *Handbook for the Recently Deceased* reveals to them their predicament. Although they are now ghosts, they can remain in their home; if they try to leave, they end up in another dimension, a desert world populated by enormous sandworms.

Their peace is soon shattered, however, when their house is sold and the new residents arrive from New York. The Deetzes – henpecked Charles, would-be sculptor Delia and their morose daughter Lydia – under the guidance of obese interior designer, Otho, begin transforming the house into a horrific piece of modern art. The Maitlands seek help from their afterlife case worker, Juno, who informs them that they must remain in the house for 125 years, and if they want the Deetzes out, it is up to them to scare them away. But the Maitlands' attempt to haunt their home proves ineffectual. Although the Maitlands remain invisible to Charles and Delia, their daughter Lydia can see Adam and Barbara and becomes their friend.

Against the advice of Juno, the Maitlands contact the miscreant Betelgeuse, a freelance bio-exorcist, to scare away the Deetzes, but Betelgeuse is more interested in marrying Lydia and re-entering the real world. It takes the combined efforts of the Maitlands and Lydia to defeat Betelgeuse and banish him to the afterlife. The Deetzes and the Maitlands decide to live together in harmony.

1989
Batman
Production company: Warner Bros
Executive producers: Benjamin Melniker, Michael Uslan
Producers: Jon Peters, Peter Guber, Chris Kenney
Director: Tim Burton
Screenplay: Sam Hamm, Warren Skaaren, story by Sam Hamm, based on Batman characters created by Bob Kane
Cinematography (colour): Roger Pratt
Editor: Ray Lovejoy
Music: Danny Elfman
Production designer: Anton Furst
Cast: Jack Nicholson (Joker/Jack Napier), Michael Keaton (Batman/Bruce Wayne), Kim Basinger (Vicky Vale), Robert Wuhl (Alexander Knox), Pat

Hingle (Commissioner Gordon), Billy Dee Williams (Harvey Dent), Michael Gough (Alfred), Jack Palance (Carl Grissom), Jerry Hall (Alicia) 126 mins. 35 mm

Gotham City is in the grip of mob boss Carl Grissom. Reporter Alexander Knox and photo-journalist Vicky Vale begin investigating the truth behind the rumours of a shadowy vigilante figure dressed as a bat, who has been terrifying criminals throughout the city.

Vale and Knox attend a benefit at the mansion of millionaire Bruce Wayne, who is taken by Vicky's charms. That same night, Grissom's second in command, Jack Napier, attempts to raid a chemical factory. When the police arrive, Napier realizes he's been set-up by his boss, angered by his affair with Grissom's girl. In the midst of the shoot-out, Batman arrives and Napier is tossed into a vat of toxic waste, later emerging hideously deformed as The Joker – his mouth twisted into a permanent grin, his face deathly white, his hair green.

After killing Grissom, The Joker takes over his empire and holds the city at his mercy by chemically altering everyday hygiene products so that those using a certain combination of products die. Batman, who is revealed to be Bruce Wayne's alter-ego, attempts to track down The Joker, who has become interested in Vicky Vale. The Joker, it turns out, killed Bruce's parents when he was a boy. The Joker holds a parade through Gotham, luring its citizens on to its streets by dispensing money, intending to kill them with a lethal gas. Batman foils his plan, but The Joker kidnaps Vicky and takes her to the top of Gotham Cathedral. After a fight with Batman, The Joker is thrown from the belfry, but his body is mysteriously absent from the ground below.

Beetlejuice: The Animated Series
Burton was executive producer of the Beetlejuice animated TV series.

1990
Edward Scissorhands
Production company: Twentieth Century Fox
Executive producer: Richard Hashimoto
Producers: Denise Di Novi, Tim Burton
Director: Tim Burton
Screenplay: Caroline Thompson, story by Tim Burton and Caroline Thompson

Cinematography (colour): Stefan Czapsky
Editor: Richard Halsey, A.C.E.
Music: Danny Elfman
Production designer: Bo Welch
Special makeup and scissorhands effects: Stan Winston Studio
Cast includes: Johnny Depp (Edward Scissorhands), Winona Ryder (Kim), Dianne Wiest (Peg), Anthony Michael Hall (Jim), Kathy Baker (Joyce), Robert Oliveri (Kevin), Conchara Ferrell (Helen), Caroline Aaron (Marge), Dick Anthony Williams (Officer Allen), O-Lan Jones (Eseralda), Vincent Price (The Inventor), Alan Arkin (Bill)
105 mins. 35 mm

In a large, gothic-looking hilltop castle overlooking a pastel-coloured suburbia, Avon lady Peg Boggs finds Edward Scissorhands living all alone. The unfinished creation of an inventor who died of a heart attack before he could complete the job, Edward has everything a human should have, except, instead of hands, he has a pair of lethal shears. Feeling sorry for Edward, Peg removes him to her suburban home to live with her family.

Edward is soon accepted into the neighbourhood, revealing himself to be gifted at topiary and hairdressing. He is attracted to Peg's cheerleader daughter Kim, but she only has eyes for her brutish boyfriend, Jim, until he tricks Edward into helping him rob his parents' house and Edward is caught by the police and thrown in jail.

Later when Edward refuses the advances of Joyce, the local nymphomaniac, she turns the community against him, and he is chased to his mansion where he fights and kills Jim. Kim convinces everybody that Edward was also killed, leaving him alone in his castle once again.

Conversations with Vincent (working title)
Documentary about Vincent Price directed by Burton.

1992
Batman Returns
Production company: Warner Bros
Executive producers: Jon Peters, Peter Guber, Benjamin Melniker, Michael Uslan
Producers: Denise Di Novi, Tim Burton

Director: Tim Burton
Screenplay: Daniel Waters, story by Daniel Waters and Sam Hamm, based on Batman characters created by Bob Kane
Cinematography (colour): Stefan Czapsky
Editor: Chris Lebenzon
Music: Danny Elfman
Production designer: Bo Welch
Cast includes: Michael Keaton (Batman/Bruce Wayne), Danny De Vito (Penguin), Michelle Pfeiffer (Catwoman/Selina Kyle), Christopher Walken (Max Shreck), Michael Gough (Alfred), Michael Murphy (Mayor), Cristi Conway (Ice Princess), Andrew Bryniarski (Chip), Pat Hingle (Commissioner Gordon), Vincent Schiavelli (Organ Grinder), Steve Witting (Josh), Jan Hooks (Jen), John Strong (Sword Swallower), Rick Zumwalt (Tattooed Strongman), Anna Katarina (Poodle Lady), Paul Reubens (Penguin's Father), Diane Salinger (Penguin's Mother)
126 mins. 35 mm

A deformed baby boy is thrown into Gotham City's river by his horrified parents. Thirty-three years later, the child has been transformed into the hideous Penguin, whose gang disrupts the ceremonial lighting of Gotham's Christmas tree and kidnaps millionaire industrialist Max Shreck. Armed with evidence of the villainous Shreck's many crimes, the Penguin blackmails him into helping him discover the identity of his parents.

When The Penguin's plight becomes news, he's propelled into running for mayor. Batman is unconvinced by The Penguin, believing that he and his gang are responsible for several child murders. Meanwhile, Shreck hurls his dizzy secretary, Selina Kyle, from the top of his company's building when she discovers his plan to build a super power-plant and drain Gotham of its electricity.

Resuscitated by a group of cats, Selina returns home and after a quick bit of needlework emerges as Catwoman. Kyle, meanwhile, is being romanced by Batman's alter-ego Bruce Wayne, a situation complicated by Catwoman's teaming up with The Penguin in an effort to rid Gotham of Batman. When Batman exposes The Penguin's nasty, demented, villainous ways, thereby ruining his political chances, the Penguin mounts an attack to kill all of Gotham's first-born infants. Batman foils his scheme and Catwoman, after killing Shreck, escapes to fight another day.

Singles

Burton cameos as Brian, a director of dating agency videos, in writer-director Cameron Crowe's movie.

1993

Tim Burton's The Nightmare Before Christmas

Production company: Touchstone Pictures
Producers: Tim Burton, Denise Di Novi
Director: Henry Selick
Screenplay: Caroline Thompson, based on a story and characters by Tim Burton, adaptation by Michael McDowell
Cinematography (colour): Pete Kozachik
Editor: Stan Webb
Music, lyrics and score: Danny Elfman
Art director: Deane Taylor
Cast: Danny Elfman (Jack Skellington's singing voice), Chris Sarandon (Jack's speaking voice), Catherine O'Hara (Sally), William Hickey (Evil Scientist), Glenn Shadix (Mayor), Paul Reubens (Lock), Catherine O'Hara (Shock), Danny Elfman (Barrel), Ken Page (Oogie Boogie), Ed Ivory (Santa)
76 mins. 35 mm

Fed up with Hallowe'en, Jack Skellington, the Pumpkin King of Hallowe'entown, discovers a doorway in the forest that leads to Christmastown. Enchanted by what he sees, Jack decides that next year he wants to run Christmas, and dispatches the mischievous trio Lock, Shock and Barrel to kidnap Santa. When Christmas Eve arrives, Jack takes off on his skeletal reindeer-driven sled to deliver the presents manufactured by the residents of Hallowe'entown, but instead of enchanting children the world over, the gifts terrify them. Eventually, Jack's sled is shot down by the police and he returns to Hallowe'entown. Santa is freed and order is restored.

Cabin Boy

Comedy directed by Adam Resnick and produced by Burton and Denise Di Novi for Touchstone Pictures.

1994
Ed Wood
Production company: Touchstone Pictures
Executive producer: Michael Lehmann
Producers: Tim Burton, Denise Di Novi
Director: Tim Burton
Screenplay: Scott Alexander, Larry Karaszewski
Cinematography (black and white): Stefan Czaspsky
Editor: Chris Lebenzon
Music: Howard Shore
Production designer: Tom Duffield
Cast includes: Johnny Depp (Ed Wood) Martin Landau (Bela Lugosi), Sarah Jessica Parker (Dolores Fuller), Patricia Arquette (Kathy O'Hara), Jeffrey Jones (Criswell), G. D. Spradlin (Reverend Lemon), Vincent D'Onofrio (Orson Welles), Bill Murray (Bunny Breckinridge), Mike Starr (Georgie Weiss), Max Casella (Paul Marco), Brent Hinkley (Conrad Brooks), Lisa Marie (Vampira), George 'The Animal' Steele (Tor Johnson), Juliet Landau (Loretta King), Clive Rosengren (Ed Reynolds), Norman Alden (Cameraman Bill), Leonard Termo (Make-up man Harry), Ned Bellamy (Dr Tom Mason)

Hollywood 1952, aspiring movie director Edward D. Wood Jr works in the plant shop of a Hollywood studio by day and puts on plays with his theatre group, The Casual Company, by night. One day on the way home from an interview for a directing job, he meets his idol and former big-screen horror star Bela Lugosi trying out coffins in a mortuary. Ed convinces an exploitation movie producer to let him write and direct a movie about a sex change and casts his new-found friend Bela Lugosi in a small part. When the film, *Glen or Glenda* – in reality the story of a man (played by Wood) who likes to dress in women's clothing – proves less than successful, Ed and his friends are forced to raise the funds themselves for another feature, *Bride of the Monster*, again starring Bela Lugosi.

Late one night Ed receives a call from Bela asking for help and he turns up to find his friend on the floor of his home. Ed checks Bela into a hospital to cure him of his morphine addiction, but when the hospital discovers that Bela has no insurance to pay for the treatment he is discharged.

Ed shoots a small amount of footage of Bela leaving his house just before he dies. Later Ed incorporates this footage into another movie, *Plan 9 from Outer Space*, the financing for which he raises from the Baptist church of Beverley Hills. *Plan 9*'s cast and crew, including Ed and his wife-to-be

Kathy, attend the première. The couple leave for Las Vegas to get married immediately afterwards, with Ed convinced that *Plan 9* will be the film he will be remembered for.

James and the Giant Peach

A live-action/animated adaptation of Roald Dahl's children's book, directed by Henry Selick and executive produced by Burton and Di Novi for Touchstone Pictures.

1995
Batman Forever

Third instalment of the Batman series, with Val Kilmer as Bruce Wayne/ Batman, Jim Carrey as The Riddler and Tommy Lee Jones as Two-Face. Directed by Joel Schumacher, produced by Burton and Peter MacGregor-Scott for Warner Bros.

1996
Mars Attacks!

Production company: Warner Bros
Producers: Tim Burton, Larry Franco
Director: Tim Burton
Screenplay: Jonathan Gems
Cinematography (colour): Peter Suschitzy
Editor: Chris Lebenzon
Music: Danny Elfman
Production designer: Wynn Thomas
Cast includes: Jack Nicholson (President Dale/Art Land), Glenn Close (Marsha Dale), Annette Bening (Barbara Land), Pierce Brosnan (Donald Kessler), Danny DeVito (Rude Gambler), Martin Short (Jerry Ross), Sarah Jessica Parker (Nathalie Lake), Michael J. Fox (Jason Stone), Rod Steiger (Gen. Decker), Tom Jones (Himself), Lukas Haas (Richie Norris), Natalie Portman (Taffy Dale), Jim Brown (Byron Williams), Lisa Marie (Martian Girl), Sylvia Sidney (Grandma Norris)

Tuesday 9 May, 6.57 p.m., just outside Lockjaw, Kentucky: a flaming stampede of cattle marks the first sign of the imminent Martian invasion of Earth. The following morning, US President Dale is informed by his advisors of a fleet of Martian spacecraft amassing in the earth's atmosphere and informs the populus of this momentous event. Three days later, Martians touch down in the Nevada desert and annihilate mankind's welcoming committee, setting off a War of the Worlds-style invasion that lays waste to countries around the globe. Despite the best efforts of the US military, it's lowly donut shop employee Richie Norris and his senile grandma from Kansas who inadvertently discover that the music of Slim Whitman can kill the Martians, thereby saving the world from total destruction.

1998
Hollywood Gum
French TV commercial for chewing-gum.

1999
Sleepy Hollow
Production company: Paramount Pictures/Scott Rudin Productions/
Mandalay Pictures
Executive producers: Larry Franco, Francis Ford Coppola
Producers: Scott Rudin, Adam Schroeder
Director: Tim Burton
Screenplay: Andrew Kevin Walker
Cinematography (colour): Emmanuel Lubezki
Editor: Chris Lebenzon
Music: Danny Elfman
Production designer: Rick Heinrichs
Cast includes: Johnny Depp (Ichabod Crane), Christina Ricci (Katrina Van Tassel), Casper Van Dien (Brom Van Brunt), Miranda Richardson (Lady Van Tassel), Michael Gambon (Baltus Van Tassel), Marc Pickering (Young Masbeth), Christopher Walken (Hessian Horseman), Michael Gough (Hardenbrook), Christopher Lee (Burgomaster), Jeffrey Jones (Rev. Steenwyck), Lisa Marie (Lady Crane), Richard Griffiths (Phillipse), Ian McDiarmid (Dr Lancaster), Steven Waddington (Killian)

New York City, 1799. Police constable Ichabod Crane is despatched by his superiors to the upstate hamlet of Sleepy Hollow, two days' journey north of the city, to investigate a series of brutal slayings in which the victims have been found decapitated, their heads taken. A proponent of new, though so far unproven investigative techniques such as finger-printing and autopsies, Crane arrives in Sleepy Hollow armed with his bag of scientific tricks only to be informed by the town's elders that the murderer is not of flesh and blood, rather a headless supernatural warrior from beyond the grave who rides at night on a massive black steed. Crane doesn't believe them and begins his own investigation, until, that is, he comes face to face with the Headless Horseman himself. Taking a room at the home of the town's richest family, the Van Tassels, Crane develops an attraction to their daughter, the mysterious Katrina, even as he's plagued by nightmares of his mother's horrific torture when he was a child. Delving further into the mystery with the aid of the orphaned Young Masbeth, whose father was a victim of the Horseman, Crane discovers within the Western Woods both the Horseman's entry point between this world and the beyond, the gnarled Tree of the Dead, as well as his grave, but finds his skull is missing. The murders continue until Crane uncovers a murky plot revolving around revenge and landrights with the Horseman controlled by Katrina's step-mother, Lady Van Tassel, who sends the killer after her. Following a fight in the local windmill and a stagecoach chase through the woods, Crane eventually thwarts Lady Van Tassel by returning the skull to the Horseman, who regains his head and heads back to Hell along with her. His job in Sleepy Hollow over, Crane, Katrina and Young Masbeth return to New York, in time for the centennial celebrations.

2000
Kung Fu/Mannequin
Two commercials for Timex I-Control watches directed by Burton for production house A Band Apart.

Stainboy
Six-part animated show for shockwave.com written and directed by Burton based on characters from *The Melancholy Oyster Boy And Other Stories*.

2001
Planet of the Apes
Production company: Twentieth Century Fox/Zanuck Company
Executive producer: Ralph Winter
Producers: Richard D. Zanuck
Director: Tim Burton

Screenplay: William Broyles Jr and Lawrence Konner & Mark Rosenthal
Cinematography (colour): Philippe Rousselot
Editor: Chris Lebenzon
Music: Danny Elfman
Production designer: Rick Heinrichs
Cast includes: Mark Wahlberg (Captain Leo Davidson), Tim Roth, (Thade), Helena Bonham Carter (Ari), Michael Clarke Duncan (Attar), Paul Giamatti (Limbo), Kris Kristofferson (Karubi), Estella Warren (Darna), Cary-Hiroyuki (Krull), David Warner (Sandar), Erick Avari (Tival), Luke Eberl (Birn), Evan Dexter Parke (Gunnar), Senator Nado (Glenn Shadix), Lisa Marie (Nova), Charlton Heston (Thade's father, uncredited)
119/120 mins. 35 mm

2029. The USAF Oberon, a space research station, uses chimpanzees rather than human pilots for its test missions. When Captain Leo Davidson's pet chimp Pericles goes missing while investigating an electromagnetic storm, Leo disobeys a direct order and heads out into the void to rescue him and finds himself caught up in the same massive electrical disturbance which propels his ship forward in time several hundred years before it crash lands in a swamp on an uncharted planet. Almost immediately, he's caught up in a manhunt through the forest; only those doing the pursuing aren't human but talking apes on horseback wearing body armour. Leo is captured and together with a dozen or so humans is taken to Ape City, where he and a female, Darna, are sold by orang-utan slave dealer Limbo to sympathetic chimp Ari whose Senator father Sandar is trying to marry her off to Thade, an evil chimp and leader of the ape army. Following a dinner party in which Ari posits her theory that humans have a soul, Leo and Daena escape, find their way to Limbo's slave market to free her father, brother, and sister, plus a few other humans, who then, with the help of Ari and her gorilla Krull escape the city using a secret route, setting off to find Leo's downed ship where he recovers his messenger device which picks up transmissions from the Oberon.

The source of the Oberon's signal is the sacred ape site of Calima, deep in the forbidden desert zone, where legend has it that the first ape, Semos, will return. There, Leo finds his spaceship, but discovers it's been half-buried in the desert for thousands of years. Meanwhile, the ape army under the leadership of Thade, who's convinced the ape senate to declare martial law, masses in the desert in preparation for battle against the hundreds of humans who have joined Leo in Calima. As both sides fight, a spaceship descends from the sky piloted by Pericles who is mistaken for the returning Semos, causing the apes to down their weapons. Leo slips into the ship, followed by Thade who is trapped by Leo inside the bridge.

Outside Attar declares that from this day forth humans and apes will live alongside one another as equals. Leo says his goodbyes and takes off in Pericles' pod, finding his way to the electromagnetic storm and then the solar system and he sets a course for Earth. As he crashes down in Washington in front of the Lincoln Memorial, police arrive on the scene, but rather than humans they're apes, and the Lincoln Memorial no longer bears the face of the former US President, but that of Thade.

2003
Big Fish
Production company: Columbia Pictures, Jinks/Cohen Company, Zanuck Company
Executive producer: Arne L. Schmidt
Producers: Richard D. Zanuck, Bruce Cohen, Dan Jinks
Director: Tim Burton
Screenplay: John August, based on the book *Big Fish: A Novel of Mythic Proportions* by Daniel Wallace
Cinematography (colour): Philippe Rousselot
Editor: Chris Lebenzon
Music: Danny Elfman
Production designer: Dennis Gassner
Cast includes: Ewan McGregor (young Edward Bloom), Albert Finney (Edward Bloom senior), Billy Crudup (William Bloom), Jessica Lange (Sandra Bloom senior), Helena Bonham Carter (Jenny young and senior, The Witch), Alison Lohman (young Sandra Bloom), Robert Guillaume (Dr. Bennett senior), Marion Cotillard (Josephine), Matthew McGrory (Karl The Giant), David Denman (Don Price) Missi Pyle (Mildred), Loundon Wainwright (Beamen), Ada Tai (Ping), Arlene Tai (Jing), Steve Buscemi (Norther Winslow), Danny DeVito (Amos Calloway)
125 mins. 35 mm

American journalist in Paris William Bloom receives a phone call from his mother, Sandra, to say his estranged father, Edward, is seriously ill. Arriving at the familial home in Ashton, Alabama with his pregnant French wife, Josephine, Will is forced to confront his troubled relationship with his father, a former travelling salesman and spinner of elaborate tales to whom he's rarely spoken in years. As William begins the awkward process of reconciliation, and attempts to find the truth behind the fiction of his father, a number of the self-aggrandising Edward Bloom's mythical adventures – his childhood introduction to a witch whose glass-eye reveals the manner of your demise; his friendship with a sheep-eating giant; his detour to the ghostly town of Spectre and meeting with the poet-cum-bank robber-cum Wall Street bigwig Norther Winslow; his time in the circus; his courting of his bride Sandra; his time in the Korean War and his rescue of Siamese twin singers – are related as fact by Edward to his daughter-in-law and son, the latter of whom again dismisses their veracity. As Edward slips closer to death, Will begins the process of settling his father's affairs and, delving into Edward's past activities and associates, he discovers that there was much more truth in the older Bloom's tall tales than he ever countenanced, and that sometimes the fantasy of a situation is preferable to the facts.

2005
Charlie and the Chocolate Factory
Production company: Warner Bros, Village Roadshow, Zanuck Company/ Plan B
Executive producers: Patrick McCormick, Felicity Dahl, Michael Siegel, Graham Burke, Bruce Berman
Producers: Richard Zanuck, Brad Grey
Director: Tim Burton
Screenplay: John August based on the book by Roald Dahl
Cinematography (colour): Philippe Rousselot
Editor: Chris Lebenzon
Music: Danny Elfman
Production designer: Alex McDowell
Cast includes: Johnny Depp (Willy Wonka), Freddie Highmore (Charlie Bucket), David Kelly (Grandpa Joe), Helena Bonham Carter (Mrs Bucket), Noah Taylor (Mr Bucket), Missi Pyle (Mrs Beauregarde), James Fox (Mr Salt), Deep Roy (the Oompas), Christopher Lee (Mr Wonka), Jordan Fry (Mike Teavee), AnnaSophia Robb (Violet Beauregarde), Julia Winter (Veruca Salt), Philip Wiegratz (Augustus Gloop)
115 mins. 35 mm

Ten-year-old Charlie Bucket lives with his impoverished mother, father, and four grandparents in a dilapidated house near the factory of eccentric confectionary genius Willy Wonka. Mr Bucket works long hours at the local toothpaste plant to feed his family who exist mainly on a diet of cabbage soup. Despite their woeful plight, they are gripped by the news that reclusive confectionary genius Willy Wonka, who hasn't been seen for many years, has secreted five Golden Tickets inside five of his chocolate bars and those who are lucky enough to find them will win a tour of his factory. Every year on his birthday, Charlie receives one bar of Wonka chocolate as his present but when he doesn't find a ticket in his bar, he is understandably disappointed, especially as the tickets begin to be found around the globe. Then, one day, Charlie comes across some money in the street and, more out of hunger than anything else, buys himself a Wonka chocolate bar. Then another. And as he unwraps his second bar, he finds something shiny and golden – the fifth and final ticket – and joins the four other winning children – Veruca Salt, Mike TeaVee, Augustus Gloop and Violet Beauregarde – and their assorted parents and guardians on the trip of a lifetime. Once inside Wonka's factory, the children fall to the wayside one by one, leaving only Charlie left. Touched by Charlie's kind spirit, Wonka offers him the keys to his factory, making him heir to the Wonka candy fortune. But Wonka insists Charlie leaves his family behind and moves into the factory alone. He refuses Wonka's offer telling him that family means everything to him. Later Wonka comes calling and Charlie takes him to see his estranged dentist father, Wilbur Wonka. Once reconciled, Wonka agrees to Charlie's request to bring his family to the factory. And they all live happily ever after . . .

Corpse Bride

Production company: Warner Bros
Executive producers: Joe Ranft, Jeffrey Auerbach
Producers: Tim Burton, Allison Abbate
Directors: Tim Burton, Mike Johnson
Screenplay: Caroline Thompson, Pamela Pettler, John August
Cinematography (colour): Peter Kozachik
Editor: Jonathan Lucas
Music: Danny Elfman
Production designer: Alex McDowell
Art director: Nelson Lowry
Character designer: Carlos Grangel
Cast includes: Helena Bonham Carter (Corpse Bride), Johnny Depp (Victor Van Dort), Emily Watson (Victoria Everglot), Tracey Ullman (Nell Van Dort), Paul Whitehouse (William Van Dort), Joanna Lumley (Maudeline

Everglot), Albert Finney (Finis Everglot), Richard E Grant (Barkis Bittern), Christopher Lee (Pastor Gallswell), Michael Gough (Elder Gutknecht) Jane Horrocks (Black Widow), Enn Reitel (Maggot), Paul Whitehouse (Paul The Head Waiter), Deep Roy (Napoleon Bonaparte)
77 mins. Shot on Canon digital still cameras

In a small, 19th century European village, Victor Van Dort, shy, only son of William and Nell Van Dort and heir to the Van Dort fish fortune, is due to marry Victoria Everglot, daughter of Finis and Maudeline Everglot who are the oldest family in town. Neither bride nor groom has met the other; they are pawns in a marriage of convenience arranged by their respective parents who hope that the union will bestow upon them wealth and respectability. Unable to remember his vows during the wedding rehearsal, Victor heads out into the forest to practice them placing the ring on what he believes to be a tree branch but it is in fact the finger of the Corpse Bride who erupts from the ground wearing a tattered wedding dress and proclaims the two of them married. She whisks Victor off to the land of the dead where Victor discovers that Corpse Bride's real name is Emily and that she was murdered on her wedding day by a highway robber. Meanwhile, in the land of the living, Victoria's parents have found her a new suitor, dastardly newcomer Barkis Bittern who agrees to marry her in place of Victor. After tricking Corpse Bride into briefly returning to the land of the living where Victoria and Corpse Bride meet, Victor feels bad for his actions after Mayhew, the Van Dort's recently deceased driver, pops up in the land of the dead and tells Victor of Victoria's wedding plans, he agrees to marry Emily properly, even if that means he must die by drinking a magical potion that will stop his heart forever. They decide to move their wedding upstairs to the land of the dead where the underworld's celebrations disrupt Barkis' and Victoria's wedding feast. Corpse Bride recognises Barkis as the man who murdered her and stole her wedding ring years before. After duelling with Victor, Barkis drinks from the chalice meant for Victor and dies. Although Victor is still prepared to go through with his wedding, Corpse Bride is unable to see Victor die for her and she leaves Victor and Victoria free to marry.

Bibliography

The Motion Picture Annual, 1986, 1989, 1991, 1993, Cine Books Inc.

Selected Interviews/Articles

Cinefex, no. 34, 1989
Premiere, vol. 2, no. 11, July 1989
Cinefantastique, vol. 20, no. 1/2, November 1989
Cinefex, no. 41, February 1990
Starburst, no. 155, July 1991
Cinefantastique, vol. 22, no. 2 October 1991
Cinefex, no. 51, August 1992
GQ (US), November 1993
Cinefantastique, vol. 28, no. 7, January 1996
Premiere, January 1997
Karen R. Jones, *Mars Attacks! The Art of the Movie,* Ballantine
    Books (US)/Titan Books (UK), 1996

Note on the Editor

Mark Salisbury is London correspondent for the US edition of *Premiere* magazine. A former editor of Britain's *Empire* magazine, he also contributes to numerous publications in the UK and US and is the author of six books, among them *Writers on Comic Scriptwriting* and *Behind the Mask: The Secrets of Hollywood's Monster Makers*. He lives in North London with his partner and young son.

Index

Numbers in *italics* refer to illustrations

204–5, 213, 216, 219, 260; passion for gadgetry, 28, 50; personality, 168; Political Correctness, 223, 227
'Burtonesque', xviii
Buscemi, Steve, 214, 216

Cabin Boy, 128, 271
Cabinet of Dr Caligari, The, 19, 40
Cage, Nicolas, 154–5
Cal Arts (California Institute of the Arts), 7–8, 167, 205, 247
Calloway, Cab, 122, 123–4, 258
Cameron, James, 187
Cannon Films, 154
Catalina Island, 2
Catwoman, 145
CG (computer-generated) imagery, 246; Big Fish and, 218; Burton on, 49, 151; in Charlie and the Chocolate Factory, 240–1; in Mars Attacks!, 149
Chaney, Lon, 56
Charlie and the Chocolate Factory (2005), xv, xvi, xx, 223–45; adapting the book, 225, 243; animals in, 241; casting, 230, 233–4, 235; filmography, 278–9; Oompas Loompas in, 242–3; previous film of, 223; scripts for, 225–6; sets for, 236–40; shooting, 242; storyline, 223; themes, 227–8
Chiodio, Steve, 16, 28, 39
Citizen Kane, 228, 233, 237
Claymation, 251
Close, Glenn, 152
Coen Brothers (Joel and Ethan), 170
Cohen, Bruce, 203, 210
Columbia Pictures, 128, 136, 137, 203
Columbus, Chris, 187
Conversations with Vincent, 98
Coppola, Francis Ford, 182
Corman, Roger, 151
Corpse Bride (2005), xvi, xxi, 225, 236, 246–61; animation, 251; casting, 254–6; drawings, 251–2; filmography, 279–80; music for, 260–1; Nightmare Before Christmas and, 246, 247, 248, 250, 256, 257, 258, 260; origins of story, 247–8; puppets, 252; scripting, 250; stop-motion in, 248, 252, 257; voices, 254–6
Crosby, Bing, 165
Crowe, Cameron, 212
Crudup, Billy, 203, 205, 212, 213–14
Cruise, Tom, 91

Cry-Baby, xi
Cushing, Peter, 167, 168, 170, 177
Czaspsky, Stefan, 143

Dahl, Felicity 'Liccy', 224, 226
Dahl, Roald, xv, xx, 223, 224, 226–7, 237
Danger: Diabolik, 239, 240
Davis, Geena, 58, 63
Davis, Sammy Jr, xii, 258, 259, 260
Day of the Dead, 253
Days of our Lives, 216
Death of Superman comic-book, 154
Deja, Andreas, 10, 12
Depp, Johnny: and Burton, ix–xii, xiv–xvii; 91–2, 132, 133, 138, 178; character, 91–2; in Charlie and the Chocolate Factory, xv, xvi, xx, 230, 231, 233, 234, 243; in Corpse Bride, xvi, 254; in Ed Wood, xiii, 136, 137; in Edward Scissorhands, xi, xiii, 85, 89, 90, 91–2, 94, 95, 176, 222; forewords by, ix–xii, xiv–xvii; in Sleepy Hollow, 167, 168, 174, 176–7, 178–9; and Winona Ryder, 92–3
DeVito, Danny, 103, 110, 111, 152, 208, 214
Di Novi, Denise, x, 100, 101, 128, 129, 145
Disney, Walt, 170, 247, 250; and Burton see Burton, Tim: Animator; and Cabin Boy, 128; Cal Arts, 7–8; and Ed Wood, 135, 136; and Frankenweenie, 39; and Nightmare Before Christmas, 117–18, 119; philosophy, 8, 10, 12–13; and The Adventures of Ichabod and Mr Toad, 165, 167, 177; and Vincent, 16–17, 24–5
Disney Channel, 26, 31
Down With Love, 210
Dr Seuss, 16, 19, 115
Dracula Has Risen from the Grave, 173
Dream Works, 251
Duncan, Michael Clarke, 194, 199, 199
Duvall, Shelly, 36, 39, 40

Earth Versus the Flying Saucers, 147, 148, 149
Earthquake, 148
Eastwood, Clint, 145
Ed Wood (1994), xii, xiii, xviii, xx, 129–43, 146, 179, 182, 222, 227, 261; background to character of, 129–30; Big Fish and, 206; in black and white, 136–8; Burton's involvement with character of, 131, 134, 139–40; casting, 138–9, 152, 161, 180;